The Heavy Metal Guita

Published by **www.fundamental-chan**

ISBN: 978-1-911267-99-7

Cover image copyright Shutterstock: Melis / Fundamental Changes Ltd.

Contents

Foreword to the Compilation

Thank you for buying this compilation of my three volumes on metal guitar! No matter where you're at in your playing there should be something of value here. Together, this is a comprehensive guide providing a path for rock guitarists with the fundamentals down to conquer all aspects of playing metal.

Taken as a whole, it would be easy to become overwhelmed by this leviathan of metal licks. If you're just starting out then following from the start to the end would serve you well, or work from the start of Heavy Metal Rhythm Guitar and Heavy Metal Lead Guitar simultaneously.

However, by dipping into relevant sections as issues arise, the wealth of information contained here can also help you to troubleshoot your pain points. Whether you want to write melodic solos, to expand your tapping technique, or are struggling to feel a new time signature, then just dive in at the appropriate point.

The technical skills are of course important, especially in such a demanding genre as metal, but the technical challenges are addressed throughout using examples that directly applicable to real musical situations.

Taking what you've learnt in the first two books, Progressive Metal Guitar stretches every facet of your playing. This section will develop your rhythm and lead ideas to include more technical and complex ideas, bringing you up to date with the modern trends in heavy metal.

There are many listening recommendations for songs that demonstrate the material covered. It's easy to prioritise instrumental practice and forget that attentive listening should be at the centre of your musical growth, so be sure to keep your ears open. While some of the classic tracks will be very familiar to you, hopefully you'll discover some new artists along the way too.

As both a musician, and as a passionate fan of this sophisticated, intelligent and primal genre of music, I hope you take as much pleasure in using this compilation, as I took in writing and recording it for you.

I'm passionate about nurturing creativity in my students, so from the start I decided to write a book to help you *understand* the way music works, rather than just teaching technical skills. Broadening your aural skills and theoretical knowledge will let you appreciate how your favourite songs are constructed, and perhaps even allow you to write your own.

Now tune up, turn up and ride the lightning!

Good luck!

Rob Thorpe

December 2016

Heavy Metal Rhythm Guitar

Published by www.fundamental-changes.com

www.fundamental-changes.com

Get the Audio

The audio files for this book are available to download for free from **www.fundamental-changes.com.** The link is in the top right-hand corner. Simply select this book title from the drop-down menu and follow the instructions to get the audio.

We recommend that you download the files directly to your computer, not to your tablet, and extract them there before adding them to your media library. You can then put them on your tablet, iPod or burn them to CD. On the download page there is a help PDF, and we also provide technical support via the contact form.

For over 250 Free Guitar Lessons with Videos Check out:
www.fundamental-changes.com

Twitter: **@guitar_joseph**
Over 7500 fans on Facebook: **FundamentalChangesInGuitar**
Instagram: **FundamentalChanges**

Get your audio now for free:

It makes the book come alive and you'll learn much more!

www.fundamental-changes.com/download-audio

Foreword

This book is a comprehensive guide for guitarists who wish to master the essential techniques and concepts in metal. It includes a wealth of material that is accessible yet challenging for beginner to intermediate guitarists.

Metal Rhythm Guitar examines the guitar playing at the roots of metal in the mid-1960s, such as Led Zeppelin and Deep Purple, and the New Wave of British Heavy Metal bands of the late '70s and early '80s like Judas Priest, Saxon and Iron Maiden. The thrash metal of bands like Metallica and Slayer will be studied, along with bands like Death, Pantera and Meshuggah who progressed the style and expanded the technical possibilities.

Where did metal come from? Who were the first real heavy metal band?

Fans and musicologists have suggested answers to both of these questions, but in my opinion, heavy metal was born in Birmingham, England in 1969 with the bell chimes, thunder, and the crashing guitar riff that opened Black Sabbath's first album.

Sabbath's guitarist, Tony Iommi, worked in the steel factories of industrial Birmingham, and the sounds of the machinery most likely influenced the ominous, dark rhythms of Black Sabbath's music. Black Sabbath's bassist, Geezer Butler wrote many of the band's lyrics. His interest in religion, fantasy, the occult and horror combined the lyrical subject matter with the industrial sounding music.

At that time, many bands had been moving in an increasingly heavy direction, but until now, the sound had remained planted in blues-rock. Black Sabbath introduced many of the ingredients that we now think of as essential characteristics of 'heavy metal', and for the first time The Blues took a back seat.

The next generation of rock musicians took the influence of Sabbath, Zeppelin, Mountain and other hard rock bands, distilling the heavier tone and darker lyrical subject matter and causing it to diverge further from rock and pop music trends.

While progressive rock explored unusual song forms and classical influences, the New Wave of British Heavy Metal (NWOBHM) bands like Judas Priest, Saxon and Iron Maiden created dramatic songs that balanced powerful instrumental music with the operatic vocal power of singers like Bruce Dickinson.

Meanwhile, musicians in San Francisco, California had been influenced by both the NWOBHM bands and the faster, more abrasive development of punk rock known as 'hardcore'. Hardcore punk exploded out of Southern California and across America in the late '70s, led by bands such as Black Flag. These musicians went on to develop thrash metal. Key figures were Dave Mustaine, James Hetfield, Jeff Hanneman and Scott Ian, who played in several notable bands before forming Metallica, Slayer and Anthrax.

Thrash metal also adopted the DIY ethic of indie record labels that characterised hardcore punk.

By the time these thrash metal bands came to record their standout albums such as *Master of Puppets* (Metallica, 1986) and *Rust in Peace* (Megadeth, 1990) their sound had become extremely polished and the complexity of compositions had developed greatly from their punk-influenced beginnings.

When thrash metal was adopted and progressed by a new generation 'death metal' was born, with important death metal scenes present in both Florida and Scandinavia. The ingredients of thrash metal (guttural singing, fast double kick drums, and intricate, technical guitar riffs) were all exaggerated in death metal music. Similarly, the bleak, lyrical subject matter developed into increasingly vivid depictions of graphic, satanic imagery.

At the same time, other bands were taking rock music in a new direction. Rather than exploring increasingly aggressive music, they built on the melodic and theatrical elements of bands like Iron Maiden. Power metal formed in the mid-'80s with European bands like Helloween, Blind Guardian and Stratovarius and was characterised by a more symphonic sound employing keyboards, vocal harmonies, orchestral elements and folk melodies to create rich textures. The lyrics frequently drew from pagan myths, or fantasy writers such as J.R.R Tolkien and H.P. Lovecraft.

Power metal's upbeat harmonies and melodic hooks were combined with the complexity and theatrical influence of the progressive bands like Yes and Rush to form progressive metal. This sub-genre raised the bar for virtuosity and featured technically demanding instrumental sections, strong vocal delivery, and complex song structures. Early pioneers included Fates Warning and Queensrÿche followed by Dream Theater and Symphony X.

No matter which sub-genre of metal you connect with, the following journey through the development of metal guitar playing will help you to understand the music and play it authentically. Understanding how the style evolved will help to turn you into a well-rounded and knowledgeable musician.

This book covers the key concepts and techniques common to *all* styles of metal and they can be applied however you wish. There is a logical progression from classic 'hard rock' through to more technically demanding modern metal ideas. Along the way we will cover all the relevant music theory including scales, rhythm and harmony, and how to apply these components to the guitar.

By the end of the book, you will have developed strong guitar technique and an understanding of the mechanics of metal guitar allowing you to write your own songs.

Have fun with these ideas but above all experiment and be creative with the information. Doing so will mean that you get the most out of this book and help you to grow rapidly as a musician.

Good luck, and have fun!

Rob Thorpe

Get the Audio

The audio files for this book are available to download for free from **www.fundamental-changes.com.** The link is in the top right-hand corner. Simply select this book title from the drop-down menu and follow the instructions to get the audio.

We recommend that you download the files directly to your computer, not to your tablet, and extract them there before adding them to your media library. You can then put them on your tablet, iPod or burn them to CD. On the download page there is a help PDF, and we also provide technical support via the contact form.

For over 250 Free Guitar Lessons with Videos Check out:
www.fundamental-changes.com

Twitter: **@guitar_joseph**
Over 7500 fans on Facebook: **FundamentalChangesInGuitar**
Instagram: **FundamentalChanges**

Get your audio now for free:

It makes the book come alive and you'll learn much more!

www.fundamental-changes.com/download-audio

Primer: Rhythm and Notation

Before we begin, it will be helpful to learn how to play and notate rhythms. This will help you to notate the music you write or transcribe, and also to practice efficiently.

Note Values and Simple Time

Musical notation combines information about both the pitch and duration of a note. Guitar tablature often misses rhythms off completely which can make the music hard to understand. Reading rhythmic notation will help you to understand how to play music without having to hear it first.

Western music is divided into *bars*, which show how the music is to be phrased. Bars are then further divided into individual *beats*. In most rock music there are four beats in each bar, and this is indicated by a *time signature* at the start of the sheet music.

Figure 1 shows two bars of **4/4** time. Each bar contains four 1/4 note beats. The numbers under the *stave* (musical notation) illustrate how to count through the bars. It may seem basic, but counting out loud when you play will help greatly later on when playing more complicated rhythms.

Fig. 1:

Some notes last longer than one beat. Figure 2 shows *whole notes* (four beats) and *1/2 notes* (2 beats).

Fig. 2:

Rhythmic notation is very logical because every note value is broken down into simple divisions of bars and beats. A time signature with a '4' on the bottom (like 4/4) means that each beat will always divide into multiples of two. The following example shows how each 1/4 note beat can be divided into 1/8th notes (two notes per beat) and 1/16th notes (four notes per beat).

Look at the counting under each stave. The basic 1, 2, 3, 4 pulse should remain at the same speed (tempo) while the shorter note values are squeezed in evenly into each beat. Each time we *subdivide* a note, we add another *tail* to the note's stem.

Fig. 3:

Dotted Notes

Dotted notes can also be used. Adding a dot next to the note head extends the length of a note by half its original value. The dotted 1/2 note in the following example lasts for three beats (1/2 + 1/4). This same concept applies to any note value.

In the second bar the dotted 1/4 notes last for three 1/8th notes each. (1/4 + 1/8)

Fig. 4:

Rests

As well as defining the length of each note that is played, we need a way to notate the space between notes when we require silence. This is the job of *rests* and every note has an equivalent rest value.

The symbols for rests are shown in figure 5.

Fig. 5:

Study the following figures to see combinations of note values that are likely to occur in real musical situations.

Clap, or strum a muted chord to play the following rhythms. They are included as audio examples so that you can hear them in context.

Fig. 6a:

Fig. 6b:

Triplets and Compound Time

A triplet is simply three notes squeezed evenly into a single 1/4 note beat.

The following example shows a bar of 4/4 with triplets on beats two, three and four. Notice how they are counted.

Fig. 7a:

Triplets have a recognisable feel that will probably be familiar to you. You can hear them in Iron Maiden's *Phantom of the Opera* and Black Sabbath's *Black Sabbath* (4:35 onwards).

If triplets are used as the foundation of a piece of music, then a different time signature might be used to simplify the notation. *12/8* is an example of *compound time* and means that there are still four even beats in each bar, but now each beat has three divisions instead of two.

Figure 7b would sound the same as a bar of triplets in 4/4, but now the beats are naturally divided into threes. To account for this, each beat is actually a dotted 1/4 note, as shown by the metronome mark.

Fig. 7b:

There can be confusion about the difference between the time signatures of *3/4* and *6/8,* as they both contain a total of six 1/8 notes. The important difference is that each beat is divided differently.

In figure 8a, there are three even beats and each one is divided into two 1/8 notes.

In figure 8b, the *6/8* time signature is broken into two beats with each beat subdivided into three 1/8 notes.

Fig. 8a:

Fig. 8b:

Put simply, 3/4 has three strong pulses that are divided into two, while 6/8 has two strong pulses that are divided into three.

This primer covers the fundamentals of reading rhythmic notation. We'll cover other bits of notation as we progress, but this section forms the basis of everything that follows.

Don't worry if this is new to you, every example in this book can be heard on the accompanying audio examples. You can download them from **http://www.fundamental-changes.com/download-audio.**

Chapter One: Roots of Metal

We will start by exploring the early blues-influenced styles of hard rock and heavy metal. The vocabulary found in the music of bands such as Deep Purple, Led Zeppelin, Cream, Black Sabbath and The Jimi Hendrix Experience set the blueprint for heavy metal's trajectory.

These bands had Rock 'n' Roll as an inspiration, but their '60s spirit of adventure and psychedelic experimentalism drew on folk, classical and jazz influences in their search for a new sound.

The first few musical examples show how the minor pentatonic scale is used in rock riffs. The five note minor pentatonic scale is the basis of most blues melodies, making it an essential sound, no matter what your taste in music.

First, we have a riff based around the E minor pentatonic scale, which is similar to ideas used by Jimmy Page and Richie Blackmore.

Example 1a:

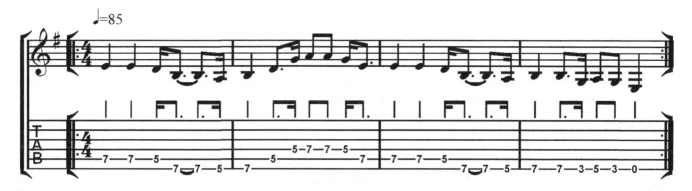

All the riffs in this book are brought to life by the way they are played so make sure to play them with plenty of attitude.

Try adding subtle grace notes, slides and vibrato to the examples in this book as I do on the audio example. It's these little details that can give simple musical phrases a lot of character.

In the next example, the 12/8 time signature means that each beat is split into three equal notes, a feel inherited from the blues origins of heavy metal. Listen to the audio and you'll hear the characteristic '**1**&a **2**&a' groove.

Example 1b:

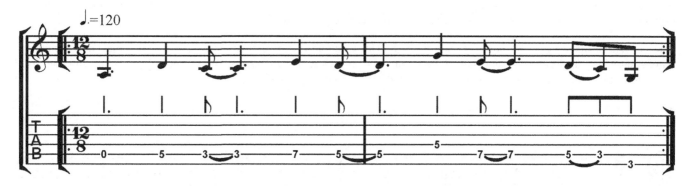

The next riff demonstrates a device called *anticipation,* which is a form of *syncopation* (playing between the beats). Pre-empting the beat gives forward motion and energy to the riff.

Compare the following example with the previous two, and try to notice why it sounds different. Compare music by Black Sabbath and AC/DC and you will hear that AC/DC uses a lot of anticipation whereas Sabbath's rhythms usually fall right on the beat.

Example 1c:

To play syncopated riffs accurately, keep your picking hand moving in a continuous down-up strumming motion, even when you're not actually playing the notes. Doing this helps you to keep in time with the pulse of the music.

Think of your picking hand as a mini conductor who keeps time for you, or as the needle on a record player so sound is only produced when your pick is in contact with the strings.

In the next example, double-stops are used to create a fatter sound. To get a bluesy feel and to help in achieving good vibrato, use the first or third fingers flattened across the fretboard to play each double-stop. Many classic riffs by bands like Deep Purple and Led Zeppelin use double-stops (such as the ubiquitous *Smoke on the Water).*

Example 1d:

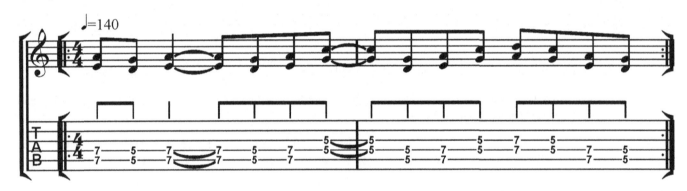

The next example teaches you how to play a low, shuffling Em riff. This idea could easily come from Black Sabbath or the later 'stoner' metal bands like Kyuss. It shows the enduring influence of early metal.

The musical distance from the root of a scale to the b5 (for example E to Bb) is called a *tritone*. When played in isolation, a tritone has a very dark and dissonant character and can create a sinister or 'evil' sound. To hear an isolated tritone interval, listen to the intro to Jimi Hendrix's *Purple Haze*, or Black Sabbath's *Black Sabbath*.

Example 1e:

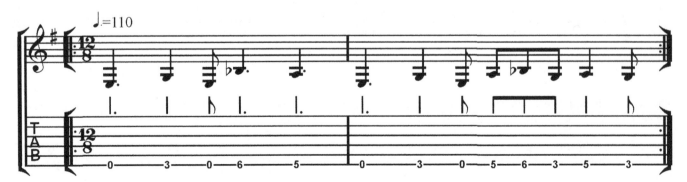

Building Riffs with Pentatonic Scales

The following ideas look at some other pentatonic scale shapes that can be used to create new riffs and ideas.

You might already be familiar with the pentatonic 'box' shapes that guitarists often use. These scales are very effective when developing lead guitar vocabulary, but they can also be used in a different way to create metal guitar riffs.

Metal guitar riffs are usually played on the lowest strings of the guitar, so for the moment we will focus there and learn to play up and down the length of these strings.

The following example shows the E Minor Pentatonic scale played on the low E string. If you learn to recognise the shape and sequence of these *intervals*, it will be beneficial for both your playing and fretboard knowledge.

Example 1f:

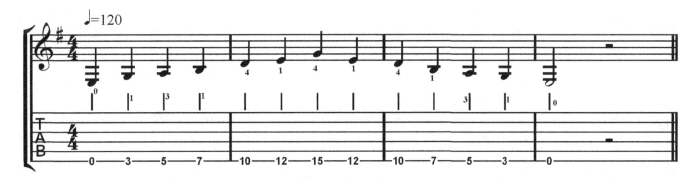

Example 1g shows how this single string approach can be used in a musical way. Notice how the subtle slides help to smooth the position shifts as well as making the riff more musical. The whole riff can be fingered with just the index and ring fingers.

Example 1g:

Staying on just the low E string helps us to keep the thick, consistent tone that is often important for metal rhythm guitar.

Many different ideas can be created by reordering the notes and using different phrasing.

Now that we know how E minor pentatonic sounds on the bottom string, we can extend the scale across the bottom three strings. Notice that each fragment contains the same five notes starting from a different point each time.

Example 1h:

Fluency in both horizontal and vertical patterns allows you to navigate all over the fretboard while staying within the E minor pentatonic scale.

Let's combine the previous two exercises and ascend from the open E string up to the fourteenth fret.

Example 1i:

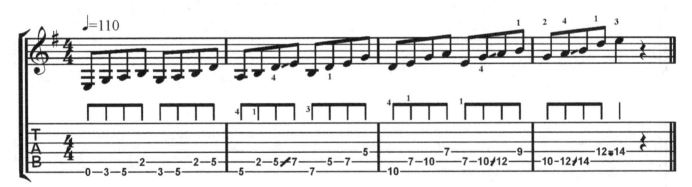

Try exploring these different pentatonic shapes by coming up with your own riffs as well as playing them as written. An interesting approach to building classic groovy riffs is to start strumming a rhythm with muted notes, and, as you repeat it over and over, gradually introduce pentatonic notes to the groove until you've got a loop that feels good and balances rhythmic and melodic interest.

The Classic Roots of Modern Metal

You can hear a strong blues and hard rock influence in Tom Morello's approach to riff writing with Audio Slave. Dimebag Darrell also used pentatonic-based writing in Pantera. This bluesy 'swagger', combined with modern guitar tone and virtuosic delivery was why Pantera had such a huge impact on metal in the early '90s.

In the following riff the movement down the fretboard in bar one can be tricky, however, most of the notes can be played with the index and ring fingers while adding the pinkie for the Bb in bar one and the middle finger for the Bb in bar two.

Example 1j:

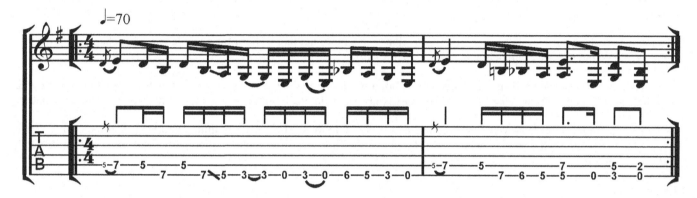

Example 1k lays down another linear riff in A minor that shifts the previous ideas up by one string and uses other ideas we've touched on, such as the b5, slides and double-stops. Be careful with the slides and pay attention to the recommended fingerings in bars three and four. This riff works in the key of D by moving it up by a string.

Example 1k:

The following examples from early '70s hard rock to modern metal all use pentatonic based riffs:

Led Zeppelin – *Heartbreaker*
Black Sabbath – *Iron Man*
Metallica – *Seek & Destroy*
Pantera – *I'm Broken*
Audioslave – *Cochise*

Chapter Two: Moving Power Chords

Power chords consist of two notes: the root and the fifth. These two notes sound extremely stable together so a power chord sounds like a denser, reinforced version of the root note.

This *consonance* (musical stability) makes power chords work well with distortion and helps to avoid the 'mushiness' that can occur when full major or minor chords are played with distortion.

Power chords are normally one of the first things that modern guitarists learn, and there are thousands of rock songs that can be played using power chords alone. As well as being used to outline chord progressions, power chords are used to thicken up single-note riffs.

Playing riffs with power chords takes more coordination than simply holding a chord for a whole bar. This chapter will discuss some exercises and riffs that will help you to develop this skill.

Aim to maintain the shape of the power chord when sliding from one to the next by locking the fingers in position and moving the whole arm from the elbow. These first few exercises may seem simple, but they are an important rhythm guitar technique.

In the first example, we're simply sliding from a G power chord up to A. The important thing to notice is that the open E string is muted with the heel of the picking hand as it's played, but the chords are allowed to ring properly. This gives a sense of depth and contrast to the part.

Example 2a:

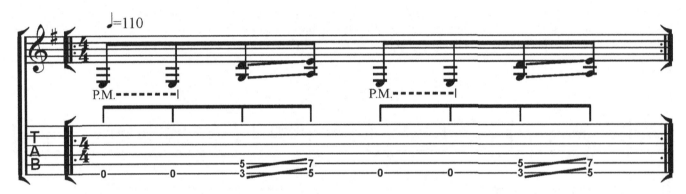

In the next example, the slide direction is reversed and the slide starts on an offbeat. Timing can be an issue with these slides because they are played *legato* (without picking) and many players rely on their picking hand to control the rhythm. Any rhythm guitar idea needs to be rhythmically tight so as to lock in with the bass and drums, so develop this accuracy early on.

Example 2b:

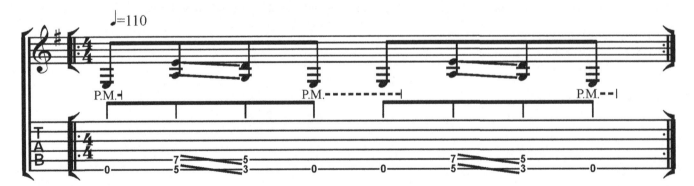

Next, we widen the intervals and include both ascending and descending slides. If you find you have difficulty stopping accurately at the right fret, it can be helpful to look at the target fret ahead of time, rather than just watching your hand play the first chord.

Example 2c:

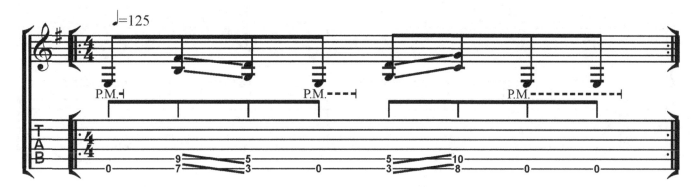

The following example groups slides together. Follow the picking directions to begin with, then for an extra challenge, pick only the first power chord in each group of four and slide each of the following ones. This approach can lose the forcefulness that metal guitar requires but it is a great way of testing your timekeeping.

Example 2d:

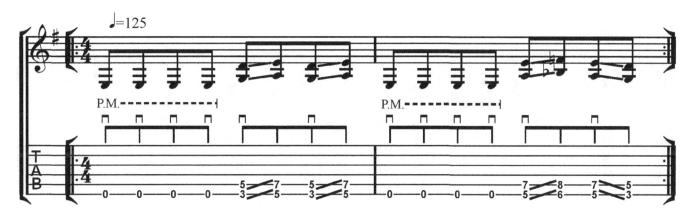

This next exercise uses sliding ideas along the length of the bottom strings. Take it slowly and remember to keep your eyes ahead of your hand if you're over- or under-shooting the slides.

Example 2e:

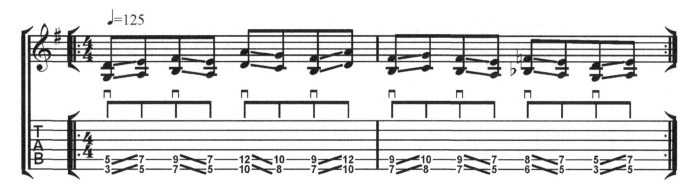

The final exercise demands some long slides up and down the neck and will help you to develop your accuracy. Dimebag Darrell had an excellent sliding technique, and could fly up and down the neck with precision while rocking out on stage. Test yourself by looking away from the guitar neck as you play and trust your ears to judge whether you've hit the right fret. This pays dividends when it's time to perform!

Example 2f:

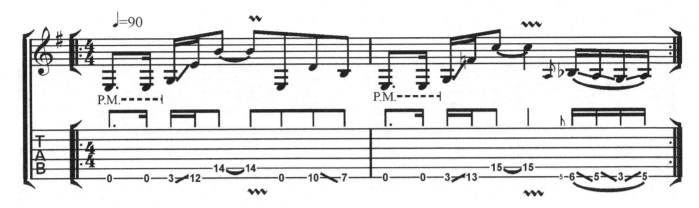

Moving Chords Across Strings

Next we will work on moving power chord shape across strings. Despite the smaller distance, this movement can be harder than moving the chord along the length of one string because when changing chords, the fingers must briefly leave the strings, although keeping the shape of the power chord intact is essential.

Example 2g:

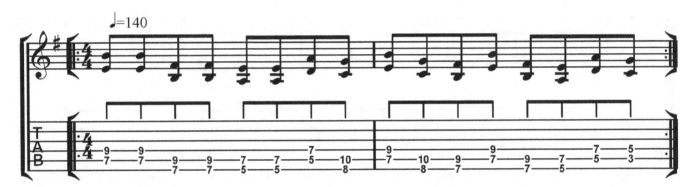

Example 2h is a slightly trickier example that builds upon exercise 2g by moving one fret *and* one string between each chord. Begin by carefully learning the chord movements at a slow tempo.

Example 2h:

You can hear ideas like this executed with speed and precision in death metal and other related genres. Aim to move the hand as little as possible. Keeping the fingers close to the strings helps with speed.

In the following example, we move along the neck in semitones while using an open E string *pedal*.

Example 2i:

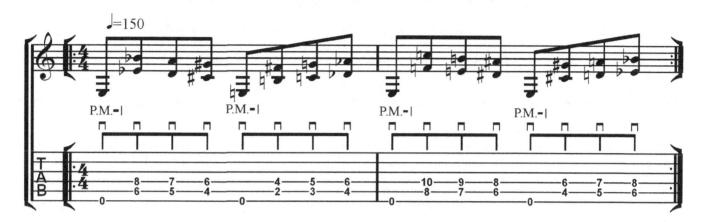

Try to *palm mute* the E string while allowing the chords to ring fully. Listen to the audio example to hear this technique in action. Down-picking the chords creates a more aggressive attack.

Finally, here's a chromatic death metal riff. Learn this idea slowly and focus on the timing. It is easy to become tense in the fretting hand, so if you feel yourself getting tight, be sure to shake it off and try again at a slower tempo. With consistent practice, stamina will build within a few weeks.

Example 2j:

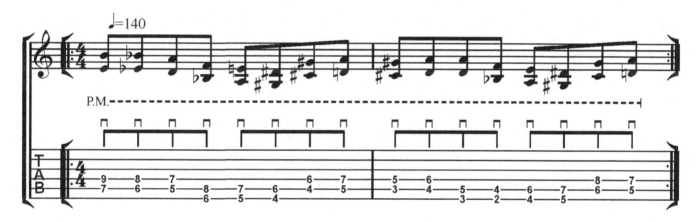

The following songs feature moving power chord based riffs:

Black Sabbath – *N.I.B.*
Metallica – *Master of Puppets* (verse)
Slayer – *Reborn*
Pantera – *A New Level*
Slipknot – *Surfacing* (bridge)
Machinehead – *Imperium* (chorus)

You can download all the audio in this book for free from **www.fundamental-changes.com/download-audio.**

Chapter Three: Developing the Picking Hand

Over the past thirty years, metal's technical demands have required an increasingly well-developed picking hand.

This chapter gives you musical examples and exercises that develop the speed and stamina to tackle rhythm parts in thrash and death metal.

There are as many variations of picking hand position as there are players, but the most successful guitarists tend to have similar approaches.

The two essential considerations of any technique are a *relaxed posture* and *good sound*. By this, I mean that you should try to reduce any tension in your arms and hands while producing a quality of sound that has good clarity and attack.

When learning to play metal, there is a temptation to play fast straight away. Many young players cramp up and hunch over the guitar in an effort to replicate the speed they hear on records, but speed is the product of regular practice over a long period of time.

Repetitive strain injuries in the picking hand are not uncommon amongst extreme metal guitarists although this risk is greatly reduced by warming up properly and keeping the muscles relaxed while playing.

The powerful string attack of players like Jeff Hanneman (Slayer) and Chuck Schuldiner (Death) is the product of *relaxed* control. Sheer aggression is no substitute for relaxation and good technique.

The motion of the picking hand should come from the wrist rather than the thumb and index finger joints. Strumming from the wrist will allow more stamina than relying on the small muscles controlling each finger to move the pick.

Experiment with the angle of the pick as it makes contact with the strings. If the angle is too flat, the string will create too much resistance. If the pick strikes edge on, the note will be less clear. Many metal players prefer a thicker, 2mm pick with a sharp tip to put momentum behind the attack and glide through the strings.

When playing rhythm guitar you (along with the bass and drums), are a part of the band's rhythm section. For this reason timekeeping is your primary concern and is actually more important than tone or even note accuracy!

In rock and metal, it is standard practice for each rhythm guitar part to be *double-tracked* when recording. The doubled recordings result in a rich, fat sound that one guitar alone cannot achieve. However, if you try to record double tracking parts by yourself, the accuracy needed to record even a straightforward riff is raised significantly.

To help develop your sense of rhythm, always practice with a metronome or drum loop. This will get you used to playing to an external beat rather than at whatever speed happens to feel most comfortable to you.

There are two components to timekeeping:

- Keeping the tempo even.

- Subdividing the beat evenly.

As your picking technique gets more accurate and confident, the accuracy of your subdivisions will get better. However, keeping a consistent *internal* pulse is much less about physical technique and can be improved with simple exercises and a slow metronome.

Internal Rhythm Exercises

Begin by strumming a simple acoustic-style rhythm to a metronome set at 160bpm. Tapping your foot can help with timekeeping by providing a regular pulse.

Fig. 1:

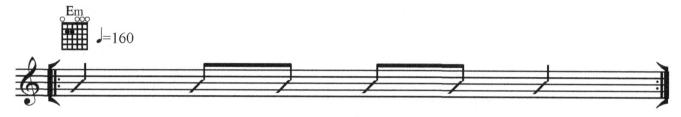

Once you feel that your playing at 160bpm is solid, set the metronome to 80bpm, but *play at the same speed.*

Fig. 2:

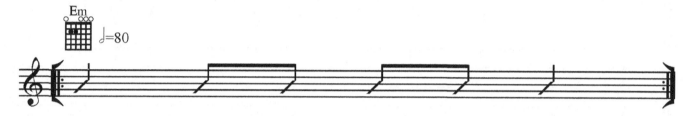

Half the click again to 40bpm. The click is now only heard on beat one of the bar and playing accurately with the slow click this slow can feel like a trust exercise. Staying in time can be hard at first but this kind of practice quickly improves your internal clock and helps you to be confident and relaxed.

Fig. 3:

Finally, set the metronome to 20bpm so that the click is only heard once every two bars. It will probably take you some time to get the feel of this exercise.

Fig. 4:

Some metronomes will not click this slowly but several smartphone apps and more expensive electronic metronomes have the option to click on only beat one of a bar.

If you can relax enough to play the previous exercises accurately without speeding up, you can feel confident in your time keeping.

Get into the habit of recording your practice and listening back to the results 24 hours later to make any timing issues more obvious. When you learn a new song, record it to objectively review your performance and to document your progress.

Picking Riffs

Now we've had a quick primer on timing and using a metronome, it's time to break out some metal riffs. These riffs have all been written to hone in on your picking hand and address the different issues that crop up in metal.

The following exercise uses constant 1/8th notes. Use all down-strokes rather than alternate picking to get an authentic, heavy metal attack.

Example 3a:

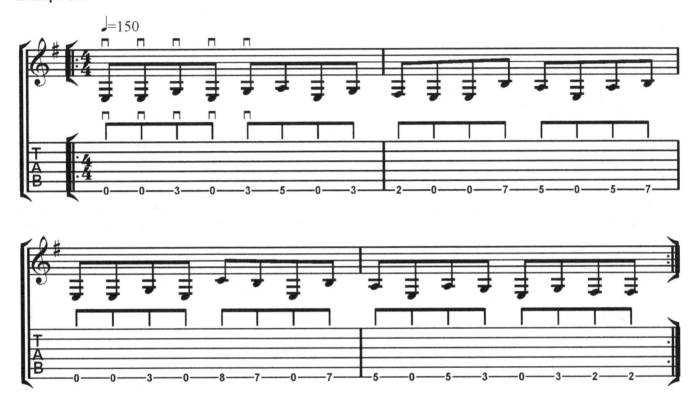

Palm muting helps to keep riffs tight and well-articulated, and to create the characteristic 'chug' sound of metal rhythm guitar. To get the right sound, keep the fleshy side of your picking hand on the bridge saddles so that they touch and slightly mute the strings. Experiment by moving your hand further forward over the strings to increasingly dampen their ringing.

This second example introduces some notes on the A string. Maintaining the even down-strokes while changing strings takes a bit more control than just thrashing away at one string, so make sure you're relaxed and the wrist is free to slide across the bridge saddles.

Example 3b:

There are limitless possibilities for this kind of riff. Just have a listen to a handful of old school thrash metal records to hear different takes on the same idea.

The following down-picked riff involves more string crossing than the previous idea so practice this example slowly and learn to play it consistently before speeding up. Use all four fingers of the fretting hand to navigate the *chromatic* notes.

Example 3c:

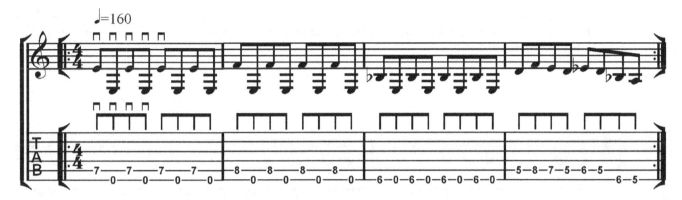

Gaining the speed and endurance needed for thrash metal takes time and repetition. Try raising the metronome speed periodically by 5bpm to see if you can maintain control at faster speeds. If you have any pain or lasting aches, you should see a doctor or a specialist. If you have any doubts, stop and get professional advice from your physician.

This next exercise is the foundation of everything that follows in this chapter so it's worth spending some time getting comfortable playing it at a moderate tempo of between 100 and 120bpm. Return to this exercise as you progress through the rest of the examples and you'll feel how your control improves.

The purpose of the exercise is to rhythmically 'lock in' and be aware of how each note subdivides the beat into four equal divisions. Start slowly, and accent the first of each four-note group to help stay in time as you begin to raise the metronome speed.

Example 3d:

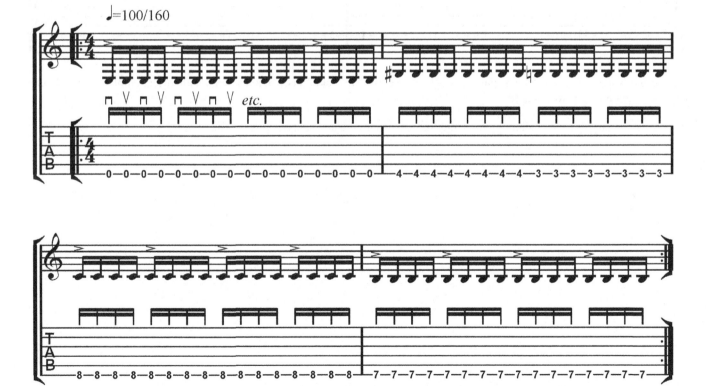

When playing the above example along with the audio, there should be unity between the bass drum hits and the guitar. The more you can concentrate on listening to the drums while you play, you more you'll be able to lock in.

Gallop Rhythms

The 'gallop' rhythm has been played by many bands but is often associated with Iron Maiden who used it as the basis for several of their most famous songs.

Single string picking works just like strumming, so maintain the 1/16th note down/up pattern of exercise 3d to help your timing, and 'ghost' over the string when a note is not required. As the second pick of each four-note group is missed out, the picking pattern will be 'Down-Down-Up' on each beat.

Example 3e:

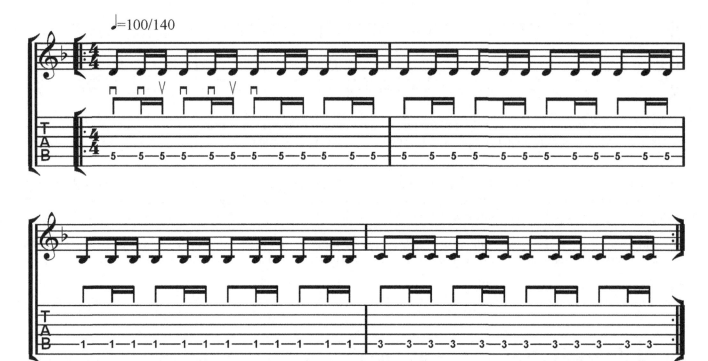

Let's use this idea to create some actual music. Using exercises to make music helps to keep us focused, enthusiastic and helps us to see a genuine creative benefit.

Adding power chords to the gallop rhythms highlights each chord change, driving the music forward.

Example 3f:

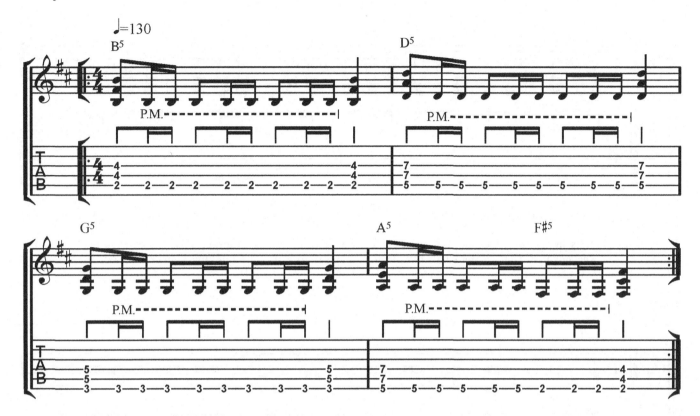

Keep the single notes tight and controlled while making the power chords big and loud. Achieve this by palm-muting the faster 'gallop' parts, but remove the palm from the bridge for the power chords and allow them to ring out fully.

Here's another riff that employs the gallop rhythm, but this time the open E string acts as a *pedal* (a static bass note) while the power chords provide melodic interest. Learn this riff slowly until both hands feel comfortable. Try to keep the power chord shape intact while sliding it around the neck and pay attention to the timing of the slides.

Example 3g:

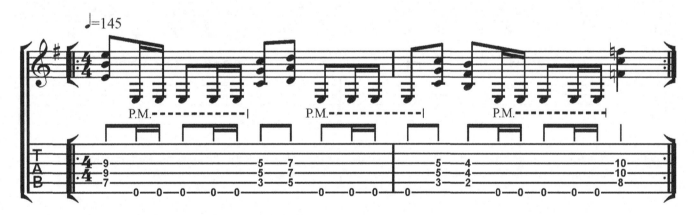

This kind of idea is common in '80s-era Metallica and Exodus, as well as with many other thrash metal bands.

Thrash metal fused together the sounds of British heavy metal and hardcore punk to create a fast-paced, aggressive new style incorporating the technical proficiency of metal. Thrash bands used a variation of the gallop rhythm known as the 'reverse gallop'.

By playing the reverse gallop pattern directly on the beat they created an energetic sense of urgency.

Example 3h:

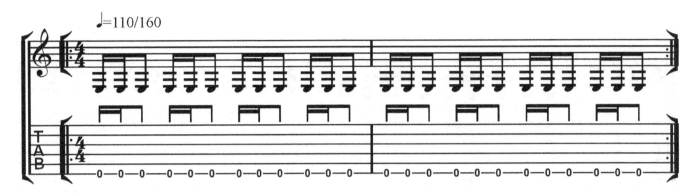

This idea may be a little more demanding, but your stamina should increase within a few weeks of playing these ideas regularly.

The next example is in 3/4 time, meaning that each bar contains three beats. More progressive bands from the early thrash movement, like Testament, as well as later bands like Death and Nevermore, use different time signatures to add variation to the thrash vocabulary. Keep the pick moving down and up in 1/16th notes.

Example 3i:

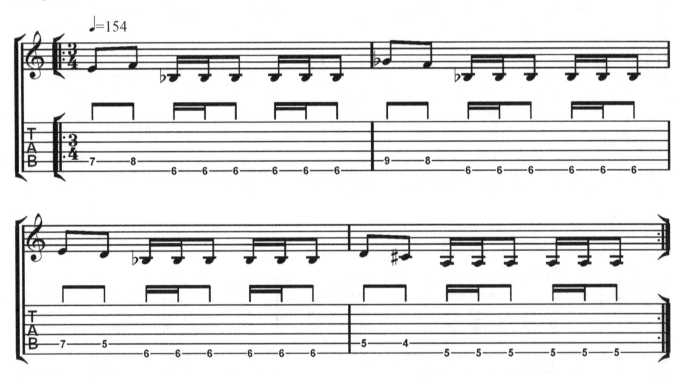

Example 3j again uses the reverse gallop pattern. Try to maintain down-strokes for the 1/8th notes on beats three and four. Down-strokes provide a more powerful tone, while the more consistent picking hand motion helps with timing.

Example 3j:

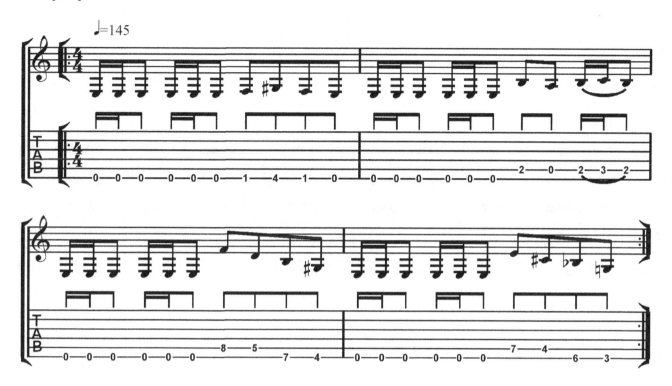

Now for a more syncopated example in the style of Pantera.

Many of the notes in the following example occur on off-beats, so use strict alternate picking and follow the notated picking directions. To articulate the syncopated rhythms properly the notes should be kept short and punchy. Listen to the audio examples to help you capture the right feel. **Example 3k:**

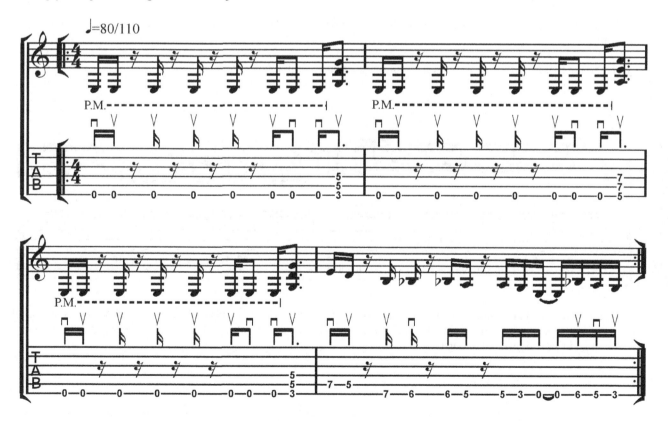

Between each note, mute the strings with the fretting hand by flattening the fingers gently across the strings. It may take some time to coordinate the hands, but go slowly and it will soon feel natural to switch between picking and muting.

Rhythmic precision was heightened by bands such as Fear Factory and Meshuggah in the early '90s and the next example demonstrates this style.

Example 3l:

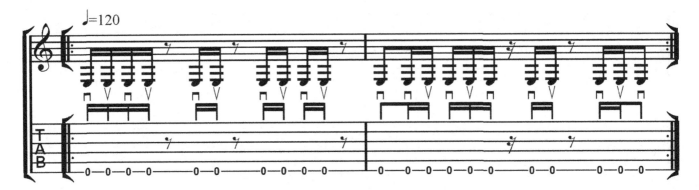

The gaps between the notes should be silent to create the proper impact.

For the most effective muting technique, rest the first finger of the picking hand on the top five strings throughout the riff and pad the remaining three fingers on to the strings to damp the sixth string during the rests. Fan the fingers to avoid accidental natural harmonics.

The technical bar for extreme metal rhythm playing was raised by Death and Cynic who both emerged from the late '80s Florida death metal scene. Cynic's debut album, *Focus* contains many technical and precise riffs.

The following two examples combine to form one musical idea that demonstrates the multi-layered approach to songwriting found across Cynic's records.

The first part shows a typical melodic idea where the motif is phrased in 1/8th notes, but each note is picked twice to create a 1/16th note pulse.

To help you hear the two parts more clearly these examples are played individually and then together.

Example 3m:

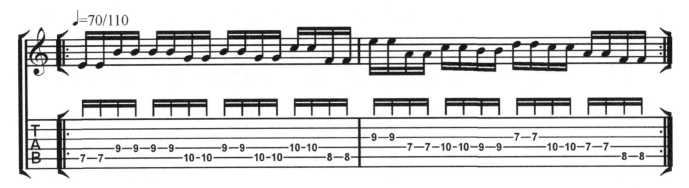

The lower guitar part, shown in example 3n, needs careful muting between the chords and single notes. The short bursts of 1/32nd notes must be given special attention too. The picking hand will need to be very relaxed to execute these rhythms comfortably and they should feel like a single, quick burst of energy.

Example 3n:

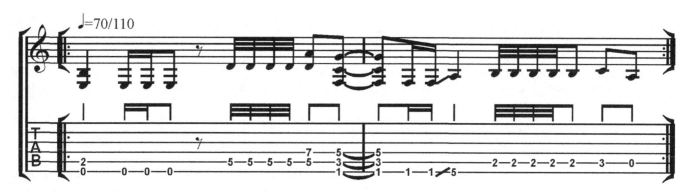

The following songs contain great examples of these picking patterns in context:

Iron Maiden – The Trooper
Anthrax – Caught in a Mosh
Metallica – Motorbreath
Megadeth – Holy Wars... The Punishment Due
Slayer – Raining Blood
Trivium – Pull Harder on the Strings of Your Martyr
Death – Born Dead
Cynic – Celestial Voyage
Strapping Young Lad – Wrong Side
Fear Factory – Self Bias Resistor

Chapter Four: Scales for Metal

Having looked at rhythmic patterns and phrasing in the previous chapters, we will now look at how scales add a melodic dimension to metal riffs.

Ever since Tony Iommi hit a tritone interval in the title track of Black Sabbath's eponymous debut album, heavy metal has been characterised by its dark, malicious-sounding music. This heavy sound created the perfect atmosphere for metal's brooding, aggressive or even satanic lyrics.

In this chapter, we will study the most commonly used scales in metal, and see how they are used by heavy metal rhythm guitarists to develop riffs and chord progressions.

Most scale dictionaries are usually designed for soloists and provide many patterns that cover the whole neck. As we are only concerned with rhythm guitar, the diagrams in this chapter teach scales on the lower (bass) strings and show how they're played horizontally along the neck. I have, however, included one 'open-position' scale shape across all six strings to help you build riffs in the lower portion of the neck.

When learning new scales, it is important to recognise each scale's defining 'character notes'. Every scale has a distinctive flavour, and knowing which notes contribute to the scale's unique mood is very important.

Most of the scales here contain the same minor chord (1, b3, 5) or minor pentatonic scale (1, b3, 4, 5, b7) within their seven notes, so the character notes are normally the remaining notes (the 2nd and the 6th).

It is useful to examine common chord progressions associated with each scale, both to help you make music, and also to see scales as a basis for songs rather than just theoretical ideas. To form chords from scales, each scale needs to be *harmonised*.

Harmonising a Scale

Chords are formed by stacking up three notes, each a 3rd above the previous one. These three-note structures are called *triads* and they are the most basic type of chord structure in music.

To harmonise a (C Major) scale start with the notes of C major written out:

C D E F G A B C

To build a chord on each step simply take alternate notes.

<u>C</u> D <u>E</u> F <u>G</u> A B C = C,E,G = major triad

As you can see, a triad is formed by skipping alternate notes in the scale, and this process can be started on any note in the scale.

The notes C, E and G form the chord of C major while the notes D, F and A form the chord of D minor. The distance from C to E is four semitones, but the distance from D to F is only three semitones.

C <u>D</u> E <u>F</u> G <u>A</u> B C

If a triad has a distance of *four semitones* between the root and the 3rd (e.g., C to E), then it is a major chord. If a triad has a distance of *three semitones* between the root and the 3rd (e.g., D to F), it is a minor chord.

Forming triads on each note in the scale creates the following sequence of chords:

C major, D minor, E minor, F major, G major, A minor, B diminished

Chords are often referred to by Roman numerals. Each chord is referred to by its relationship to the root of the parent scale.

In Roman numerals the Major scale is written in the following way:

I   ii   iii   IV   V   vi   vii°

Capital letters indicate major chords and lower case letters indicate minor chords.

In the above diagram, you can see that chord I is major, (capital letters) but chord vi is minor (lower case).

Every Major scale has the same pattern of intervals therefore the sequence of major and minor triads will be the same in every key. This means the Roman numerals can represent the notes found on the steps of any scale.

Diminished triads (chords built from two minor thirds) are indicated by a small circle and *augmented* triads (chords built from two major thirds) are shown by a plus (+) sign.

Other scales are formed with a different pattern of intervals, so later you will see chords being referred to by sharps and flats (#'s and b's). For example, you may see chord bIII. This symbol tells us that the third step of the scale is a minor third from the root and that the chord formed on it is major.

Using this system, I'll illustrate the chords formed when each of the scales in this chapter is harmonised and also suggest some chord progressions for you to experiment with.

The Natural Minor / Aeolian Mode

Aeolian or 'Natural' minor has a sombre yet majestic quality and is the most common seven-note minor scale used in metal. Guitarists such as Gary Moore, Richie Blackmore and Uli Jon Roth started using this scale in the '70s to expand the bluesy vocabulary of hard rock at that time.

The natural minor scale provides many strong chord progressions and is usually the basis for minor-key songs. The sombre quality of the scale occurs because the harmonised scale creates a minor v chord, rather than the major V chord provided by the closely related Harmonic Minor scale.

The character notes are the natural 2nd and b6th of the scale. Moving from the 2nd up to the b3rd, or from the b6th to the 5th step of the scale with a melody or riff will help you to hear Aeolian's dark mood clearly. Our musical examples home in on these specific intervals.

E Aeolian/Natural Minor: Formula 1 2 b3 4 5 b6 b7

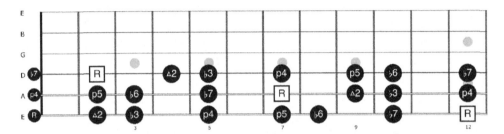

E Aeolian/Natural Minor

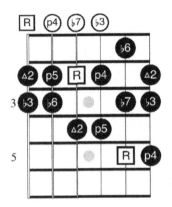

The Aeolian mode harmonised:

i	ii°	bIII	iv	v	bVI	bVII
Em	F#dim	G	Am	Bm	C	D

Common Chord Progressions:

34

Songs that use the Aeolian mode:

Metallica – Fade to Black
Iron Maiden – The Loneliness of the Long Distance Runner
Judas Priest – Breaking the Law
Ozzy Osbourne – Crazy Train
Muse – Time is Running Out
Rammstein – Reise, Reise
Slipknot – Sulfur

The first example is written in the style of British heavy metal bands like Iron Maiden and Judas Priest. It outlines a common rock guitar progression and ends with a scale fill that highlights the character notes of the Aeolian mode.

Example 4a:

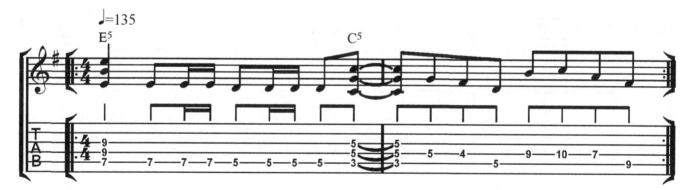

The following riff is a repeating, one-bar pattern that outlines the Aeolian mode while a second guitar uses power chords to play an Aeolian chord progression.

When playing with another guitarist, take the time to arrange complementary parts rather just playing in unison.

Example 4b:

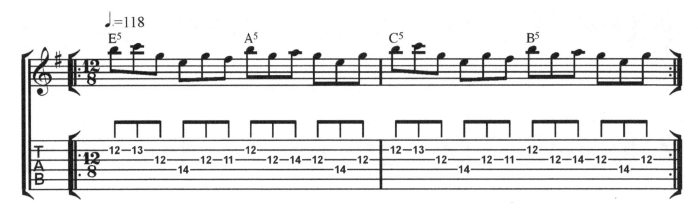

Listen to the way Hetfield and Hammett use the two guitars to complement each other in classic Metallica songs, creating a more interesting texture.

The third Aeolian riff is in the style of more melodic bands like The Offspring or Rufio, who mixed melodic post-hardcore punk and metal in the '90s. Use downstrokes for a driving rhythmic sound. Some palm muting on the bass notes will help to emphasise the melody.

Example 4c:

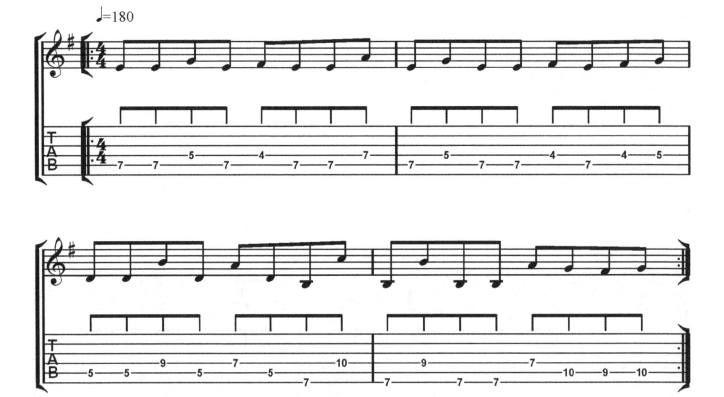

Notice also how the lowest note changes throughout the riff while the overall rhythmic pattern stays the same. This implies a sense of moving harmony through the riff, which could be further developed by effective bass guitar writing.

The Harmonic Minor Scale

The Harmonic Minor scale is very popular in the neoclassical style that was pioneered by Uli Jon Roth, Richie Blackmore and Yngwie Malmsteen in the '80s. These players combined metal guitar with a vocabulary drawn from classical composers such as Nicolo Paganini and J.S. Bach. The neoclassical style influenced heavy metal, and the Harmonic Minor scale is now used by many players.

The Harmonic Minor scale provides a sense of classical influence, as well as a hint of exoticism created by the tone-and-a-half interval between its b6 and 7th degree. Harmonic Minor differs from the natural minor scale by only one note (the 7th note is raised), but this causes a dramatic change in its flavour and the chords generated when it is harmonised.

The raised 7th turns the previously minor v chord into a (dominant) V7 chord, and the V7 – i chord progression is a big factor in the neoclassical sound of the Harmonic Minor scale. A diminished chord exists on the second degree of the scale (ii°), so diminished arpeggios are often heard in Harmonic Minor tunes. The character notes of Harmonic Minor are the b6 and the 7.

Be careful when playing the wider stretches found in this scale. Spreading your first and fourth fingers across five frets may seem uncomfortable at first, but your fingers will limber up with practice. Just be careful not to overstretch and damage your tendons.

E Harmonic Minor Formula: 1 2 b3 4 5 b6 7

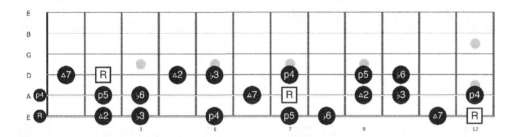

E Harmonic Minor

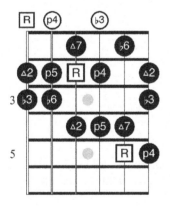

The Harmonic Minor scale harmonised:

i	ii°	bIII	iv	V7	bVI	vii°
Em	F#dim	G	Am	B7	C	D#dim

Common Chord Progressions:

Songs that use the Harmonic Minor scale:

Yngwie Malmsteen – *Vengeance*
Muse – *New Born*
Pantera – *Revolution in My Name* (bridge)
Children of Bodom – *Bed of Razors*
Trivium – *Entrance of the Conflagration* (pre-chorus)
Sonata Arctica – *8th Commandment*

Our first riff moves from an E5 power chord to a D#5 to capture the flavour of the E Harmonic Minor scale. The short sequence of thirds in bar four helps to accentuate the neoclassical sound. Listen to the audio example and check out how I vary the palm muting throughout the riff.

Being able to control and vary your palm muting is an important skill and which helps to bring your music to life. The power chords should be unmuted, the repeated Es should be heavily muted, and the final phrase should be lightly muted so that the pitches are still clearly audible.

Example 4d:

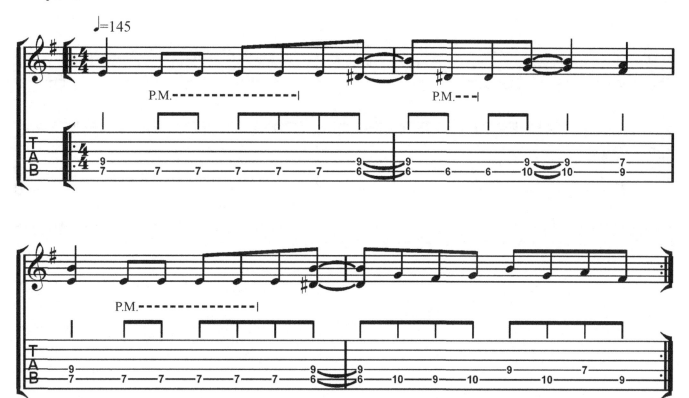

This next neoclassical-style riff is a great picking workout. Although the triplet feel gives the riff something of a swagger, the picking still needs to be precise and controlled. Note the inclusion of the diminished arpeggio in the last two beats of bar two. The Harmonic Minor scale can be implied by combining the tonic arpeggio (in this case E minor) with a diminished arpeggio played either a tone up or a semitone below the tonic (F#dim or D#dim).

Example 4e:

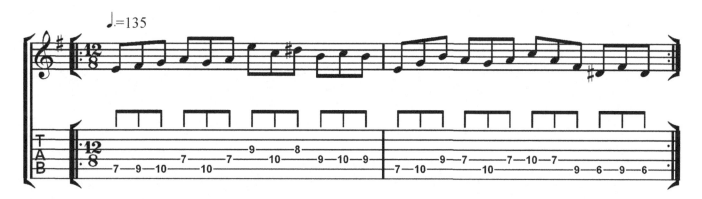

In the next riff, you may find the legato notes a little difficult to control at first, but these phrases help to break up the tonal consistency of the picking.

The semitone ideas target the b6 and natural 7th character notes of Harmonic Minor. In the second bar, the tension comes to a head as the accented notes form a descending B7 arpeggio (B A F# D#) that implies a progression of Em – B7 (i-V7)), typical of the Harmonic Minor harmony.

Example 4f:

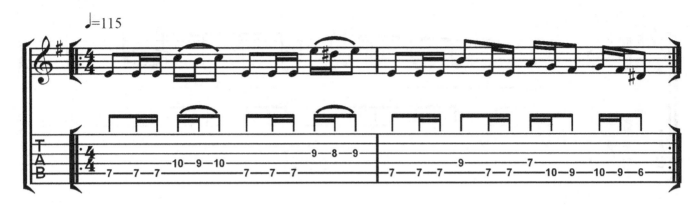

While the Harmonic Minor scale can be very effective in bringing a sense of drama to your playing, its distinctive flavour can become over-familiar if you're not careful. Be responsible and use in moderation!

The Phrygian Mode

The Phrygian mode is similar to Aeolian except that the 2nd note of Phrygian is flattened. This small difference creates a unique character. The Phrygian mode is often found in Persian and Indian music and provides an exotic Eastern sound when used in metal.

E Phrygian Formula: 1 b2 b3 4 5 b6 b7

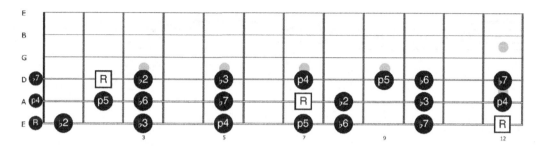

E Phrygian

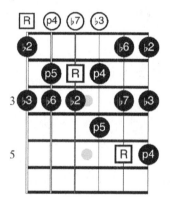

The Phrygian mode harmonised:

i	bII	bIII	iv	v°	bVI	bvii
Em	F	G	Am	Bdim	C	Dm

Common Chord Progressions:

Songs that use the Phrygian mode:

Slipknot – *Duality*
Mastodon – *Blood and Thunder*
Megadeth – *Take no Prisoners*
Al di Meola – *Race with the Devil on a Spanish Highway*
Metallica – *Wherever I may Roam*
Kreator – Violent Revolution

Here is a thunderous, heavy riff that exploits Phrygian's brooding b2 interval. The heaviest riffs are often the slow, dragging ones, rather than the ones that are fast and 'shredding'.

Dig in hard with your pick, and heavily palm mute the two 1/16th notes in bar one. Use wide vibrato on the final F and play it with attitude!

Example 4g:

Now for a typically aggressive riff akin to bands like Slayer and Exodus. Let the power chords ring clearly but palm mute the open low E string. The last beat could be picked but the legato provides a tonal contrast.

Example 4h:

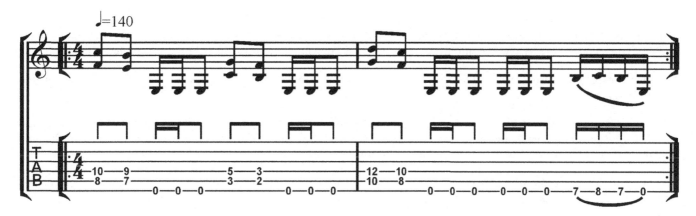

In the next example, try to keep the fretting hand locked into the octave shape when sliding around the fretboard just as we did with power chords in chapter two. The picking should be a loose strumming motion, so keep the other strings quiet by flattening the fretting hand index finger over the unused strings and releasing the pressure for the muted notes.

Example 4i:

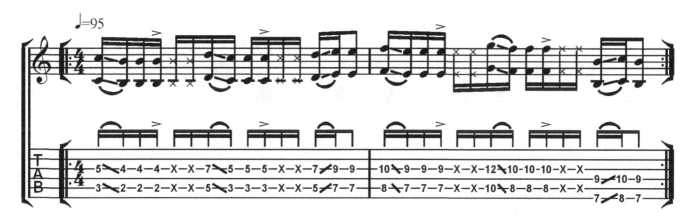

The Phrygian Dominant Mode

The Phrygian Dominant mode was popular with the original crop of neoclassical rock guitarists, but can also be found in thrash and death metal due to the far-reaching influence of players like Yngwie Malmsteen, Marty Friedman and Jason Becker.

Phrygian Dominant is closely related to the Phrygian mode, the only difference being the presence of a major 3rd compared the minor Phrygian mode.

The name Phrygian *Dominant* arises because the scale is built on the *dominant* (5th) degree of the Harmonic Minor scale. Phrygian Dominant contains the same notes as the Harmonic Minor scale but beginning on the 5th. For example, E Phrygian Dominant contains the same notes as A Harmonic Minor, but E is heard as the 'home' note, rather than A.

It can be difficult to hear the difference between modes just from playing scale shapes. The flavour really becomes apparent when you play them over the appropriate chords.

The sound of this scale is more tense and restless than the Harmonic Minor scale.

E Phrygian Dominant Formula: 1 b2 3 4 5 b6 b7

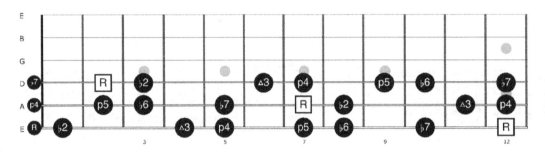

E Phrygian Dominant

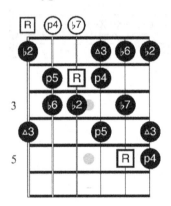

The Phrygian Dominant mode harmonised:

I7	bII	biii°	iv	v°	bVI⁺	bvii
E7	F	G#dim	Am	Bdim	Caug	Dm

Common Chord Progressions:

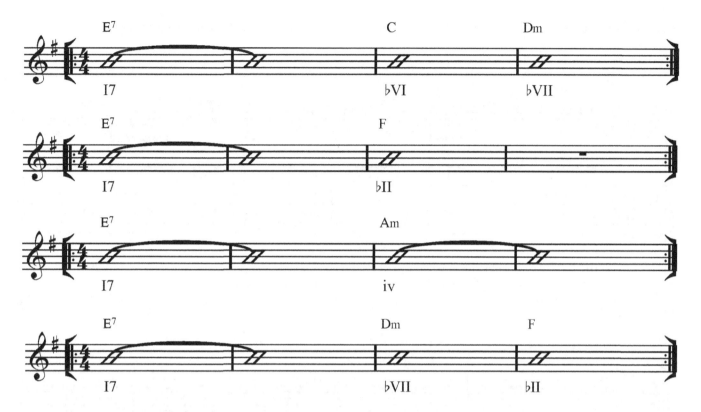

Songs that use the Phrygian Dominant mode:

The Scorpions – *Sails of Charon*
Symphony X – *Inferno (Unleash the Fire)*
Metallica – *Wherever I may Roam*
Death – *Pull the Plug*
Iced Earth - *Birth of the Wicked*
Dream Theater – *In the Name of God (main riff)*

The heavily distorted guitar tones used in metal can make full chords sound muddy and undefined when they are strummed, so using *arpeggios* to break up chords is a great approach. The following riff moves between some of the triads contained in the Phrygian Dominant scale.

Example 4j:

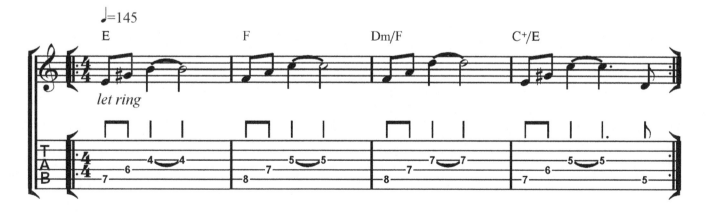

With slower arpeggios, note separation is less important than in melodic riffs, and allowing the notes to bleed into one another can be a useful creative effect. Roll down the volume on the guitar to make your amp/pedal provide less distortion for a bit more clarity.

The next riff is similar to Uli Jon Roth's work with The Scorpions. The 3, b2 and b6 of the scale are emphasised.

Example 4k:

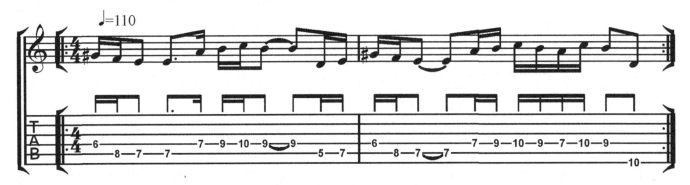

Our last Phrygian Dominant example highlights the adjacent major thirds (E-G# and F-A) contained within the scale. It then targets other major thirds in the scale before ending with a typical melodic turnaround.

Example 4l:

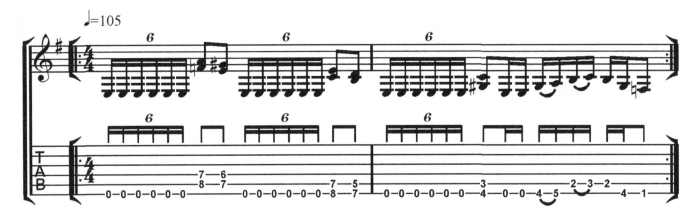

Keep the wrist loose for the fast picking 'cells'. You'll find that the sextuplets will take care of themselves if you focus on landing the final downstroke on the following beat. Angle the pick forward slightly to help slice through the string more easily.

The Locrian Mode

The Locrian mode is often neglected in the study of music. It is not used in popular music due to its dark and dissonant harmony, although this dissonance and instability can be exploited to create menacing, demonic-sounding riffs!

The Locrian mode does not contain a natural 5th interval from the root, instead having a diminished 5th or *tritone* (during the middle ages the tritone was superstitiously known as the devil's interval) and because of this inherent instability, the Locrian mode is normally used in combination with other minor scales such as Phrygian or Aeolian. Mixing these related modes provides a whole spectrum of tensions.

The Aeolian, Phrygian and Locrian modes represent a wide range of stability and dissonance although just one note changes between each scale.

E Locrian Formula: 1 b2 b3 4 b5 b6 b7

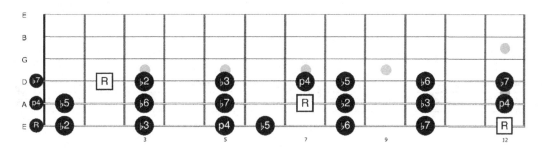

E Locrian

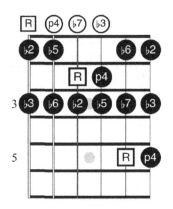

The Locrian mode harmonised:

i°	bII	biii	iv	bV	bVI	bvii
Edim	F	Gm	Am	Bb	C	Dm

Having said earlier that character notes are not normally found in a scale's tonic chord, it's worth noting that in this case it's the presence of the b5 that differentiates Locrian from Phrygian, and creates Locrian's unresolved flavour.

Common Chord Progressions:

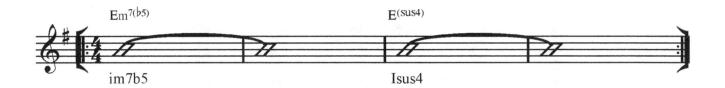

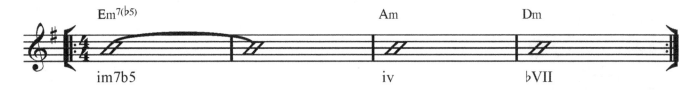

Songs that use the Locrian mode:

Metallica – Seek and Destroy
Slayer – Angel of Death
Metallica – Blackened

In example 4m the *tritone* (a distance of three tones) between the root and b5 is emphasised to bring out the full dissonance of the Locrian mode. The final bar uses two four-note patterns. First starting on the b5 and then on the b2.

Whether you decide to use down-picking or alternate picking, be sure to get the string crossing accurate.

Example 4m:

Norwegian Black Metal bands in the early '90s had a 'punk rock', lo-fi aesthetic to both their production and their playing. While these bands would have tremolo-picked the following riffs with less control, the bands that they influenced, such as Strapping Young Lad and Cryptopsy were much more technically precise. Aim for exact semiquavers here to lock in with the drum part.

Example 4n:

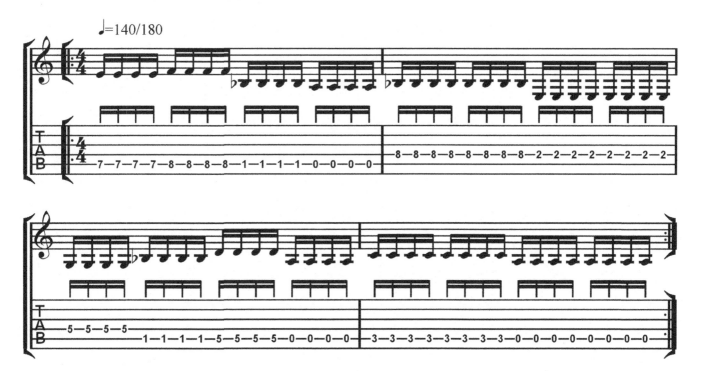

After that warp speed use of the Locrian mode, the following straight-ahead nu-metal inspired riff slows things down and focuses on groove and simplicity while leaning heavily on the tritone interval. The key to making this riff work is to really dig in with the pick to create a percussive sound. Lock in rhythmically with the drums to make it groove. It's almost like a heavy version of a funk guitar riff.

Example 4o:

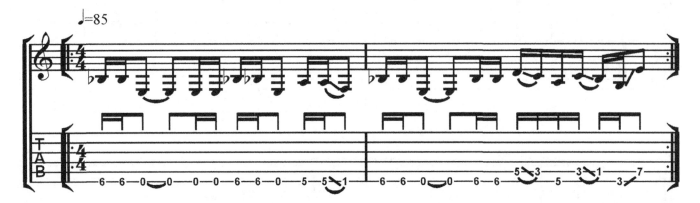

The nu-metal bands had the heaviness of metal but drew from alternative rock and grunge's sense of songwriting so they often avoided overly technical riffs, or lengthy instrumental sections. Many heavy metal fans and guitarists write off this whole subgenre but the change of aesthetic allowed a different range of influences to seep into metal.

Diminished Seventh Arpeggios

The word 'arpeggio' is just a posh was of saying 'play the notes of a chord separately'. Arpeggios are treated as melodic devices just like scales and modes, except they have wider intervals between each note.

A *diminished seventh* chord (different from the diminished triad found in the Locrian mode) is a four-note chord with the intervals 1, b3, b5, bb7. All of the notes in the chord are a minor third apart.

When the notes in a chord are all the same distance apart it is referred to as a *symmetrical* chord. The musical benefit of this characteristic is that any diminished motif can be shifted up or down in minor thirds while still staying within the tonality.

Diminished arpeggios are not found in the major scale but occur in both the Harmonic Minor and Phrygian Dominant scales. Given their symmetrical nature, there are only three possible different diminished arpeggios before you repeat one in a different inversion.

E Diminished Arpeggio: Formula 1 b3 b5 bb7

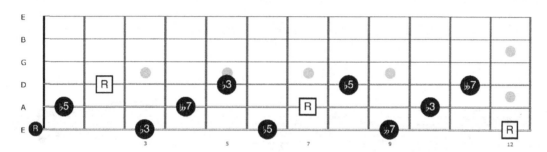

E Diminished Arpeggio

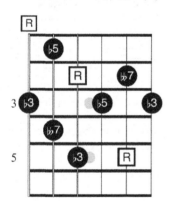

Songs that use diminished arpeggios:

Symphony X – *Seven*
Yngwie Malmsteen – *Arpeggios from Hell*
Nevermore - *Born*
Arch Enemy – *Nemesis* (bridge)
Necrophagist – Diminished to B

The following example shows that music theory is quite flexible when dissonance is the objective, and the strongly recognisable sound of the diminished arpeggio allows you to combine them at will without worrying about a parent scale or tonality. There are only three different diminished arpeggios (because each *inversion* is still a diminished arpeggio.) Rather than using all three, try picking two out of the three to maintain a cohesive but dissonant sound.

Example 4p combines the diminished arpeggios of E,G,Bb,C# and F#,A,C,D#, spending two beats on each before shifting from one to the other.

Using legato should help with the string crossing here but keep an eye on your timing!

Example 4p:

Jeff Loomis frequently used diminished ideas during his time with Nevermore, and this next riff is inspired by their earlier albums. In the next example, I wasn't thinking about a specific scale, even though the open E string gives a sense of tonal centre. The ear accepts the overall effect because of the distinct, recognisable pattern of each diminished arpeggio.

Example 4q:

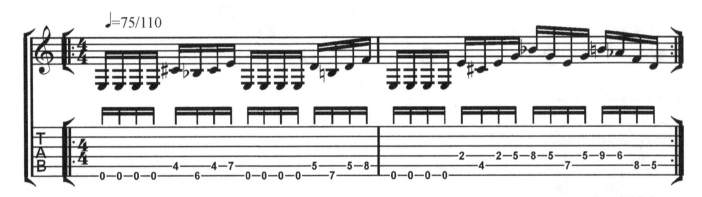

In example 4r, we use just one diminished arpeggio but move the same pattern up and down through its different inversions.

Although the pattern stays the same, notice how it is re-fingered in bar three to make the position shift at the start of bar four easier. The added open Es in bars three and four help with the position change, as well as providing variation to the riff pattern.

Example 4r:

To learn to use the diminished arpeggio with other scales, try combining riff ideas from Harmonic Minor or Phrygian Dominant with diminished arpeggios. From the harmonising and chord progression sections of each scale subchapter we can see that a diminished arpeggio is actually hidden within both those scales, so you should find that they flow one into the other nicely.

Good combinations to experiment with would be A Harmonic Minor with D diminished, or B Phrygian Dominant with C diminished.

Mixing Scales

In practice, musicians often mix together several scales to create riffs from a chromatic palette of notes, and in thrash and death metal it is common to take a motif or a single interval and move it up or down in semitones.

Given that making interesting and exciting music is our goal, combining elements of different shapes and scales without worrying about 'correct theory' is as much of a legitimate approach as playing within the confines of one scale.

In the end, the only judge of good or bad is your ear and, to use an old cliché, 'if it sounds right, it is!'. Whether your compositions are built on theoretical understanding or not isn't really that important.

Songs that mix scales or shift motifs up and down:

Slayer – *Raining Blood*
Metallica – *Disposable Heroes*
Meshuggah – *Straws Pulled at Random*
Slipknot – *Surfacing*
Cynic – *Veil of Maya*
Megadeth – *Rust in Peace... Polaris*
Building on the previous diminished arpeggio examples (that strayed from the confines of a single key), the following examples are only concerned with the *effect* of each note over the E pedal.

It is possible to view our first example in terms of where the parts are borrowed from: Locrian (Bb, F), the Blues scale (B-Bb) and Aeolian (F#-G), but it makes more sense to just see semitone pairs moving around the root and to let your ear decide what works best.

Example 4s:

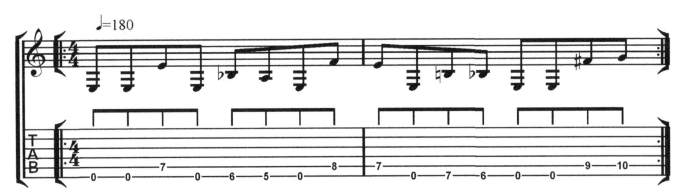

The next example is a James Hetfield inspired riff featuring power chords and down-picking. The riff includes chromatic movement but still outlines an E minor pattern.

Practice moving the power chords around accurately at a slower tempo because they can easily get out of control during long, fast phrases.

Example 4t:

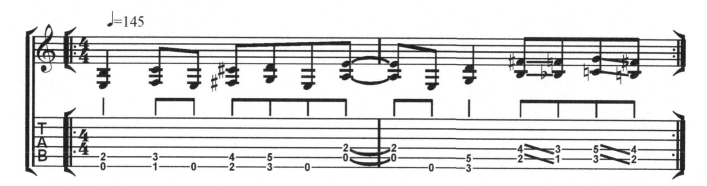

Our final example is in the style of bands like Slayer and Exodus. The motif in bars one and three is moved chromatically in the answering phrases in bars two and four. Getting the fingering tidy here can be a little tricky, so take it slowly to ensure you're using the most comfortable approach for you.

Example 4u:

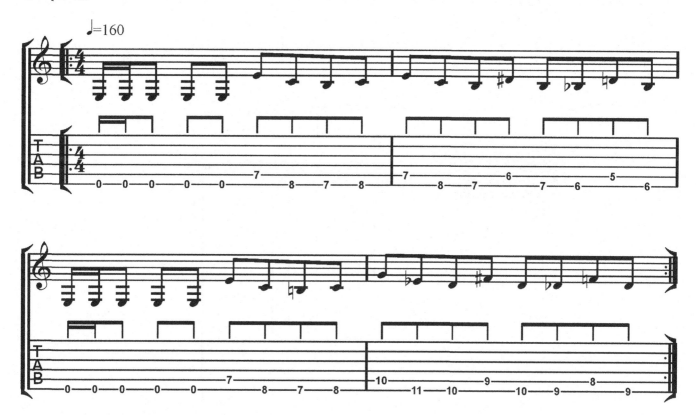

Hopefully this inspection of the various scales and arpeggios found in metal has given you a better understanding of how riffs are constructed, and why certain riffs sound the way they do. It's worth trying to think creatively and emotionally about this information, rather than getting swept up by all the theory. What does each scale's flavour make you think of, and does it makes you feel?

Keep your ears open for scales and modes as you work through the other chapters and identify the melodic devices used.

Chapter Five: Harmonics

After all those chugging rhythms and sludgy power chords it's time for some contrast. When listening to metal, you've probably heard some high-pitched, piercing notes interspersed between the low riffs. These notes are called *harmonics*, and in this chapter we'll discuss different types of harmonics and how they're achieved.

Rhythm guitar playing can sometimes sound a bit sludgy and nebulous, particularly when the guitars are down-tuned to a lower register. Harmonics can break up this wall of sound and help to accentuate important beats.

A brief physics lesson...

A guitar string vibrates to produce the sound we hear, and the rate at which it vibrates dictates the pitch of the note. However, to create the *tone* that you hear, strings also vibrate in a complex combination of higher frequencies simultaneously. These frequencies are known as harmonics or overtones.

The relative loudness of each overtone defines the perceived *timbre* of an instrument and allows our ears to distinguish the characteristics of notes played on different instruments (or between different strings on the guitar). This is why a clarinet sounds different from a cello when playing the same pitch.

The wavelength of the fundamental note is equal to the length of the string. The harmonic overtones vibrate in divisions of this length.

Without getting too scientific, a harmonic can only be found at *node* points along the string where the scale length can be divided into equal divisions or ratios. The following diagram illustrates why the harmonics fall where they do on the fretboard.

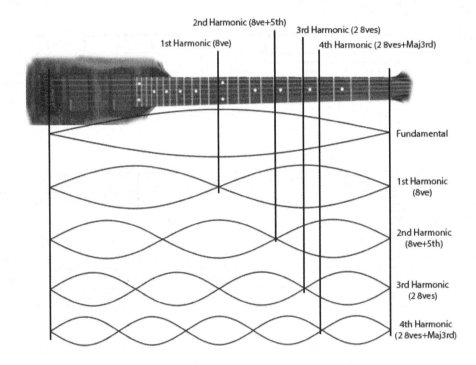

Harmonics are played by isolating the higher frequency overtones and removing the fundamental pitch of the open string by manipulating the strings at node points.

On the guitar, it is possible to create a range of natural and 'artificial' harmonics and these will be discussed in turn.

Natural Harmonics

Natural harmonics are the most widely used harmonic and also the easiest to play. Natural harmonics are not found on every fret, they are only available at the *node* points as shown in the diagram. The strongest ones are at the 12th, 7th and 5th frets.

To perform a natural harmonic, gently touch the string at the 12th fret, but don't press down onto the fretboard. Make contact directly over the fret wire rather than behind it. When you pick the string the sound should be pure and bell-like.

Here is a preliminary figure to help you isolate the technique before working through the riffs. In the first bar lay the index finger across the whole fretboard, making sure that all the strings are ringing out and are not muted accidentally. In the second bar try to keep each harmonic separate by just using a smaller area of the pad of the finger. Remember, you are not fully fretting the note, just gently touching the string above the fret.

Fig. 1

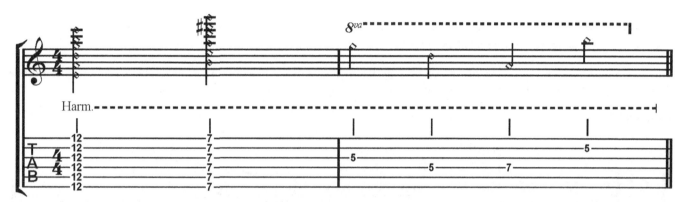

Our first riff is inspired by Slayer's South of Heaven/Seasons in the Abyss period and contrasts a chugging, muted riff with chiming bell-like natural harmonics.

Ringing harmonics can be beautiful when played with a clean tone, but they can easily get out of control when distortion is added. When combining riffs with harmonics, it's very important to mute the unplayed strings and learn to deaden harmonics after they have been played.

Use the palm of the picking hand and the unused fingers of the fretting hand to mute them.

Example 5a:

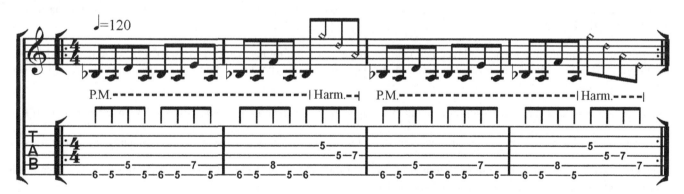

Use the pad of the first finger to play the fifth fret harmonics, aiming to place it across the strings so that it mutes the B while you play the G. It should also move to mute the G when playing the D string. Repeat the process with the ring finger on the seventh fret.

In the following example, we alternate a low, single-note riff with two different harmonics to build your control.

Example 5b:

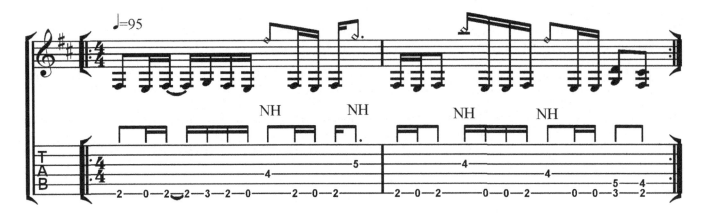

Use the pinkie to catch the harmonics while the first finger is laid across the bass strings to keep them silent. Take the time to find the position that works for your hand and neck profile.

The menacing feel of the following riff is enhanced by the inclusion of the haunting harmonics. The low E string can drone throughout and the harmonics will benefit by being allowed to overlap to create a suitably dark dissonance!

Example 5c:

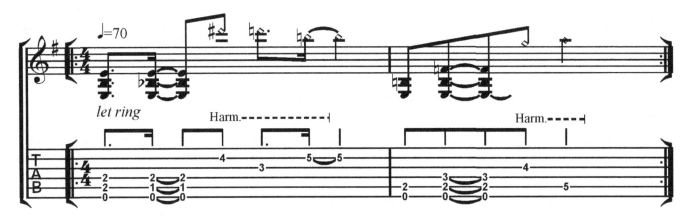

Harmonics at the fourth fret and below can be more difficult to execute than those at the 12th, 7th and 5th frets, but using distortion, the bridge pickup and picking near the bridge will all help the harmonics ring out successfully. These higher harmonics are demonstrated in example 5c.

The third-fret harmonic in bar one is played just in front of the fret wire, rather than directly over it because that is where the harmonic node falls. This slight mismatch between fret position and the harmonic node is a good illustration of how true intonation and our equal tempered system diverge.

The next harmonic idea is more of a sound effect than a proper riff so this technique is often used as an embellishment or fill.

We are going to play a series of natural harmonics by lightly brushing the E string between the neck pickup and highest frets.

Dimebag Darrell and Mark Tremonti (Alterbridge) have used this effect, and bassist Billy Sheehan often uses this idea in his unaccompanied bass solos with Mr Big and other bands.

Example 5d:

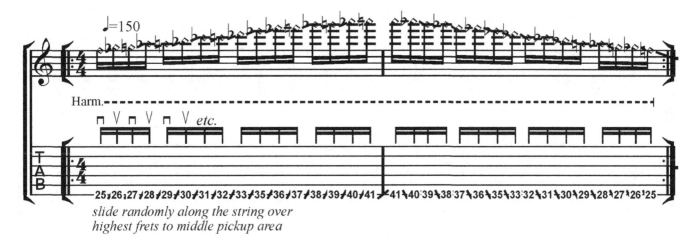

slide randomly along the string over
highest frets to middle pickup area

Pinch Harmonics

Pinch harmonics (also affectionately known as 'squealies') are the most aggressive sounding harmonics. Unlike natural harmonics, they are created entirely by the picking hand, leaving the fretting free to add vibrato and bends to the pinched note. When combined with rock vibrato, pinch harmonics are a great way to accentuate notes in solos.

The pinch technique itself can be tricky to grasp initially, so be prepared for some trial and error before it clicks. In essence, pick the string with a downstroke aiming to push the pick *through* the string so that the outside edge of your thumb touches the string immediately after the pick does. It helps to leave only a small amount of the pick's tip protruding from your fingers.

As soon as the thumb has made contact with the string remove your hand, otherwise you will deaden the string completely.

Changing where you pick the string will change the pitch of the harmonic produced. Higher pitched harmonics will be found closer to the bridge pickup and lower pitched ones are created over the neck pickup. Experiment by moving your hand up and down the string between the bridge pickup and the neck.

Fig. 2

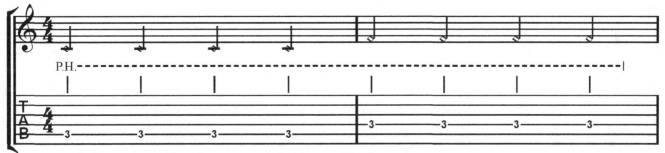

pick from over neck pickup towards bridge and back again

Our first pinch harmonic riff example is slow and heavy, allowing you plenty of space to focus on the pinch harmonics.

Example 5e:

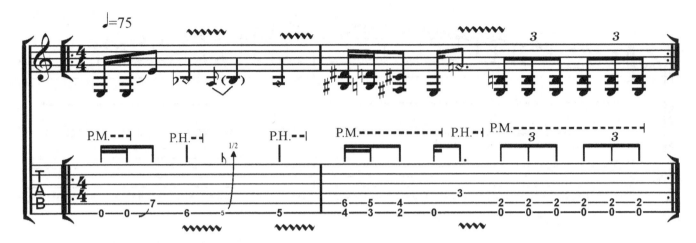

The bend in bar one should be slow and exaggerated and the palm muting should almost deaden the completely to get a very percussive sound. Accentuate the wide vibrato.

The next example is in the style of Slipknot's guitarists Mick Thompson and Jim Root and combines tight staccato rhythms with pinch harmonics.

Getting a strong vibrato on the harmonics really helps them to sing out. I chose to pick the first harmonic near to the bridge to create a higher pitch, and to pick the second harmonic over the neck pickup to produce a lower pitch.

Example 5f:

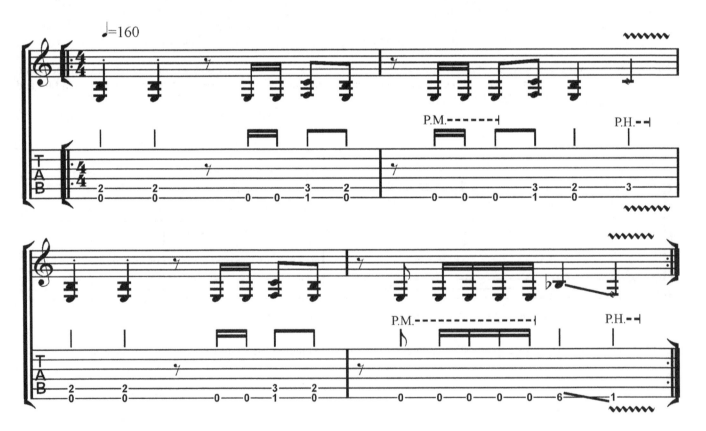

The above riff contrasts cropped low chugs with harmonics, so be sure to mute carefully with the fretting hand and keep the first few notes between each power chord detached.

The repeated harmonics in the following riff can be hard to nail, especially if pinched harmonics are new to you. The principle is similar to example 5d, but now we are using the thumb of the picking hand to touch the harmonic points instead of the fretting hand.

As you pick down through the string to catch the pinched harmonics, move the picking hand along the area from the bridge to the top of the fretboard to bring out different pitches. Revert back to normal picking for the power chords.

Example 5g:

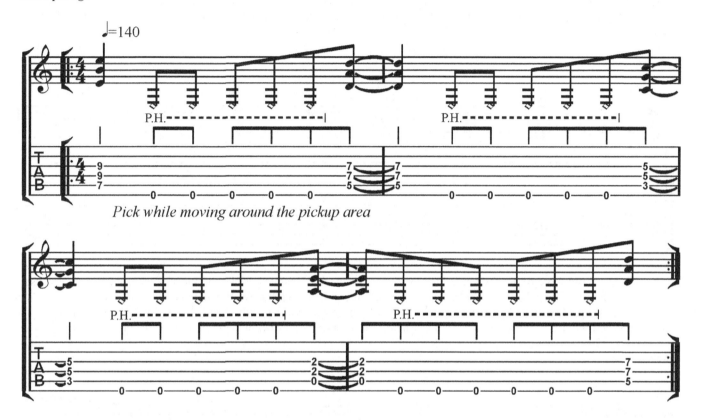

Pick while moving around the pickup area

The final example involves both hands and demonstrates how to move from alternate picking to pinch harmonics. Perfect the string crossing slowly, and keep the first finger of the fretting hand flattened to mute unused strings.

Example 5h:

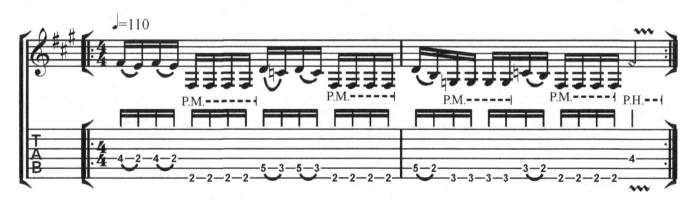

Tapped Harmonics

Tapped harmonics are less common than the previous techniques but sound great when played with distortion. They are a fun way to decorate a note *after* it has been picked. The idea is to play a note normally and then to quickly tap on the fret wire 12 frets above the fretted note. The tapped note is not held: instead you should aim to bounce off the string as quickly as possible.

Vibrato, bends and whammy can all be added after the harmonic is achieved. Try some tapped harmonics in isolation to start with. Remember the bracketed fret number in the tab corresponds to the tapped note and the previous note should still be held down.

Fig. 3

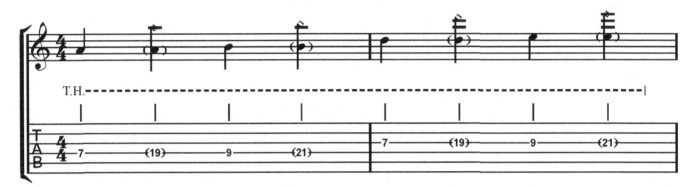

In example 5i, a 16th-note triplet rhythm is interspersed with tapped harmonics. Make the most of these harmonics and use a slow, wide vibrato. Good vibrato will enhance the 'scream' effect of the harmonic. When changing between rhythm and lead ideas, be sure to quickly mute the unused strings. Generally, the palm of the picking hand should cover the bass strings when playing lead and the fretting hand fingers should lie across the treble strings when playing rhythm on the bass strings.

Example 5i:

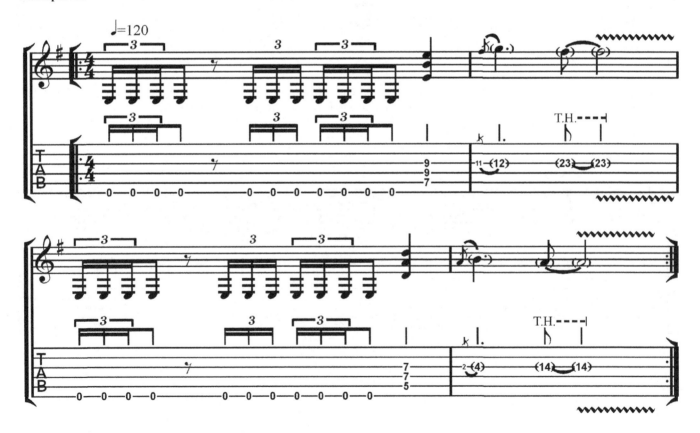

Example 5j shows how tapped harmonics can be used to embellish a sustaining chord as well as single notes.

The first four harmonics are tapped 12 frets above the fretted note. In the second shape, the tap is 7 frets higher than the fretted note producing harmonics an octave and a fifth higher.

Example 5j:

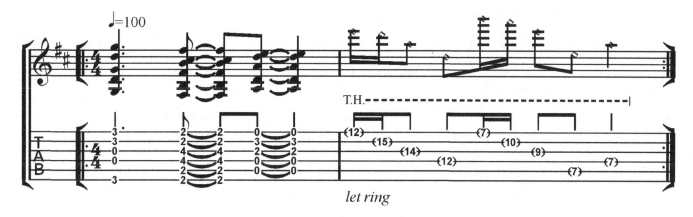

Note that the fret numbers in bar two of the tablature signify the frets that the *picking* hand should tap to create the harmonics, while the final Dsus2 chord remains held from the previous bar.

Dream Theater bassist, John Myung can be heard using harmonic ideas like this on *Images and Words* and *Awake,* and they work equally well on guitar. Moderate distortion will provide 'glisten' to the harmonics without turning them into poorly defined mush. Try rolling the volume pot on your guitar down to about seven to get less distortion from your amp.

Harmonics are a great way to widen your palette of sounds, but also think about their placement within the song when writing riffs. For example, a riff that is accompanying a strong vocal melody may not be the best place to let rip with squealing pitch harmonics. Likewise, a held chord under a keyboard or drum embellishment may be all that's needed and the addition of touch harmonics would clutter the texture. Knowing when to hold back will help make your writing more dynamic and effective.

Songs that use Harmonics:

The Dixie Dregs – *Take it Off the Top* (intro)
Ozzy Osbourne/Jake E. Lee – *Bark at the Moon* (half time bridge)
Megadeth – *Tornado of Souls* (intro)
Dream Theater – *Erotomania* (final intro reprise)
Pantera – *Cowboys from Hell* (post-solo riff)
Machinehead – *Imperium*
Black Label Society – *Suicide Messiah*
Slipknot – *Duality* (pre-verse/bridge)
Racer X – *Superheroes* (pre-chorus)

Chapter Six: Riff Writing

So far we have looked at the many technical and theoretical aspects of playing metal guitar riffs. These should help you tackle your favourite songs and work on any technical challenges that arise.

My goal in writing this book was to help you develop the creativity and musical understanding to start writing new music. I want to continue now by focussing on the compositional aspect of metal guitar.

Once we have absorbed musical information (such as scales and technique) we must learn how to apply that knowledge and form a musical vocabulary. In this section of the book I'll be using the techniques and scales we've already looked at, but with an emphasis on using them creatively. I will examine how metal riffs are commonly constructed and look at some ideas you can use to get writing authentic sounding riffs yourself.

Most rock and metal riffs are built from a small melodic idea that is varied on repeating phrases. The purpose of a riff is to be a memorable, instrumental idea that energetically drives the song forward. Riffs can support vocal sections or instrumental solos where complex melodic ideas would be cluttered and distracting.

We will look at several compositional tools that are at your disposal such as pedal point, sequences and odd time signatures.

Pedal Point Riffs

Pedal point is the technique of alternating a constant note with other notes or a changing melody. The pedal could also be held throughout as a drone while other notes move against it.

The term 'pedal point' originates from classical music, and is a reference to organ music where the lowest notes are played using the foot pedals rather than the keyboard. It is normal for the pedal note to be the bass note in the texture, but a high pedal is also possible, this is called an 'inverted' pedal.

There are plenty of classical motifs that are actually quite 'metal', and pedal point is definitely a common factor. Listen for pedal points in the intro to *Summer - Presto* from Vivaldi's Four Seasons and J.S. Bach's much loved Toccata and Fugue in D Minor (which were undoubtedly influences on neoclassical rock guitarists.)

Pedal tone riffs were particularly popular with the thrash metal bands of the '80s and our first example clearly illustrates the concept. In example 6a we alternate the notes of the A Natural Minor scale with the open A string.

Take care to keep the unused strings quiet throughout the exercise by gently dampening the higher strings with spare fingers.

Try to use down-picking throughout to get the best tone and attack.

Example 6a:

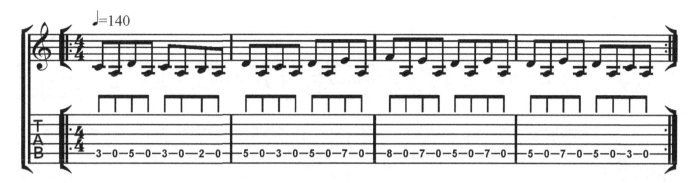

The next idea is similar, but the moving pitches are all on the off beats. Changing rhythmic emphasis can make a huge difference to how a riff feels to play. Master these first two examples so that you can comfortably place the fretted notes either on, or off the beat.

Example 6b:

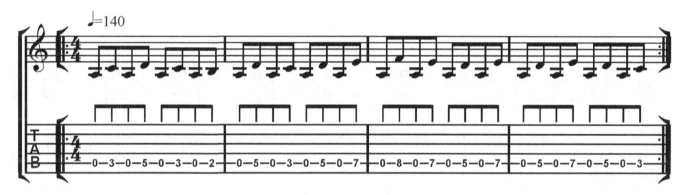

These riffs are also a great way to learn scales along the length of each string while also practicing picking control and stamina. Try playing different scales along the length of each string to create pedal point riffs.

In example 6c, we add extra open strings to the idea so that the fretted notes occur on a mixture of on and off beats. By creating less predictable rhythmic patterns for the melody, you can maintain the listeners' interest.

Example 6c:

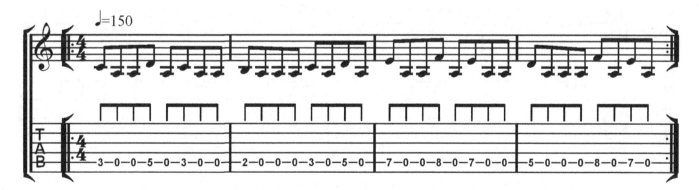

Try to create your own riffs in this style by varying the pitches and the rhythms.

The previous examples alternate between a single note and the pedal tone, but now we will alternate *two* notes with the pedal tone. Pay attention to the rhythmic phrasing here; the two fretted notes combined with one pedal note means that the pattern repeats every three notes. This creates what is known as a *cross-rhythm*.

Listen to the audio example to help you to feel the rhythm correctly.

Example 6d:

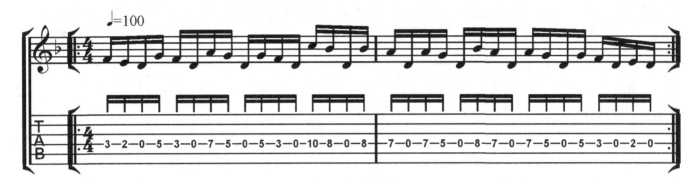

While the *motif* in the previous example was the moving part, the next example uses a pedal motif that alternates with a moving single note. This example is a great string crossing exercise to develop alternate picking, and will quickly help you to increase your accuracy and control.

Example 6e:

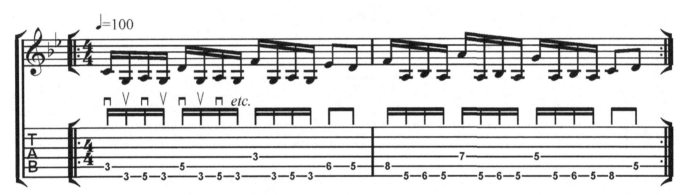

The pedal point in example 6f is combined with the reverse gallop rhythm. Be careful to synchronise your hands to ensure that the melody is heard clearly. Try to maintain an 1/8th note pulse of down-strokes, and use alternate picking for the 1/16th notes.

Example 6f:

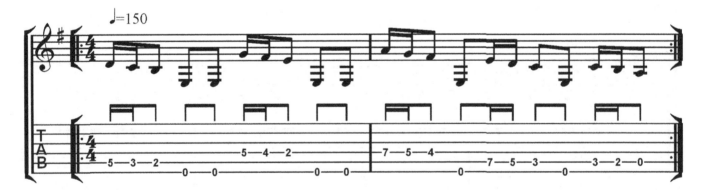

Most metal riffs are in 'open string' keys such as E and A, however, this next example is in the less common key of Eb minor.

The lack of open strings in this key makes riffing more difficult. The more complex fingering needed is a worthwhile challenge as it allows you to re-arrange existing songs and transpose ideas to different keys. To illustrate, example 6g is, in fact, example 6a transposed from E minor to Eb minor.

Example 6g:

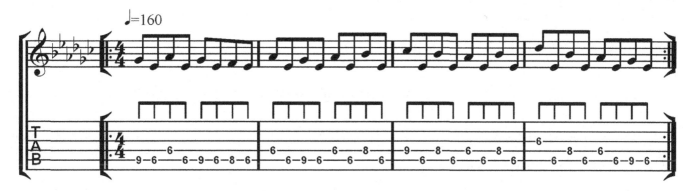

The following example requires relaxed alternate picking to play the fast 1/16th notes. Keeping the arc of the pick motion as small as possible will help to achieve the speed. It is common for this kind of idea to be played in unison with the double kick drum pattern so you must be rhythmically accurate to stay locked in time. The accenting technique discussed in chapter three will pay dividends here.

Accenting the fretted notes will help you to keep time. Using legato for the last two beats of bar two varies the tone of the riff and also gives the picking hand a brief rest to reduce the risk of cramping up.

Example 6h:

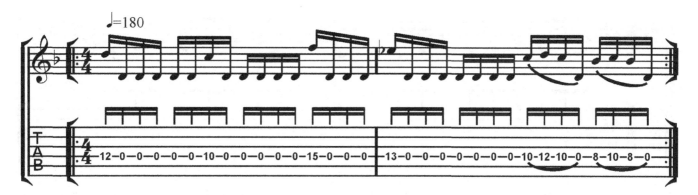

Example 6i is another death metal riff using an open E pedal tone against a short chromatic motif. Again, try to accent the motif with the picking hand once you have developed enough control to play it accurately. Accenting certain notes brings riffs to life by adding a sense of light and shade.

Example 6i:

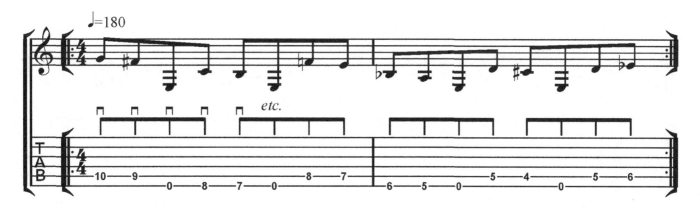

Riffs that feature pedal point:

Iron Maiden – *Wasted Years*

Ozzy Osbourne – *Crazy Train* (verse)
Metallica – *Damage Inc.* (bridge)
Yngwie Malmsteen – *Vengeance*
Dream Theater – *Panic Attack* (intro)
Muse – *Stockholm Syndrome*

Sequencing Riffs

Music with the most powerful impact strikes a balance between unity and variety. In other words, it should be able to hold the audience's interest by developing in new way, while still relating to what has already been heard. Sequences are a great way to achieve this kind of structure and are a popular device in all styles of music.

Baroque harpsichord music was full of sequences, and this proved to be a great influence on rock soloing in the '70s and '80s. If this interests you, I can recommend the inventions of J.S. Bach, and sonatas of Scarlatti to improve your understanding of scale patterns.

The following simple rock riff uses the A minor pentatonic scale. The triplet feel synchronises with the descending sequence of three notes. If you use legato, be careful to get the timing as precise as if you were picking.

Example 7a:

Our second example uses a pattern of three notes in B natural minor but now the example is played with a straight feel. This means that the start of each group of three falls on a different part of the beat each time to create a commonly used cross-rhythm.

If you take some time to internalise the rhythm, you will start to feel both the three-note groupings and the 1/4 note pulse simultaneously. Accent the first note of each three-note motif and tap your foot on the 1/4 note pulse.

Example 7b:

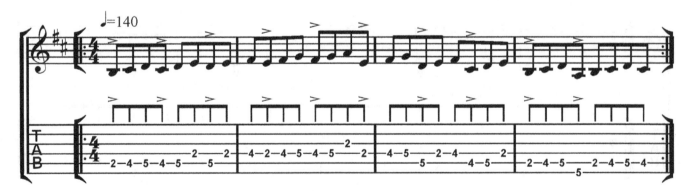

Now try mixing fragments of this scale sequence with picking cells on an open string pedal note. Notice how the timing of the riff becomes syncopated by varying the length of each sequence pattern. Take your time to get the rhythm memorised accurately before speeding up.

Example 7c:

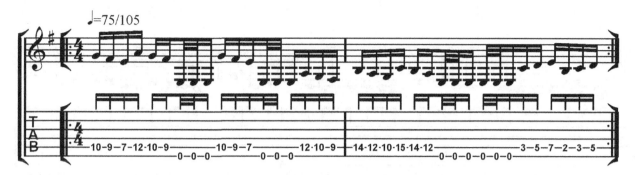

In example 7d, a two-bar pedal point idea is sequenced through several steps of the C# minor scale. Although the chord symbols show power chords, the double-stops in the riff change to accommodate the expected major or minor tonality of each pedal note.

Consistent down-picking would normally be used to play this idea, but you may like to try using hybrid picking. Plucking the high double stops with the middle and ring fingers together helps them to jump out with more twang and attack.

Example 7d:

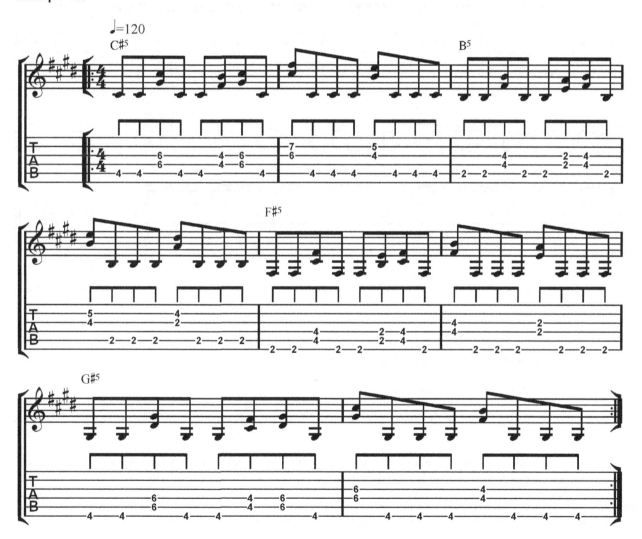

Example 7e is a long phrase in E Phrygian that moves through different positions on the neck. The initial phrase is adapted to fit the notes of the scale in each shape.

Example 7e:

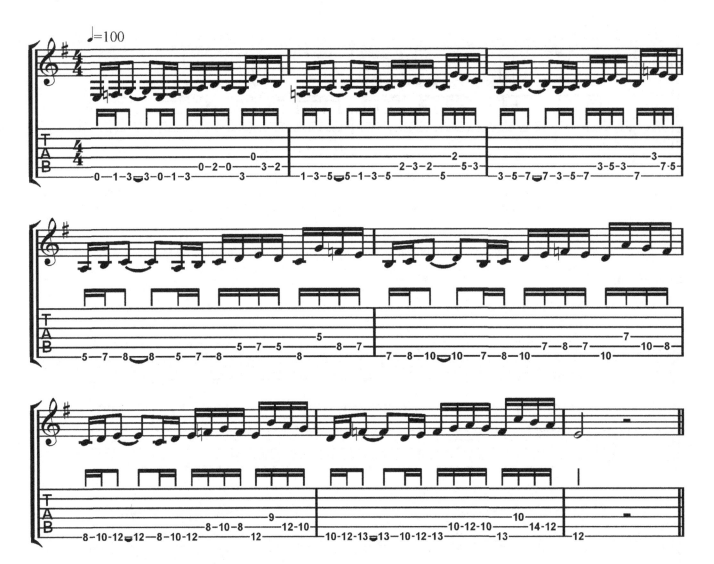

This idea could be played by moving across the strings in one position, but there are three main advantages to shifting it along the neck.

- It is easier to visualise for the fretting hand

- The picking part remains the same for every iteration in the sequence

- The tone of the notes remains more consistent

Always try to play on the lowest strings of the guitar when a thick rock tone is desired because they provide more bass and midrange frequencies.

It is possible to create interesting rhythmic variations by applying mathematical rules to the development of a musical idea. Example 7f contains an idea characteristic of progressive metal bands like Dream Theater and Spastic Ink.

There are two sequences at work in the following example. Firstly, the melodic notes move up through the E Aeolian scale with each repetition of the phrase. Secondly, we gradually truncate our original four-beat pattern, so the repetitions get shorter in length.

In bar three, the final four notes of the original riff are discarded. Two bars later, the first four notes of the pattern are removed, and again at bar seven another four notes are lost, leaving the final two repetitions containing only four notes from the original sixteen. Count carefully to avoid getting lost.

Example 7f:

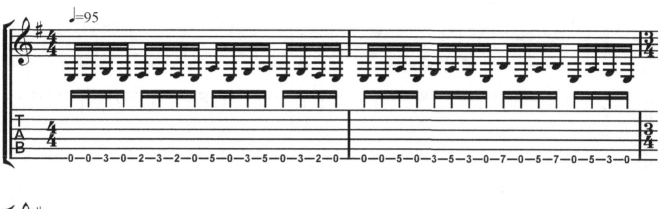

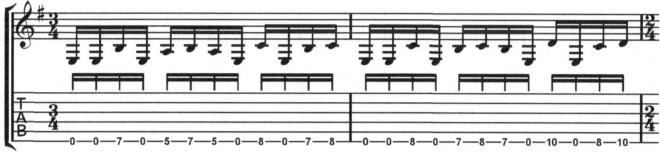

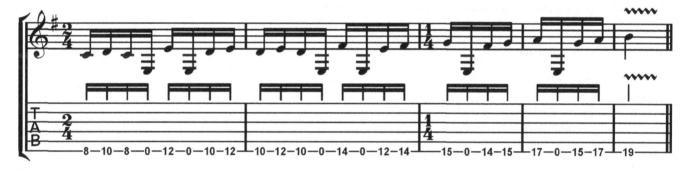

This gradual shortening of the pattern delivers a sense of speeding up, although the tempo does not change. The effect of this developing musical idea is to build to a strong climax after the tension of the rhythmic and melodic sequences.

The next example develops the idea of 'subtractive' rhythmic sequences. This time we have a scale pattern that lasts for eight 1/16th notes. Every time the phrase repeats we lose a note until only one is left. The process then reverses and adds one note at a time to grow again to the original motif.

To help with timing and control use alternate picking, but be aware that the phrase will sometimes start on a down-stroke and sometimes on an upstroke because of the changing phrase lengths. It is good to practice phrases starting on both an upstroke and a downstroke to prepare you for these uneven types of riffs.

Example 7g:

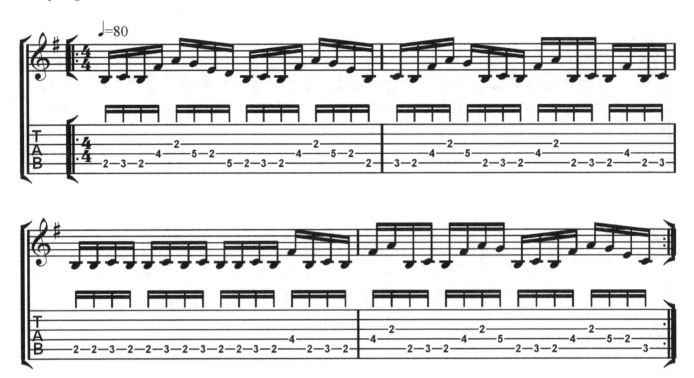

The piece *Coming Together* by contemporary American composer Frederic Rzewski is a great example of this kind of pattern based writing

Riffs that Contain Sequencing:

Racer X – Technical Difficulties
Nevermore – Born
Lovefist – Dangerous B*stard (bridge riff)
Black Sabbath – Symptom of the Universe
Pantera – Cowboys from Hell
Dream Theater – Fatal Tragedy (structure of guitar/keys solos)
Angra – Speed

Odd Time Signatures

The last few examples delved briefly into the world of odd time signatures, but so far nearly all of the examples in the book have been written in 4/4. The vast majority of music you have ever heard is written in 4/4, which is why it sounds so natural. However, depending on your cultural heritage, other metres like 5/4, 7/4 or 7/8 may also feel completely natural and easy to dance to.

Odd time signatures are particularly common in traditional Balkan and North African music.

Many metal bands, particularly those influenced by world music or progressive rock, have used odd time signatures for entire songs without any unbalancing effect (for example Tool's *Jambi*, or Alice in Chains' *Them Bones*), although odd time signatures normally do create a sense of musical tension.

Just as dissonant harmony creates a tension that needs to resolve, uneven rhythmic phrasing also creates a 'metric dissonance' that is resolved by moving to an even time signature.

The key to playing in any time signature (and developing a strong sense of time in general) is learning to feel the rhythm of the music instinctively. Counting out loud is a good start, but repetition and listening to a lot of music in different metres are both vital if you are to master odd time.

Let's recap how rhythms can be divided so as to help understand how odd time signatures are phrased and felt.

As you know, a bar of 4/4 is divided equally into four 1/4 notes. Each 1/4 note is divided into two 1/8th notes and these can be further divided into 1/16th notes:

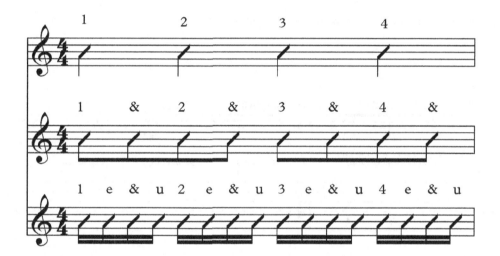

A bar of 6/8 is divided into six 1/8th notes with the accents on the first and fourth 1/8th note. Although a bar of 6/8 is the same length as a bar of 3/4, 6/8 feels like two groups of triplets. 3/4 feels like a single, slower group of three.

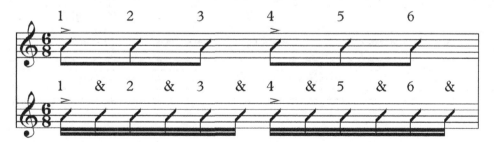

Learning to feel combinations of triple and even times opens a new rhythmic vocabulary. This kind of feel is common to the traditional music of several Balkan countries, and in the work of 20th Century classical composers like Bartok and Stravinsky, who were inspired by the music of other cultures. In fact, many metal musicians cite Stravinsky as an inspiration, so check out a recording of his bombastic orchestral masterpiece 'The Rite of Spring' – it's pure metal!

To begin our look at odd time signatures, we will start with 6/8. Though not an 'odd' time signature, 6/8 is less common than 4/4, and exploring its possibilities will help you get to grips with other, more complex meters.

Tap your foot on the first and fourth beats of the bar. Listen to the click in the audio to help you feel the three note phrasing.

Example 8a:

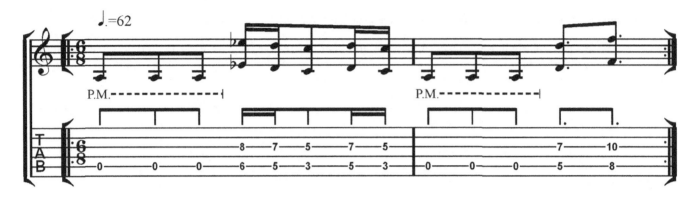

If you find yourself struggling, tap your foot on all six 1/8th note beats to help you internalise the subdivisions and become comfortable with the rhythm.

The next example highlights the subtle difference between 6/8 and 3/4. A classic example of this rhythm is *America* from Leonard Bernstein's *West Side Story*, later covered by early progressive rock group The Nice.

Keeping those lyrics in mind will help you connect to the shifting pulse of the music.

Example 8b:

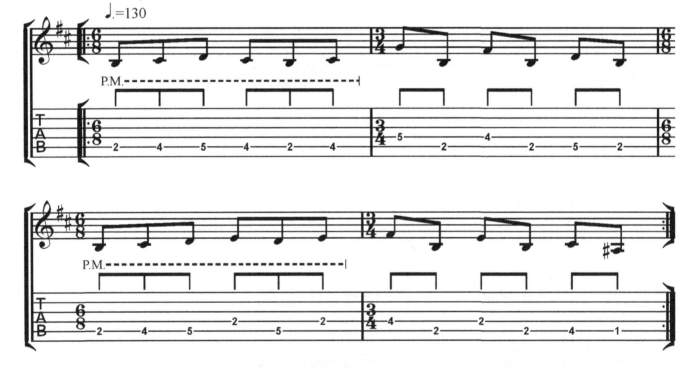

This next riff in 7/4 features many sliding power chords. Very often there are different ways of notating a musical idea that subtly change where the rhythmic emphasis lies. This riff could also have been notated as alternating bars of 4/4 and 3/4.

Example 8c:

1/8th Note Odd Time Signatures

7/8 is half the length of 7/4 and can be felt like a bar of 4/4 with the last 1/8 note removed to leave three and a half beats per bar. The effect is that the pulse now feels rushed as beat one comes earlier than expected and this sense of instability builds rhythmic tension.

Example 8d:

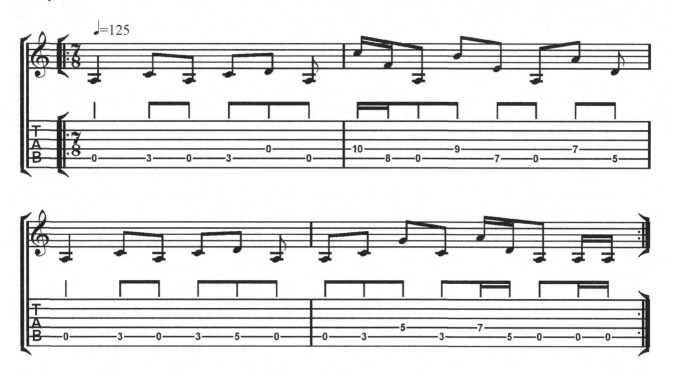

7/8 can be heard in the intro to Steve Vai's *The Attitude Song.*

The time signature of 5/8 can be felt like 6/8 with the final 1/8th note removed. Compare example 8e with example 8a and you will see that the phrasing is similar.

To feel 5/8, count to five while accenting beats one and four. Once you have begun to internalise the sound and feel of the following riff, you can stop counting and it should feel like one long beat followed by a shorter one.

Example 8e:

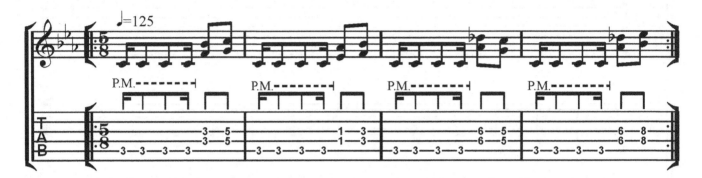

5/8 can be heard in the middle section of Dream Theater's *Octavarium.*

Combining Time Signatures

Just as we varied melodic motifs by transposing them to different pitches in the sequencing chapter, we can vary the time signatures of riffs by adding or subtracting notes.

In this example, both bars are essentially the same but an 1/8th note is added to the end of the second bar.

Example 8f:

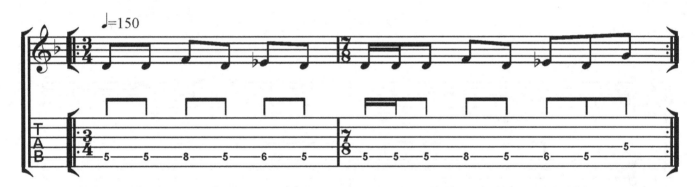

A similar example of this 'additive' process is heard in the bridge section of Mastodon's *Blood and Thunder.*

Another example of the same concept begins with a bar of 4/4, but this time we *subtract* an 1/8th note and create a bar of 7/8. The first bar is then repeated and answered by a bar of 9/8 (this time *adding* one 1/8th note).

Example 8g:

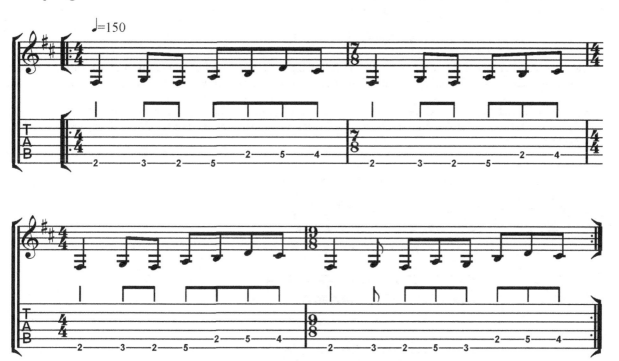

This type of metric variation is found in the intro to the Symphony X song *Inferno*.

Odd time signatures can be mathematically confusing, so when writing riffs it is often more creative to play the idea as you hear it, and figure out the time signatures later.

Next we combine both pitch *and* metric variation. This is a common idea in progressive rock, metal and fusion. Work through each bar carefully and memorise it in isolation. It can be easy to lose your place, especially when you are new to these kinds of ideas. Try clapping along with the audio to internalise the pulse.

Example 8h:

Use consistent alternate picking to play this example, but be aware that some bars will start on an upstroke because of the odd bar lengths. Accentuate the start of each bar with a harder pick stroke, even if it is an upstroke.

1/16th Note Odd Time Signatures

While 5/8 and 7/8 were based around 1/8th note divisions, the following time signatures divide the beat at a 1/16th note level. 1/16th note time signatures can look intimidating on paper, but the principle of subdividing the beats remains the same.

The next example is written in 11/16 which is formed from two 1/4 note beats and three 1/16th notes. To follow along to the audio you should count the 1/16th notes. Counting in 11/16 can be difficult at faster speeds, but the following figure shows how to count through the bar.

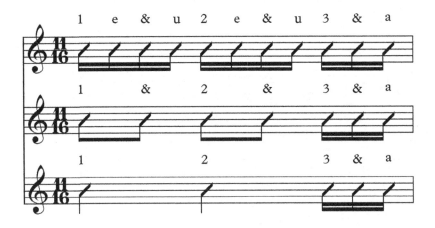

Example 8i:

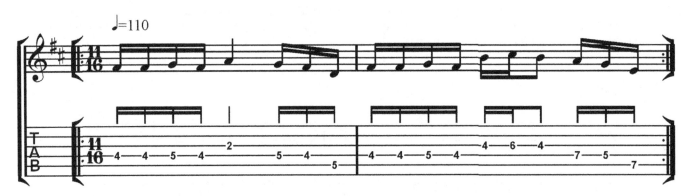

The next idea is written in 15/16. A good way to practice these riffs is to slow them down and tap your foot in 1/8th notes to provide more reference points.

Try splitting the bar of 15/16 up into smaller portions to make things more manageable. For example, the first two 1/4 note beats can be practiced separately from the remaining seven semiquavers. (The feel of seven should be familiar from the examples in 7/8).

Pieces the second bar together in a similar fashion, and when all the parts are comfortably under the fingers, combine the two bars to form the full riff.

Example 8j:

These 1/16th note based time signatures occur in the music of bands like Planet X and Sikth and can be disorientating at first, but that is often the intended musical effect!

Odd time signatures could fill a whole book by themselves and the possibilities of combining and layering them is almost infinite. However, this chapter should have helped you start to recognise them when listening to music, and understand how they can be broken down logically.

Songs that feature odd time signatures:

Tool – *Vicarious* (5/4)
Metallica – *Blackened* (7/4, 3/4)
Dream Theater – *The Test That Stumped Them All* (7/8)
Mastodon – *The Wolf Is Loose* (7/8)
Machinehead – *Days Turn Blue to Grey* (7/8)
Cynic – *Textures* (9/8)
Pantera – *I'm Broken* (7/8)
Slipknot – *Welcome* (10/8)
Planet X – *Snuff (5/4, 7/8, 11/16)*
Gojira – *The Art of Dying* (21/16)

Chapter Seven: Drop D Tuning

Up until now every example has been played in 'standard' EADGBE tuning, however, it is common for metal guitarists to use a number of other tunings. Using different tuning offers new musical possibilities and they can help to break out of creative ruts by forcing you to abandon tired patterns and fingerings.

Most alternate tunings in metal lower the pitch of the strings to create a heavier sound, but they can also be used to transpose open-string riffs to a key that is more comfortable for the singer.

As a string's pitch is lowered, the string will become floppy due to the lack of tension making accurate picking more challenging and possibly resulting in a poorly defined attack. If you intend to use a lower tuning for a prolonged period, switch to a heavier gauge of strings. Many string manufacturers produce sets designed for down tuning.

Alternate tunings is a very broad topic, and the range of tunings available could fill a whole book. In this chapter, we'll look at how metal guitarists use the most common alternative tuning, *Drop D*.

Most alternate tunings in metal are transposed forms of either standard or drop D tuning. This means that the intervals between the strings will remain the same while the tuning of whole guitar is shifted down. For this reason, most players will still be thinking in terms of standard tuning, no matter what pitch they've actually tuned to.

Drop D was particularly popular with the nu-metal and alternative rock groups of the '90s and early 2000s to create thick power-chord based riffs.

Drop D tuning lowers the low E string by a whole step to D so that the interval between the lowest two strings is now a fifth. This means that power chords can be played easily by simply barring across the bottom three strings. Power chords riffs that might otherwise be too difficult to execute cleanly are now easily achievable. Check out the middle section of Slipknot's *Surfacing*, where a fast chromatic single note riff is repeated as power chords using Drop D tuning.

In example 9a, play the power chords in the example using either the first or third finger of the fretting hand as if you were playing a single note, but flatten the finger down across three strings. Experiment with finger angle and pressure so that you keep the higher strings silent by muting with the underside of the fingers.

Example 9a:

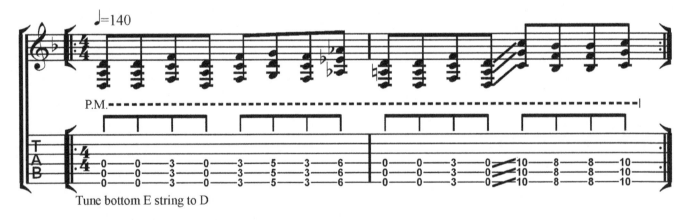

Tune bottom E string to D

These kind of grinding Drop D riffs combined with a disco influenced drum beat helped create Rammstein's distinctive sound.

Having the low E string tuned down a whole step changes how its notes relate to the notes on the other strings. In Drop D tuning, the higher octave D is now located at the fifth fret of the A string, whereas in standard E tuning, the octave E is located at the seventh fret. Metal players in Drop D tuning make great use of this octave jump, so know its location is very important. This idea is shown in the following example.

Example 9b:

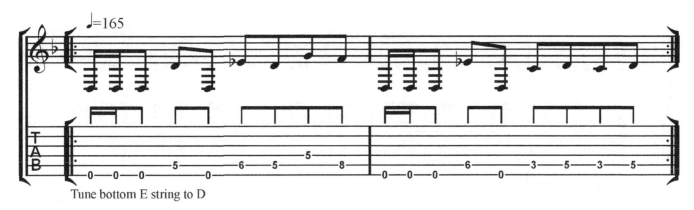

Tune bottom E string to D

The following example uses Drop D tuning to play in E minor. This riff would be impossible in standard tuning because of the use of the b7 (D) below the root.

Example 9c:

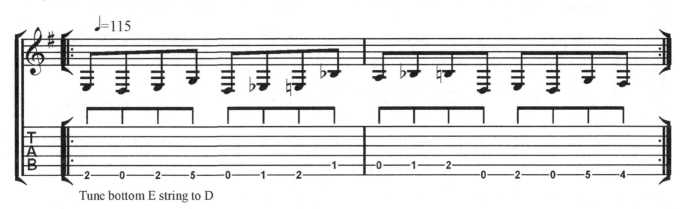

Tune bottom E string to D

In Drop D tuning, both the sixth and fourth strings are tuned to the note D, which lets us play with some cool new ideas. Here's a pedal point riff on the 4th string, repeated on the 6th string.

Watch out for the 5/4 time of this example. Listen to the audio to get the rhythm firmly in your head.

Example 9d:

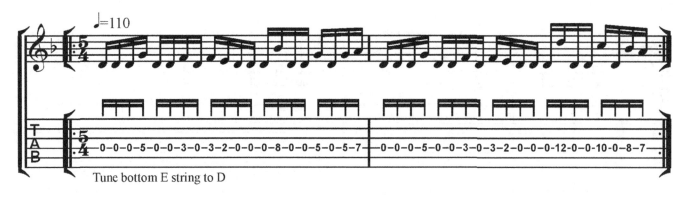

Tune bottom E string to D

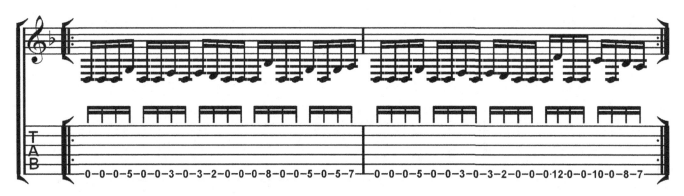

The first line of this riff could form an effective intro to a song, starting out with a single guitar playing the line on the higher D string before the whole band joins in and the riff jumps down an octave to the low D string. Thanks to the Drop D tuning, the riff can easily drop an octave while the fingering remains the same.

Experimenting with other tunings that break up the standard tuning intervals can produce great and unexpected ideas. Try detuning one or two strings by a tone and playing normal chord shapes to hear what happens! Let your ear guide you in deciding whether you like the results. You can always figure out the names of your new chords or scales later.

The use of seven- and eight-string guitars is becoming increasingly common among technical and progressive metal guitarists, having been first popularised by Steve Vai and nu-metallers KoRn in the '90s. These instruments allow access to lower pitches without sacrificing the normal note range of standard tuning. They can also create interesting chordal opportunities by moving bass notes up the neck.

Bands that use Alternative Tunings:

Rammstein – Drop D
Killswitch Engage – Drop C (CGCFAD)
Between the Buried and Me – C# standard (C#F#BEG#C#)
Slipknot – Drop B (BF#BEG#C#)
KoRn – 7 string guitars, Drop A (ADGCFAD)
Black Label Society (BADGBE on *Low Down*)

Chapter Eight: Getting a Great Sound

After examining so many elements of metal guitar, we should talk about how to get the best sound when we play. The wide range of guitars, amps, pedals and pickups on the market can make finding the right gear a long and potentially expensive process. In this chapter, I'll discuss gear and effects to help you to make informed choices when buying equipment.

I've also included some pointers to help you get the best tone out of your fingers and equipment.

Guitarists often find that when they first play with a band after practicing alone, their sound is not as they would like. Often, the guitar seems too quiet or too mushy and thin. The most common cause for this is too much distortion and destructive EQ settings, although it's often blamed on the amp being too small or a need for different pedals.

While good quality gear helps to create a professional sound, it is also easy to create a bad sound on a top-of-the-range amplifier. Knowing *how* to set an amplifier is a big factor. The most important thing to understand is that a great, low volume tone in your bedroom will sound very different on stage or in the rehearsal room.

Thankfully all amplifiers work on the same principles, so by learning how to use the features on one amp you will understand what to expect from the others that you will come across in future.

Equalisation (EQ)

EQ is the most important tool for altering the tone of your guitar, and everything from your guitar's tone pot to your wah-wah pedal is a form of EQ because they all filter the frequency of the guitar in some way. Some of the most important changes to your tone however, are created by the equalisation controls on your amplifier.

Whether your amp has simple controls for bass, middle and treble or a full multi-band graphic EQ, the amp's tone controls separate the guitar's sound into separate tonal 'bands' allowing you to independently alter the relative volumes of each band.

One common misuse of EQ is to 'scoop the mids' by turning down the mid EQ tone control on the amp. This sound has been often emulated since it was heard on early thrash recordings. The problem is that while this scooped tone works great in the bedroom (or even on recordings where the guitar has been tracked on its own), these middle frequencies form the main body of the guitar's sound. Cutting the mids can cause the guitar to disappear entirely when played alongside bass and drums. This issue is exacerbated by lower priced beginner amps having less pronounced mid frequencies to begin with.

If you're not cutting through in the mix try boosting the middle frequencies on your amp to create a more prominent rhythm tone. Rock guitarists often use an external EQ pedal to further boost their mid-range which helps solos cut through the mix.

Valve or Solid-State?

Traditional valve amps use vacuum tubes to amplify your guitar's signal. They are typically more expensive and considerably heavier than transistor amps. Valve amps are characterised by warmer, more pronounced midrange frequencies. The tone of a valve amp changes as its volume increases because the valves compress the guitar signal to produce a type of distortion known as *overdrive* when they are worked harder.

Although a rich, valve-generated distortion is very desirable, having to find different settings depending on the volume can be irritating.

In contrast, solid-state or *transistor* amplifiers, are usually cheaper, lighter and more robust than valve amps so they are better suited to the wear and tear of gigging.

The distortion and overdrive channels on a solid state amp may sound harsher and more brittle than a valve amp. However, there are guitarists who have favoured this sound, most notably Dimebag Darrel in the Pantera years.

It can be tempting to buy large, impressive looking amps, especially if it is the model a favourite guitarist uses. However, the nature of valve amplification normally means that a big amp used at a low volume delivers a less desirable tone than a small amp that is working hard. Be realistic! If you're playing in your bedroom, do you really need a 100-watt stack?! A 15-watt, all-valve amplifier can more than handle the average bar gig.

Amplifier vs. Rack/Amp modelling?

In recent years, the quality of multi-fx and amp modelling hardware has developed rapidly. Whether through laptop software, pedals or dedicated rack units, you can quickly replicate the sound of whatever amp you desire at a fraction of the cost of acquiring the original. This is a tempting option, especially for guitarists who want to create a diverse range of tones.

Modelling devices often work on a *patch* based system, meaning that all the parameters of a sound (amp type, settings, booster, effects, signal chain etc) can be changed simultaneously with just one button, rather than tap-dancing across a whole pedal board mid-song.

The trade-off to this flexibility is that the sound produced is still an emulation of 'real' gear, and only the very best amplifier modelling equipment responds well to dynamic changes in your playing. If you can achieve the range of sounds you need with just the channels on the amp and a modest number of pedals, then it could be better to invest in one quality amplifier rather than a multi-fx or modelling amp.

Boosts, Distortion and Noise gates

Unlike a distortion pedal which adds 'artificial' distortion to the guitar, a boost pedal simply makes the input signal to the amp louder so the amp's tubes will provide more compression and natural distortion.

Many players will use a boost pedal in conjunction with their amp's overdrive to create their rhythm tone. A secondary boost pedal is often used to raise the signal and add gain when soloing. The most popular boost pedal is the Ibanez Tubescreamer, whose name nicely describes the pedal's purpose.

When you increase the level of gain on a signal there is likely to be an increase in the electronic noise created along the signal path resulting in a hum or buzz through the amp. This hum can be especially problematic when playing loudly at gigs or band rehearsals. This hum is avoided by using a *noise gate*.

Noise gates set a *threshold* volume for the signal. The noise gate closes when the input signal from the guitar drops below the threshold and stops all signal passing through, including any buzz from the pedals. When you start playing, the signal will exceed the set threshold and the gate will open allowing all sound through, however the hum is now lost under the guitar signal.

Tone is in the Fingers

Great guitarists are as identifiable by their 'sound' as by the actual notes that they play. Owning all of your favourite player's equipment often won't make you sound at all like them because tone is as much about touch and articulation as it is about guitar and amp choice.

It makes sense to develop a great touch on the instrument before considering how you will then process the signal with effects or the amp. The idea is to enhance a strong tone, rather than have to make up for inadequacies in your playing.

Practicing unplugged or through a clean amp is often very revealing because distortion can mask a multitude of sins. Experiment by varying the angle of the pick, and where on the strings you are playing to find different tones. Picking close to the bridge will give more treble while picking over the fretboard will accentuate the bass and mid-range frequencies.

An electric guitar can be adjusted at the bridge, saddles and truss rod to make the guitar feel as comfortable to play as possible. A good setup can often transform an inexpensive guitar into a very playable one.

The distance between the strings and the fretboard is known as the *action* and the action is mainly adjusted on the bridge of the guitar. A low action will feel easier to play as it requires less energy and movement to fret, but there is often a loss of tone.

Try to keep the action as high as possible while still being able to execute your ideas perfectly and not having to work too hard. Since the '80s, the norm is for metal guitarists to play with very low actions (to the point of the strings almost buzzing against the frets), but the tone of these players can sometimes be lacklustre when it comes to sustaining long notes.

Strings and Picks

A small change in strings or picks can have a radical effect on the tone and the feel of your guitar. Thicker strings produce a beefier tone because there is more metal vibrating over the pickups, and because the strings are held at a higher tension.

The trade-off with thick strings is that they take more strength to bend so wide bends may prove difficult. As rock guitarists are usually expected to play both rhythm and lead parts, you may find it best to compromise by trying .10 gauge strings, as these are only slightly thicker than average. If you play rhythm guitar exclusively then you could consider something thicker for a beefier tone.

High tension on the strings can help with picking consistency at faster speeds. Heavy strings are quicker to react to a pick stroke whereas thin strings vibrate in a wider arc and produce a less defined tone.

The same logic also applies to picks: a more rigid pick will not be bent by the string and will produce a quicker, more consistent attack. Choosing a pick with a sharp (rather than a rounded) tip can also help to create a well-defined attack.

Many rock guitarists known for their picking prowess use picks that are at least 2mm thick, although there are always exceptions to the rule: Yngwie Malmsteen uses light gauge strings with thin picks and clearly has no issues with speed or consistency!

Closing Words

Phew, there we have it! That concludes our tour of metal rhythm guitar. Though we've only scratched the surface of a hugely diverse genre of music I've tried to create a guide that encourages further learning and listening. With the skills gained by studying these pages, you should now be able to learn songs by yourself and apply these techniques in different situations.

As parting advice, I would say that the key to being a competent musician is to work evenly on the skills that combine to make you a well-rounded player.

Technical proficiency, aural awareness, theory, and playing with other musicians should all be practiced equally because each element supports the development of the others. There are many transcription books available, plus 'learn to play' DVDs and YouTube lessons that will spoon feed you information. However overdependence on these sources can mean that your ears remain underdeveloped. Make time to transcribe songs by ear too.

Transcribing riffs from records will connect the placement of notes on the neck to their sound. The ultimate goal is to be able to play something as soon as you hear it.

A strong ability to aurally interpret music will increase your pleasure both as a musician and as a listener. The tuition of foreign languages never neglects listening practice in the way that music tuition often seems to!

When you're listening to music, try to focus on the rhythm guitar parts and identify how the part is being played. Is it muted? Does it involve fast picking or are there hammer-ons and pull-offs?

Progress with aural skills is harder to measure than metronome speed or theoretical information, but every time you actively listen to music, transcribe, and sing melodies, you are training your ears. Every piece of experience will accumulate to make you a more aurally aware musician.

Thank you for reading this book, I hope it is helpful on your journey into metal guitar playing.

Rock on!

Rob

Heavy Metal Lead Guitar

An Introduction to Heavy Metal Soloing for Guitar

Published by www.fundamental-changes.com

www.fundamental-changes.com

Introduction

Welcome to Heavy Metal Lead Guitar!

This book provides the developing intermediate guitarist with a comprehensive course in all aspects of playing metal lead guitar.

As both a student and a teacher, I find that many books and articles focus on developing guitar technique outside of a musical vocabulary. This book's main goal is to help you understand the musical vocabulary of metal. We will of course examine the techniques needed to execute each idea along the way, but only as a means to facilitate musical expression.

Modern metal soloing is a tapestry of the different trends and innovations throughout rock and heavy metal's history. This started in the 1950s with the pentatonic language inherited from electric blues players like Albert King, Eric Clapton and Jeff Beck.

We'll begin our journey by building a strong foundation in classic rock vocabulary, including string bending and pentatonic licks. Metal players like Zakk Wylde, Paul Gilbert, and many others have kept this bluesy influence alive and relevant in modern rock.

One of the main changes as rock grew out of electric blues, was the guitar's tone. The development of equipment in the '60s, such as the Marshall stack, fuzz and wah-wah pedals, of which blues-rock players like Jimi Hendrix and Alvin Lee were able to take advantage, meant that the guitar could sustain and feedback more easily, enabling a new way of playing.

Throughout the 1970s, many great rock and metal guitarists adapted the approach of Hendrix, Clapton and Page, refining the blues influenced rock vocabulary with increasing technical prowess.

Several guitarists from that decade started exhibiting progressive ideas, like Richie Blackmore and Uli Jon Roth, but arguably the next player to have universal influence was Eddie Van Halen. Van Halen achieved international fame by the late '70s, and Eddie's groundbreaking style proved highly influential throughout the '80s. While his famously gymnastic tapping technique stole the limelight, EVH's fluid and expressive style was heavily based on melodic blues licks and great phrasing. The successful integration of the two approaches secured his lasting appeal.

The following decade served up a hitherto unheard of level of technical ability with many players raising the bar for guitar virtuosity. Central to this new trend, dubbed 'shred', was the Shrapnel record label run by Mike Varney, who sought out rising guitar virtuosos and showcased them on instrumental releases on his label.

The figurehead of this movement was a Swedish guitarist named Yngwie Malmsteen who had moved to America after sending a demo tape to Varney. While opinion on Yngwie is polarised, his influence on rock guitar cannot be overstated. Armed with a vocabulary of licks influenced more by classical composers like Bach and Paganini than by rock and heavy metal guitar, Yngwie's flawless speed and singing tone took the genre by storm.

I hope you enjoy this comprehensive introduction to heavy metal soloing and find it helpful in your quest to develop as a lead guitarist.

Grab your guitar, and let's get started!

Rob

Chapter One: Early Metal Licks

Let's start with some stalwart licks that have stood the test of time. These are to be found in the playing of everyone from Eric Clapton to Slash, Kirk Hammett and Steve Vai.

Sometimes, cliché ideas are shunned on principle due to a desire to be new and innovative, but noble as this outlook is, don't forget that ideas usually remain popular because they sound great! Knowing the clichés gives you a strong footing for developing a personal style. When learning a foreign language, one clings to a well-thumbed phrasebook and listens carefully to native speakers, before attempting to reassemble the acquired fragments into a vehicle of self-expression.

The earliest hard rock and metal players used predominantly blues based ideas. Previous to rock n' roll's explosion, electric blues had been the loudest, most hard-hitting form of popular music.

Blues is a very expressive form of music. Central to this, is the way pitches are manipulated by bending and vibrato to create a vocal delivery, so it is worth noting that the most successful metal guitarists include plenty of blues phrasing in their playing. Metal solos can become overly technical and lose this sense of expression, so tempering the shredding with some blues is a great way to balance the adrenaline and excitement with more emotive ideas. Listen to Pantera's Dimebag Darrell, Joe Satriani and Paul Gilbert to hear great shred metal playing steeped in the blues.

To kick things off, we start with a common repeating pentatonic lick. To execute the string bend with the most control, play the bend the ring finger supported by the middle finger, and bend with a twisting motion of the forearm while locking the fingers in place.

Throughout this book I'll repeat the mantra of keeping the thumb on the back of the neck. In many situations this helps flatten the fingers to mute the unused strings, however, when string bending, you should let the thumb creep over the top of the neck to produce a grip more akin to holding a baseball bat rather than a thick book.

Example 1a

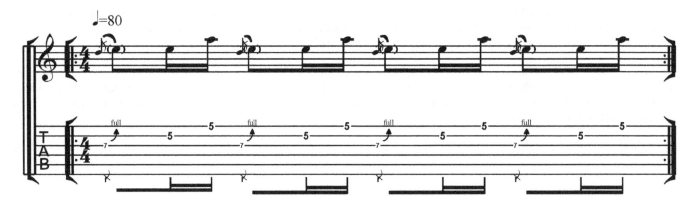

In the next example, this concept is expanded to include a descending pentatonic phrase. The resulting 'cell' of six notes lends itself to being played as triplets (three notes in the time of two). I would recommend using the pinkie to play the 8th fret on the B string. Some might use the third finger but given the dexterity required for some of the more gymnastic licks ahead of us, it makes sense to train the pinkie from the beginning.

Example 1b

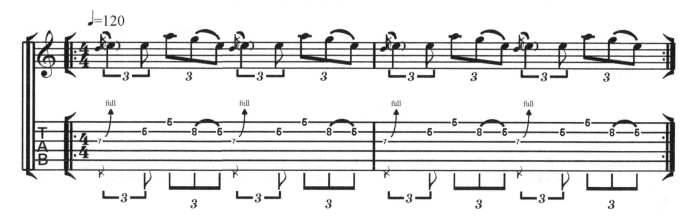

Next, here are two bends for the price of one! In this variation I contradict the advice given in example 2! As it is important to apply as much strength as possible in the following bends, I would use the ring/middle finger combo to achieve the necessary speed and intonation.

Example 1c

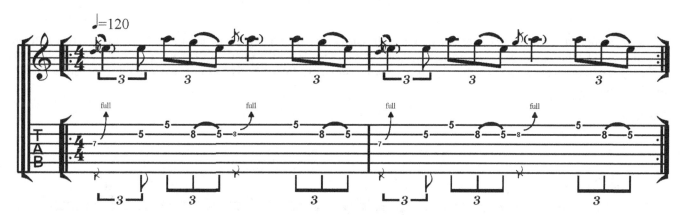

The final variation expands on the initial lick by introducing a short scale pattern. Unless you're Zakk Wylde you'll probably want to use pull-offs here as alternate picking this string crossing can get cumbersome. Practice mixing these first four repeating licks in different combinations and integrating them with your soloing. The more you create variations and use licks in a musical context (either with backing tracks or with a band), the sooner they'll become malleable pieces of your vocabulary rather than fixed phrases.

Example 1d

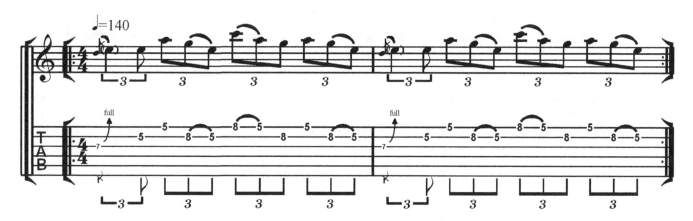

Example 1e is an effective yet straightforward lick in the style of Kirk Hammett. We're repeating the high E note but alternating between playing it as a bend and a fretted note. The lick ends with a short melody using the E minor pentatonic scale.

Use a wah pedal if you have one to get the best results. By slowly sweeping across the wah pedal as you play the repeating lick you can add another dimension of musicality.

Example 1e

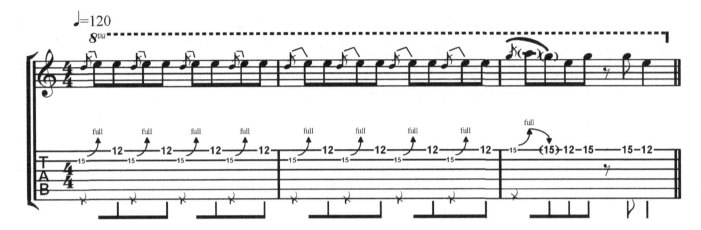

Our next example takes a short bending lick similar to the earlier examples and moves it up the neck one fret at a time. Moving in semitones like this is known as a *chromatic* movement. Once we leave the safety of the pentatonic scale shape behind, the difficulty is to know when to stop! In this lick we're moving chromatically while visualising the A minor barre chord at the 17th fret as our target.

Example 1f

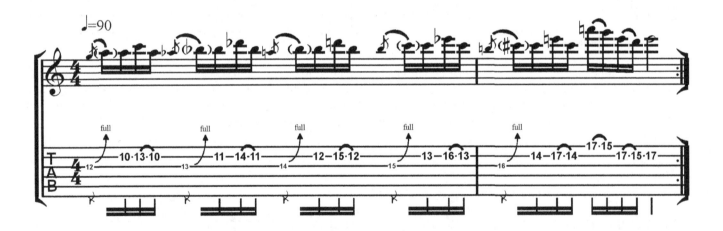

Now here's a more melodic idea. It employs the 'blue' note (Eb) as an addition to the A minor pentatonic scale and introduces a rake into the first note. The rake is achieved by muting the strings and pushing the pick across the lower strings before finally picking the B string. This action should produce a percussive sound. Don't be afraid to dig in hard with the pick, but make sure the other strings are well muted.

Example 1g

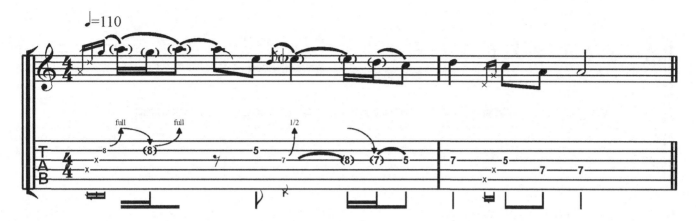

Doublestop Licks

The next four licks all involve *doublestops*. A doublestop simply means playing two notes simultaneously. Jimi Hendrix blurred the traditional distinction between lead and rhythm guitar playing by incorporating chordal licks into his solos and lead fills into his rhythm playing. Doublestops have a particularly crunchy sound compared to single notes, and when played with distortion bring a tonal contrast to your solo.

Notice how the first doublestop is bent slightly sharp giving it a more expressive quality. Fret it by barring your first finger across both strings and squeezing the hand closed to raise the pitch.

Example 1h

Our second doublestop lick is an ascending sequence through the E Minor pentatonic scale. It is the same as playing single notes but the doublestops provide a thicker texture. Apart from the fourth doublestop in bar two, the whole lick can be played with just the first and third fingers.

You could play this lick with either downstrokes or alternate picking. If you choose alternate picking, the motion is more like a small strum that catches both strings. Providing the timing is accurate the strumming can be quite loose and percussive.

Example 1i

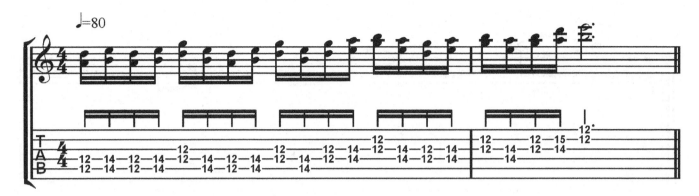

The lick in example 1j involves bending both strings together to create a bluesy 'curl', so don't be overly concerned with bending up to a specific note. Flatten the third finger across both strings and twist the wrist downwards from the forearm as if you were turning a doorknob.

The final bend is a little different. Here the top note remains at a constant pitch while the lower note is bent up a tone. Use the ring finger for the high note and bend with the second finger, backed up by the index finger.

Example 1j

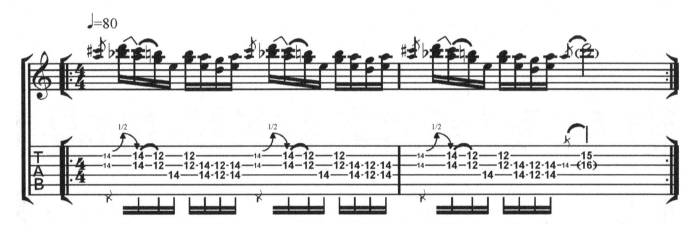

The fourth type of doublestop lick is a 'unison' bend. We fret two notes a tone apart and then bend the lower one up until the strings are in unison. Distortion emphasises the dissonance in the major second interval and consonance of the unison. To achieve the most secure hold on the lower string whilst bending, make sure to use both the first and second fingers together to push the string up.

When two notes or more are played simultaneously with distortion the sound becomes muddy before resolving as you bend into the unison interval. Using the bridge pickup and a wah pedal will accentuate the screaming nature of these bends.

Example 1k

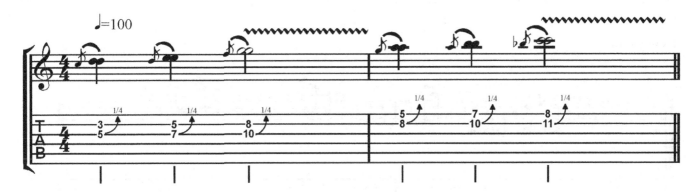

Pentatonic Patterns

We now move on to learning some pentatonic-based scale patterns. To start off simply, we will play a three-string pattern that moves across the neck. Runs like these are important tools for soloing as they help you transition smoothly from one area of the guitar neck to another.

All of the pentatonic ideas in this section will be in the key of E minor but it's worth spending time practicing them in other common keys like A minor, B minor and D minor by moving the whole shape to different frets.

Example 1l

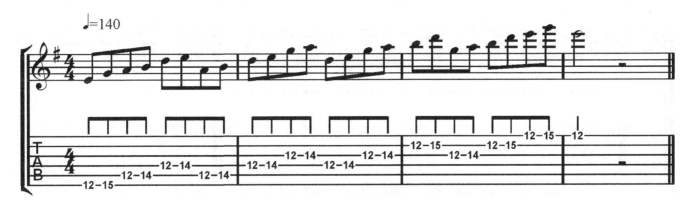

Here's the descending version of the previous example. Get familiar with examples 1l and 1m before you start playing more complicated patterns involving aspects of both examples.

Example 1m

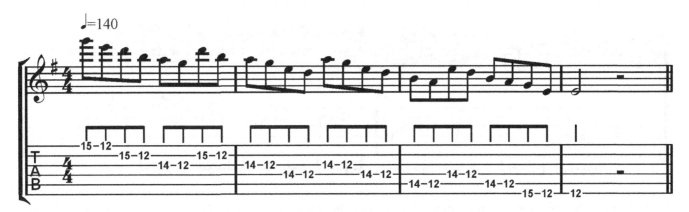

Now we'll ascend the shape in a similar fashion using a pattern of eight notes. Notice that we're using hammer-ons and pull-offs to help make the faster speed more manageable. Feel free to experiment with using more, or less legato to see how it changes the sound.

Example 1n

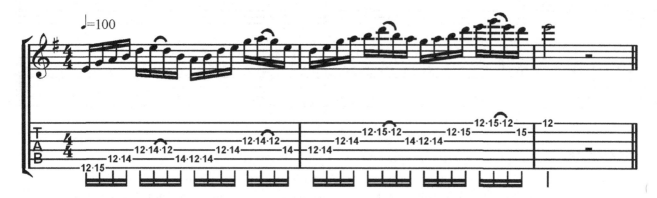

As well as constructing runs, fast repeating pentatonic scale fragments can be great for building energy and excitement during a solo. You could use picking or legato to play next example, but either way, a little palm muting will help to articulate the rhythmic contour and produce a percussive sound. Zakk Wylde often uses palm muted pentatonic riffs in his soloing.

Example 1o

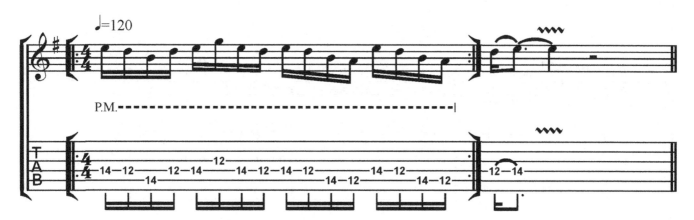

One more variation on this theme comes courtesy of Slash (though British readers might well recognise it from a certain TV comedy panel show theme tune!). Here we double pick the first note of each beat. I've used pull-offs wherever possible to make things easier and more dynamic.

Example 1p

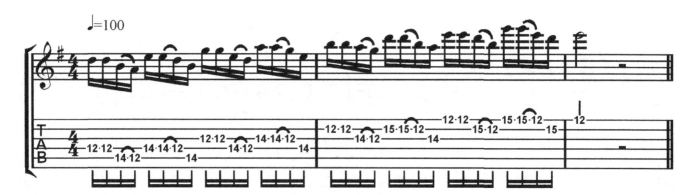

To break out of the confines of the minor pentatonic 'box', you need to be familiar with this scale all over the fretboard.

The following figure shows the notes of the E minor pentatonic scale all over the neck.

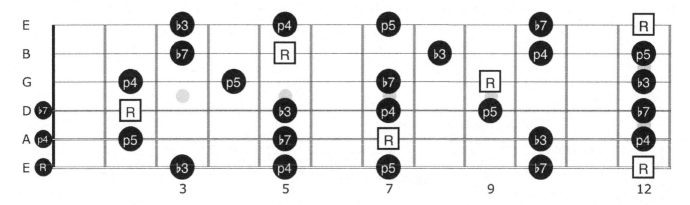

The second figure shows just the second position of the scale that starts at the 15th fret. If you play the shape used in example 1l followed by this one you will be able to see how they connect.

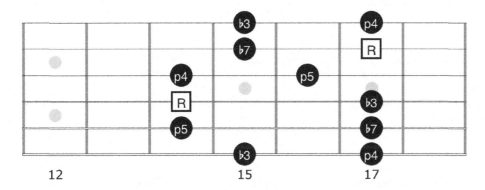

Using different shapes allows us to move around the guitar neck while playing within one scale. To demonstrate this, the fragment from example 1o is now cycled through the scale to arrive at the top E note in position two.

It helps to target a destination note when playing runs like this, and a good way to start is to target the root note in each position of the scale and aim for it as you play. This way, even if you stray off the path en-route, you will still be able to land safely on an E to finish.

Example 1q

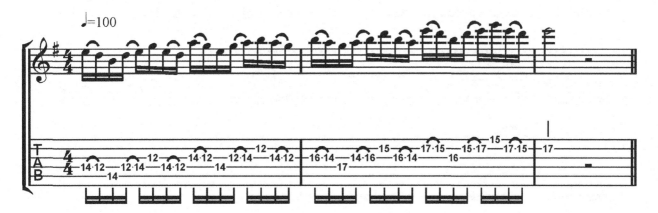

Instead of moving across the strings, this example ascends the neck on only the top two strings. This lick is a great way to learn the scale all over the neck by memorising the sequence of smaller two-note shapes.

Notice there are five different shapes before repeating the first one twelve frets higher.

Use the full-neck E minor pentatonic diagram to help you play this type of pattern on different string pairs. Starting on any root note, the following sequence is identical all over the neck.

Example 1r

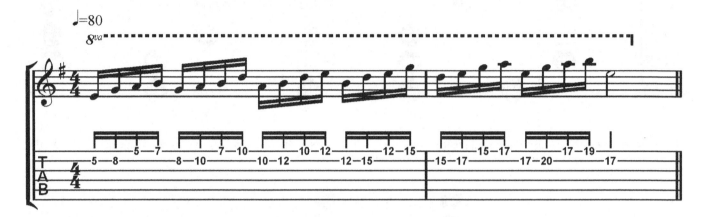

The shapes in example 1r provide many possibilities for creating variations and patterns. The following example shows an eight-note pattern applied to each scale position in turn. Initially, it can be tricky to change position smoothly.

Practice slowly, and aim to move the first finger up the B string just as you pick to avoid hearing the slide when shifting position.

Example 1s

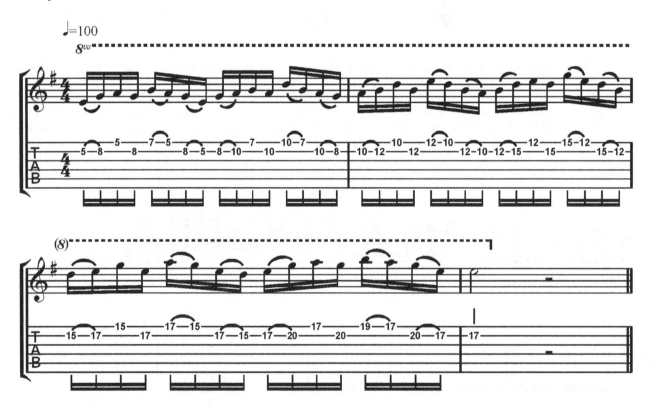

What goes up must come down! We now have a descending lick that uses only the top two strings. Aim to make the position shifts as even and accurate as possible. The listener shouldn't be able to hear your shifts. A great way to practice all the scale positions is to work on ideas like this on different strings pairs.

Example 1t

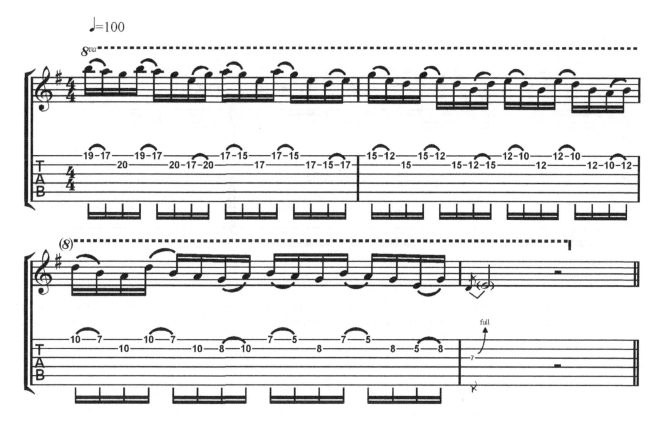

The final few licks in this chapter are a little faster. They involve plenty of pull-offs, to help achieve the speed although it may take a little time to build up the necessary stamina. Use the index, middle finger and pinkie, and follow the suggested picking directions for the best results.

I remember first learning this lick from the glam-metal band Poison, but variations on it have been played by everyone from Lynryd Skynyrd to Machinehead.

Example 1u

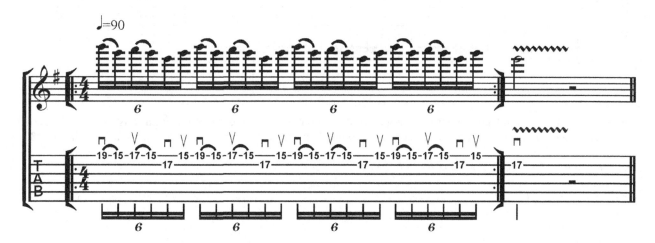

Here's another fast pentatonic lick courtesy of thrash metal lead guitarists like Dave Mustaine and Kirk Hammett. Nearly every guitar solo on Metallica's early albums uses a variation on this type of lick! Try to keep the fretting hand as relaxed as possible to improve the stamina of the pinkie and ring fingers. Moving the fretting hand thumb lower on the back of the neck will help with the wider stretch between the 12th and 17th frets.

Example 1v

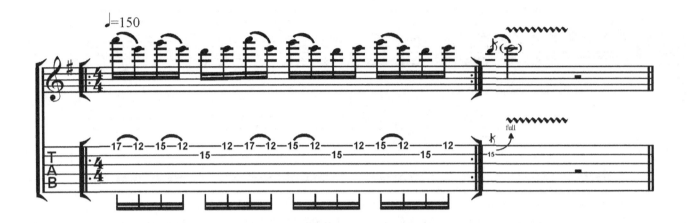

The final lick in this chapter provides a more technical variation on the previous pentatonic licks, combining faster legato with picking. Listen to the audio instead of worrying about the compound tuplet on beat one. The first three notes are just a faster 'flick' before settling into the triplet rhythm.

Example 1w

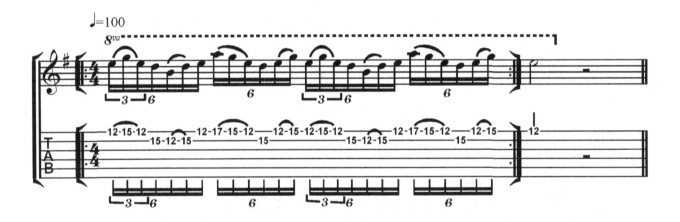

You can hear this kind of idea in Paul Gilbert's playing as well as in the music of the thrash metal guitarists mentioned earlier. Gilbert's perfect balance of bluesy expression and vibrato, along with his searing speed helped him rise to fame in the late '80s.

Recommended Listening for Classic Rock and Blues Influence:

Led Zeppelin – *Stairway to Heaven*
Deep Purple – *Hush*
Black Sabbath – *Paranoid*
Motorhead – *Ace of Spades*
Iron Maiden – *The Trooper*
Guns 'n Roses – *Paradise City*
Metallica – *Sad But True*
Pantera – *5 Minutes Alone*
Mastodon – *Oblivion*

Chapter Two: Melody and Phrasing

Much of this book describes ways to create licks and runs using different techniques. Metal lead guitar playing is often about creating a sense of energy through fast and dramatic vocabulary, however, at the same time, it's important not to lose sight of a powerful melodic component to your playing. Beautiful melodies can engage a listener and give a memorable tune to latch onto. Most well-loved rock and metal guitar solos balance exciting fast licks with simple, strong melodic phrases.

In this chapter we will attempt to break into the notoriously elusive and intangible skill of creating good melodies. Melody writing is a subject that is certainly less definable than more technical skills.

Some people write off the gift of great melodies writing as a 'stroke of genius' although I believe that it is simply a case of regular practice, just like any other element of music. With daily exercise, the brain gets better at creating the seeds of ideas that you can then develop.

An exhaustive study of the all the expressive techniques available when articulating a melody is beyond the scope of this book. Instead, we will focus on some of metal's melodic clichés, and the expressive techniques commonly used so that you can apply them to your own melodies.

Think about melodies as having a *contour*. Imagine the notes on a stave and then draw a line that intersects them. Some melodies go straight from low to high, or high to low with a 'ramp' profile, others peak then fall. When you're listening to music try to think about the contour of the melody and how the contour relates to the emotional content; does the melody build in excitement or does it die away after a climax?

As an aside, it's interesting to question whether melodies that stay on one note (such as The Beatles' *Lucy in the Sky with Diamonds*, or *De Do Do Do, De Da Da Da* by The Police) are melodies at all. In these cases, the absence of contour causes a type of tension because of the denied expectation of melodic movement. Melody can be quite subjective.

It's also worth considering how the important notes in the melody (usually the long ones), relate to the underlying chords. Starting on the root every time will guarantee consonance but can quickly become bland and boring, so try starting your melody on the 3rd or the 5th of the chord and listen to the different flavours. Without getting too 'jazzy', it is possible to start on non-chord tones like the 6th or 9th too. These notes can give richer harmonic depth to your melody.

Of the myriad sub-genres of heavy metal, the most melodic bands are found in power and progressive metal. Following in the wake of Judas Priest and Iron Maiden, they feature prominent vocal melodies as well as keyboards and orchestral instruments. There is also a significant folk influence, particularly with European power metal bands. Just like in metal, folk melodies tend to stay in a single diatonic mode so are great to use for inspiration. Listen to bands like Nightwish and Blind Guardian to hear perfect examples of a symphonic metal sound.

Practice the following activities on a regular basis to develop your sense of melody:

- Playing along with the vocal melodies of songs on your guitar. Copy anything with a strong melody, but power metal, pop, or even country songs are particularly good.

- Singing a melody and then trying to play what you sang is particularly beneficial to your overall musicianship skills. You don't have to be a great singer, but the simple act of connecting your ear and imagination to the fretboard will help you immeasurably.

- Experiment with drawing contour lines and writing melodies to fit over them. Setting unusual limitations is an effective practice tool as it forces you to think in new ways. This exercise will stop you simply repeating the same melodic patterns that your imagination regurgitates. Once you've written them, you should definitely sing the result!

The following bending licks are well-worn melodic devices that have been employed by everyone from Slash to Randy Rhoads but still sound great as melodic interjections into your solos or as an exit phrase after a faster run. You can let the bent note ring into the high note to produce a satisfying scream when played with distortion, or keep each note separate and preserve the clarity of the melody.

Example 2a

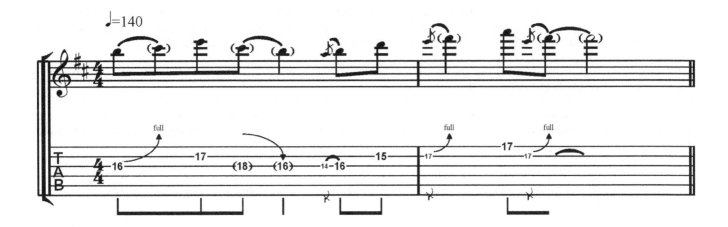

String and keyboard instruments, including the guitar, are capable of producing a constant stream of notes without having to pause. This is unlike wind instruments where players must keep pausing to breathe. The silver lining to this human limitation is that wind players are forced to break up their solos into logical phrases, separated by moments of open space.

By singing what we play, guitarists can impose this enforced phrasing on ourselves. An audience needs space in between phrases to react to what they hear, so be sure to give it to them.

Here the melody is composed of two contrasting phrases, known as 'call and response'.

Example 2b

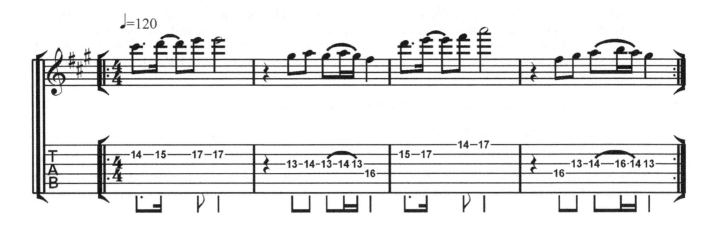

In the previous call and response lick we used a change in rhythm to provide the contrast between phrases. This time the melody's phrases are separated by *range*; Variations on a single melodic idea are transposed between higher and lower octaves.

I recommend keeping melodies simple by using just a few different notes to keep them easily memorable to the listener. See how I've managed to create four different two-bar phrases out of the same starting idea.

Experimenting with subtle changes in rhythm and phrasing breathes life into a simple melody, and avoids mere repetition.

Example 2c

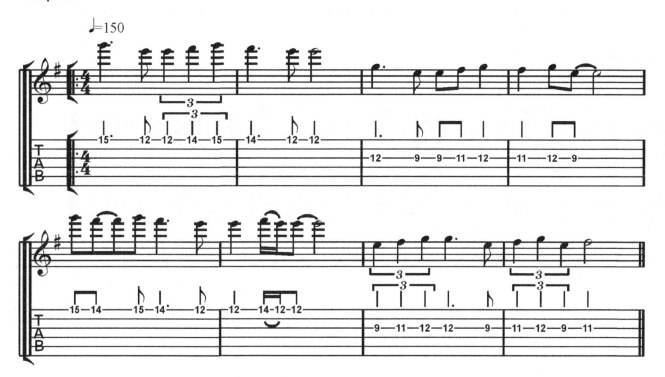

There are many ways to form effective call and response phrases by contrasting different musical attributes. In the following call and response lick we're contrasting two different scales. The 'call' uses D natural minor whereas the 'response' limits itself to the D minor pentatonic scale, lending the answer a bluesier flavour in comparison to the more classical-sounding seven-note scale.

Example 2d

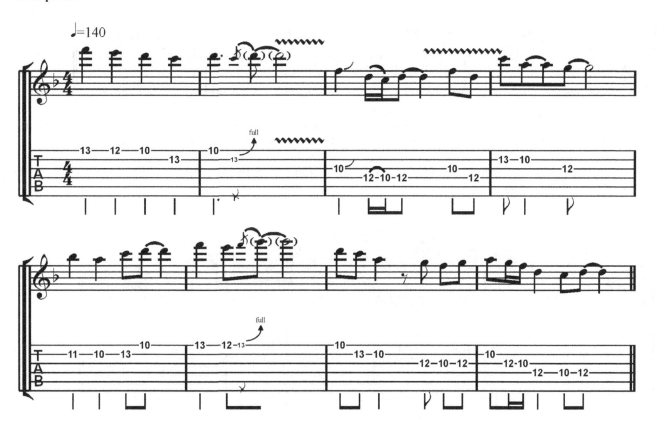

The harmonic strength of triads makes them satisfying to hear as the backbone of melodies. Transposing arpeggio-based ideas as the chord progression moves will provide a predictable hook that the listener can follow. A clear pop example is *Enola Gay* by Orchestral Manoeuvres in the Dark.

Example 2e

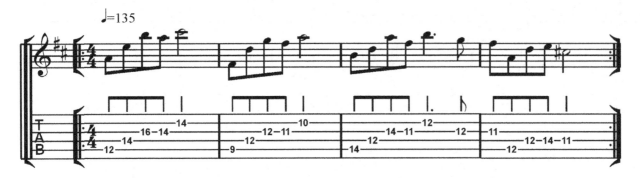

The use of wider intervals can provide ear-catching features. In this next lick, the main feature of each melodic phrase is a leap of a sixth transposed through the scale.

Sixths, like thirds, have a harmonically sweet sound, but if you seek something more angular you could apply the same principle to fourths, sevenths or ninths.

Example 2f

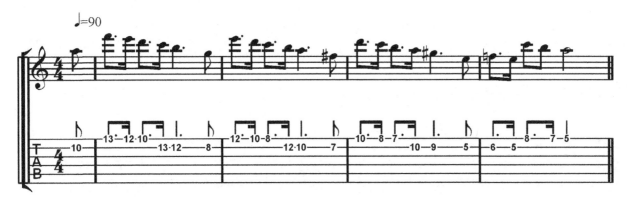

Rhythmically anticipating the change to a new chord can make for a more composed feel to a solo and gives the impression of the soloist leading the band through the changes. Rock guitarist David Gilmour particularly favours this device.

See the coda section of Dream Theater's *About to Crash* from the *Six Degrees of Inner Turbulence* suite for a very clear example from a metal band. **Example 2g**

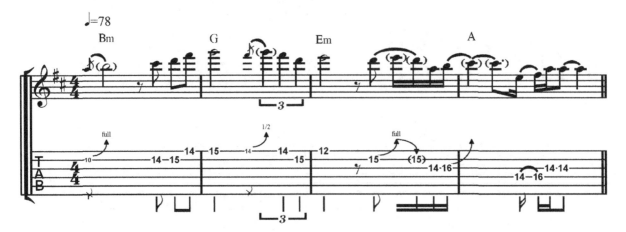

Transposing a motif to different pitches while maintaining its contour is an effective melodic tool. It helps give both soaring melodies and shred licks a more memorable structure. Balancing predictability with development ensures we keep things fresh while not overloading the listener with too much new information.

A composition tutor once instilled in me that everything boils down to balancing *unity and variety*. A simple idea, but if you keep it in mind when writing any kind of music, you won't go far wrong!

Notice that we don't constrict ourselves to the same relative intervals, or move the motif by the same distance each time. Simply maintaining the general shape for each iteration of the melody gives an adequate degree of unity.

Example 2h

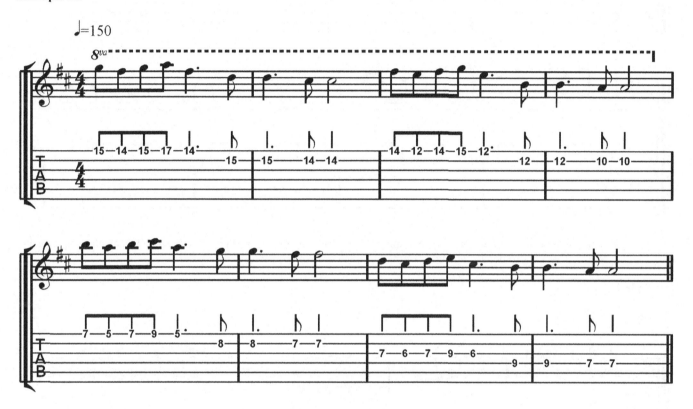

This up-tempo, bluesy melody adds an interesting little twist to the idea of sequencing. The second and fourth repetitions of the initial two bar phrase are *inverted*. This means that wherever the original melody ascended it now descends and vice-versa. Even though everything is inverted, the phrase is still recognisable.

How you play your ideas is important. Good articulation can lift a lick beyond being a string of notes and actually make it carry emotion, much like the tone of a speaking voice.

Bends emulate the human voice and make a melody 'sing' with expression. Consider the vibrato you add to notes. It can be effective to let the note sustain for a moment before adding vibrato, rather than rushing and wobbling the note all over the place straight away. Uncontrolled vibrato is a telltale sign of a beginner guitarist.

Example 2i

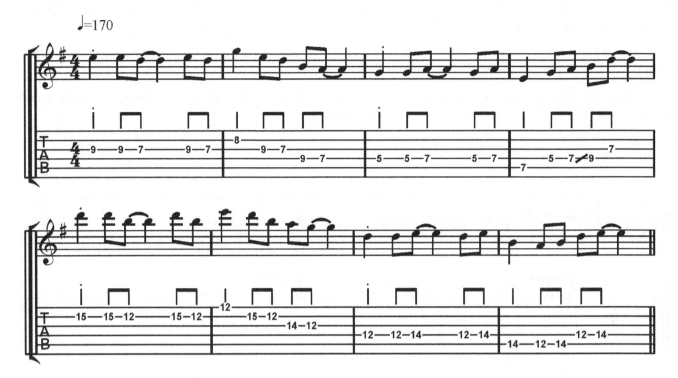

Marty Friedman often makes a common phrase sound unique with his very personal 'Japanese Koto' inspired approach to bending. He frequently uses pre-bends and bends from chromatic non-scale tones.

Example 2j

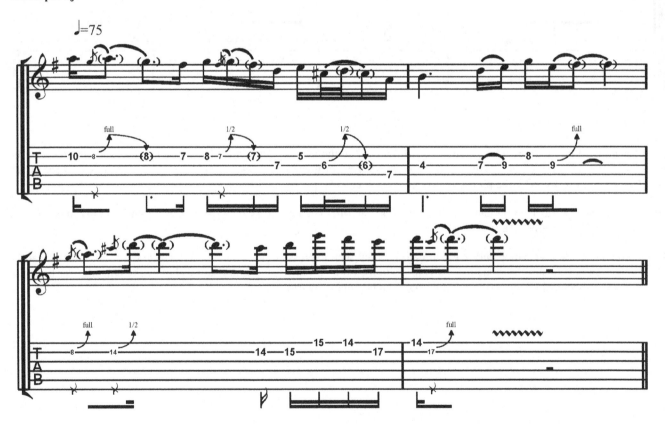

Listening to singers' vocal delivery can be a great source of inspiration when developing your articulations. Attempting to replicate the bends and inflections that singers use will train your ears and make you a more expressive guitarist.

Grace notes are notes that rush into the next note without having their own rhythmic value. To achieve this effect, the next lick uses an almost immediate hammer-on to the main melody note after playing the grace note. It is important to know which scale you're playing so you can grace from either a tone or a semitone away, depending on which is diatonic to the key

Example 2k

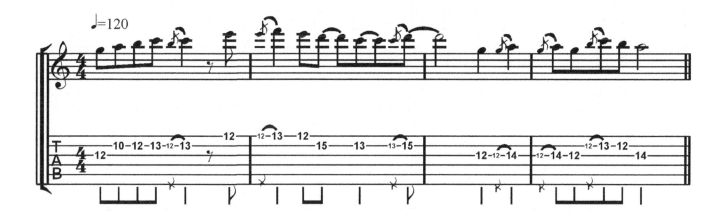

Slides are used in two main ways. The next example includes slides between two notes, each of which has their own rhythmic value. By sliding from the first, the destination note doesn't need to be picked, making it sound more legato.

Example 2l

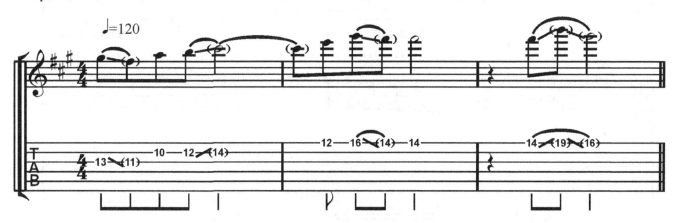

Here's the second type of slide. This slide has no rhythmic value of its own and is just an effect added to the destination note. In this respect it is similar to the grace notes in example 2k.

Each note is slid into from below (the starting fret of the slide is unimportant), and the pitch rushing up into the target note is the desired effect. This technique gives a sense of ascension and climax to the rising melodic line in bars three and four.

Example 2m

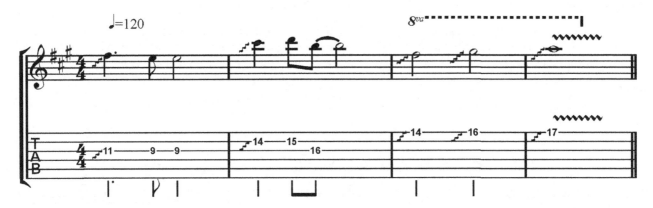

Just as the grace note slides add to the intensity of the melody note, so do short scale runs when played in a more controlled and 'classical' style. The next example uses different positions of the A natural minor scale to anticipate some of the melody notes.

Example 2n

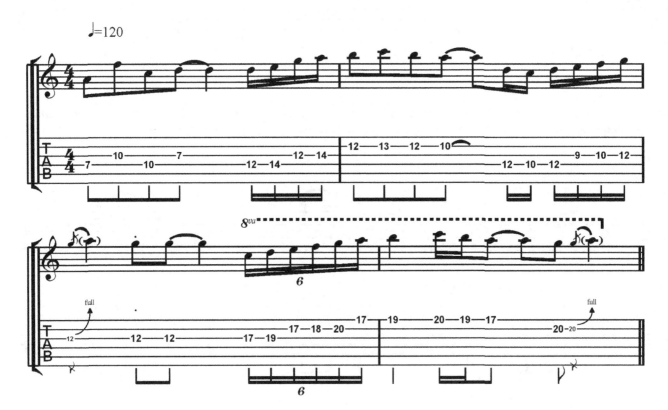

There are many ways to achieve a similar effect. For example: rather than ascending you could try descending to, or surrounding the destination note before finally playing it.

Recommended listening for melodic solos:

Ozzy Osbourne – *Crazy Train*
Boston – *More than a Feeling*
Bon Jovi – *Livin' on a Prayer*
Poison – *Every Rose Has Its Thorn*
Metallica – *Nothing Else Matters*
Megadeth – *Tornado of Souls*
Avenged Sevenfold – *Bat Country*

Chapter Three: Scale Primer

Most of the material in this book deals with scales that are arranged with three notes per string so it will be beneficial to have a working knowledge of this system and understand why it has been adopted by so many rock and metal guitarists.

In this chapter we'll learn how to interlink scale shapes and develop fluency across the whole neck, and to see scales in relation to their all-important root notes and chord shapes.

To start with, let's examine the difference between using "three-notes-per-string" shapes and traditional position-based scales. Figure one features two fingerings of the C major scale. The first is laid out so that it remains roughly around the 7th fret. The second rearranges the same notes so that we play three notes on every string and forces us slightly up the fretboard.

C Major Scale – Position fingering

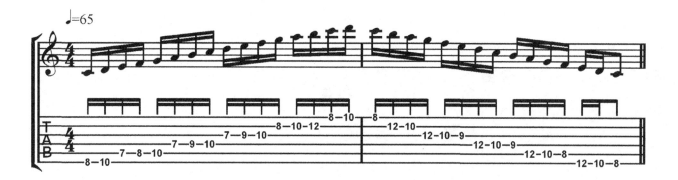

C Major Scale – Three notes-per-string fingering

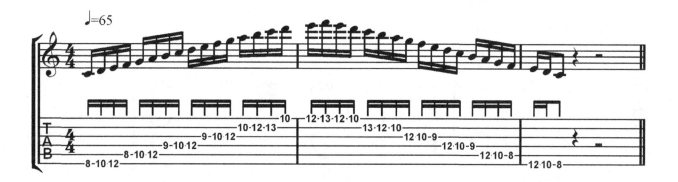

Laying scales out with three notes per string gives uniformity to every scale. The patterns for picking and fingering you use to play the above major scale are easily transferable to any mode, or to other scales like harmonic or melodic minor.

In Chapter One, we introduced the *second position* of the minor pentatonic scale, where the same notes as in position one were laid out on the adjacent area of the fretboard.

The same idea is now applied to the major scale. Each of the scale shapes below contains the same seven notes, although the lowest note changes from shape to shape. The root note of each scale is always C.

It's important to be aware of where the root notes lie in each position. I've notated the note C in each shape as a square to help you locate the root notes. It's also very helpful to be able to see scales in relation to familiar chord shapes, therefore the black notes in each diagram form a common open chord shape which you should try to visualise when playing through the scale.

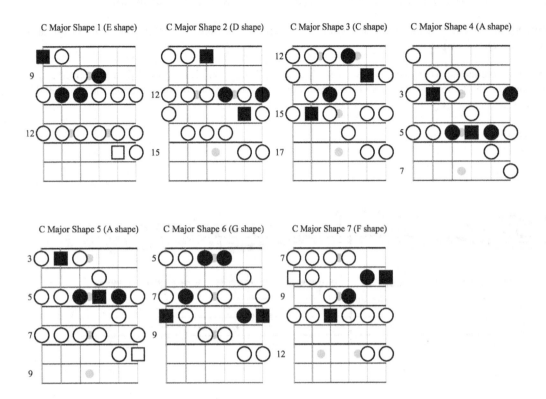

The seven shapes above connect together to cover the whole neck, and this can be seen in the diagram below. It may look complicated at first, but try to see how it can be broken up into the positions we looked at above.

C Major Scale Full Fretboard Diagram

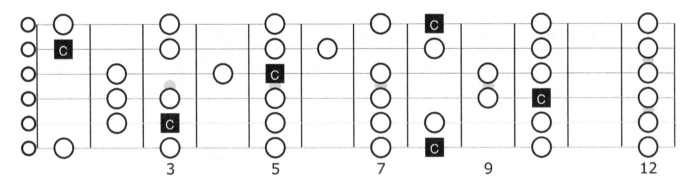

Memorising these shapes can be challenging, and to internalise how they all connect can take a lot of practice. Learning the licks and ideas contained in the rest of this book will help you to learn these connections as many of the ideas are based around three-notes-per-string shapes.

Here are a few examples to help you find ways to connect the seven shapes together.

This first example takes the pattern of notes on the first two strings of shape one and then plays the same six notes an octave higher. We've simply shifted the notes up the neck rather than staying within the confines of shape one. These repeated notes are a part of shape two.

The third set of six notes repeats the transformation again by moving the middle two strings of shape two up an octave to land us in shape three. Try this with any shape, for example starting with the bottom two strings of shape four and moving up through shapes five and six.

Example 3a

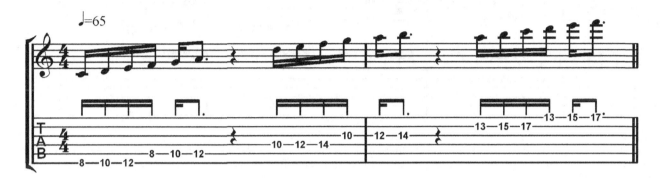

A slightly more involved variation of the same concept is shown in example 3b. This time we transpose the two-string fragment up by a fifth instead of an octave. Practicing moving between the different scale shapes using the middle strings, rather than just practicing ascending and descending each one in turn, will dramatically fast forward your fluency along the length of the fretboard.

The benefit of these exercises and the knowledge they're helping to cement is that you'll be able to create your own versions of the licks we'll look at in the rest of the book more easily. Being able to transform and reinterpret my licks is the key to you developing your own personality and self-expression as a guitarist.

Example 3b

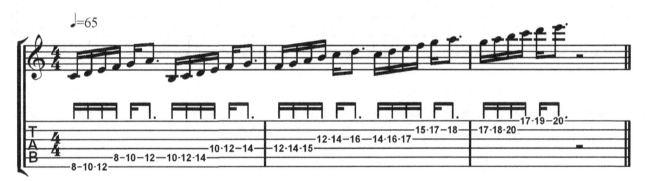

Once you've played through the different positions a couple of times, you should notice that the same sequence of fingerings occurs every time. After you've worked through the licks in this book, you'll be very familiar with the recurring patterns inherent in three-note-per-string phrasing.

This is particularly helpful once you start moving between different positions. Knowing this pattern is an easier brain process than trying to recall full six string shapes after you've just made an octave shift to the middle of a new position (as in example 3a).

The idea in example 3b can also be applied in a descending direction. Before you play through the example, try to imagine the first six notes as part of shape 3, starting at the twelfth fret, then as you move through each group of six notes, repeat the same process: picturing them within the relevant scale shape (next would be the 2nd shape, 1st, then 7th, 6th etc.).

Example 3c

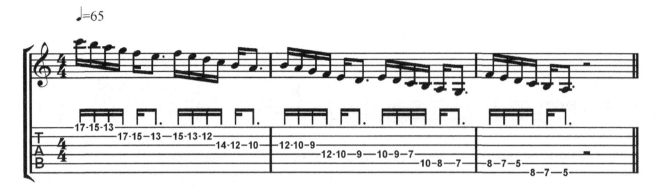

A final exercise to help you visualise how the scale shapes cover the neck involves playing *four* notes on each string. This exercise requires frequent position changes, and prevents you from sticking to the safety of one scale shape. Using your ear and trying to sing the next note in the scale will help you try to navigate up the neck even if you get lost.

Example 3d

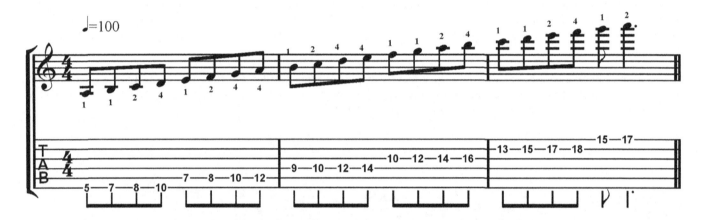

Using a position shift and three fingers helps to keep the hand in a more natural closed position, minimising unnecessary tension. However, experiment with fingerings for example 3d. I've included the most logical and ergonomic one in the notation but some players may choose to use a stretched out '1-2-3-4' fingering.

Modes

Though a full exploration of modal theory is beyond the scope of this chapter, I would like to help give you some understanding of the different musical colours that the modes most commonly found in heavy metal can create, and how you can start to use them.

A mode is treated as a scale in its own right, but is in fact formed by playing the major scale over different chords.

To explain this, let's discuss the major scale. The unique character of the major scale is the result of the sequence of tones and semitones between each of the seven notes in the scale, and the series of *intervals* they form. When the seven notes of the major scale are played unaccompanied we've been conditioned by western music to hear these notes in a certain way, and to recognise one note in particular as being the most stable and resolved. In other words, your brain will always arrange the notes of an unaccompanied major scale in a particular way and assign one note (the root) as 'home'.

However, if we play the same group of notes over a static chord from within the key, the ear interprets the notes according to the new harmonic context. In other words, you hear the root of the new underlying chord as 'home' and you subconsciously reorganise the notes in to a different order of importance. The root note of the new chord becomes the starting point for the scale. The special series of intervals that previously identified it as the major scale has been reshuffled, and when heard organised around the new starting point create a different musical feel.

For example, playing the C major scale over a D minor chord means the ear interprets each note based on its relation to D, rather than to C. You will find that the overall quality of the scale sounds more 'minor' because the notes of the scale when beginning from a D root note have a different pattern of tones and semitones than when the same notes begin from a C.

We can create the sound of each mode by changing the accompanying chord under a major scale; our playing will be more musical if we also try to phrase our solos around the new root note too.

You will notice that the following figure is identical to the C Major diagram on page 108, except that now E is labelled as the root note. To be thinking in E Phrygian, we would view the scale shapes around the note E, and E minor chord shapes.

E Phrygian Full Neck Diagram

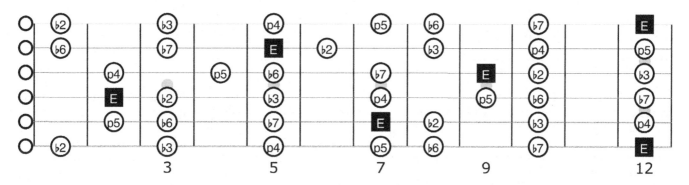

Each mode should be viewed as an independent scale with a unique set of intervals. However, the seven different modes, being drawn from the major scale all use the same set of scale shapes. In the following set of neck diagrams all seven modes are shown from a C root note, making it easier to compare the differences between each mode. The Modal name for the Major scale is The Ionian mode.

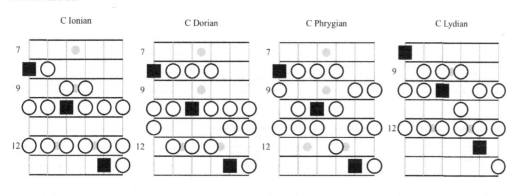

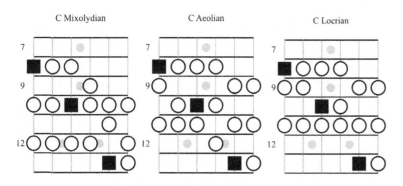

The minor modes (mode that contain a b3) are Aeolian, Phrygian and Locrian. These are the modes most commonly heard in metal, so we will begin by learning these scales. Although a minor mode, Dorian is less common in metal because it contains the brighter sounding major 6th.

Playing the first seven notes of each scale shape will show you the characteristics that make each mode unique. The following table shows the seven scale tones of all four minor modes.

If you move downwards through the scales from Dorian to Locrian, you'll see how the number of flattened tones increases between each scale. Each flattened note changes the flavour of the mode and causes it to sound darker or 'more minor'.

Mode Name	R	2	3	4	5	6	7
Dorian	R	2	b3	4	5	6	b7
Aeolian	R	2	b3	4	5	**b6**	b7
Phrygian	R	**b2**	b3	4	5	b6	b7
Locrian	R	b2	b3	4	**b5**	b6	b7

The remaining examples in this chapter play through the three most 'metal' modes, as well as demonstrating a lick that is characteristic of each one. To help make the clearest comparison of each mode, we'll be playing them all starting from an E root note at the 12th fret.

On the audio examples, you'll hear an accompanying chord pad that brings out the modal flavours more clearly, as each modal flavour is set up by the harmonic backdrop.

The first mode is E Aeolian, so the accompanying chord is E minor. Singing the notes while playing the mode makes you more aware of the unique tension each interval creates against the underlying chord.

Example 3e

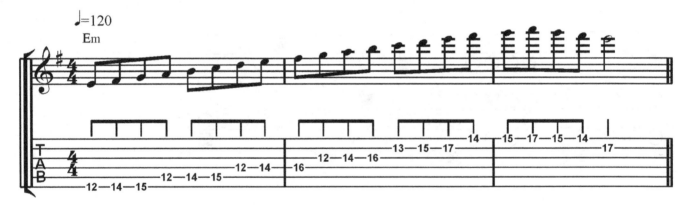

Next, we have a phrase in E Aeolian. The character notes that bring out the unique flavour of the Aeolian mode are the natural 2nd and the flattened 6th (in this case F# and C respectively)

Example 3f

The next mode is Phrygian, which differs from Aeolian by having a flattened second degree. Compare example 3g with 3e, and you'll find that all the F#'s are now F naturals. The backing chord remains E minor for Phrygian. However, we would no longer be able to use an Em add9 chord

Example 3g

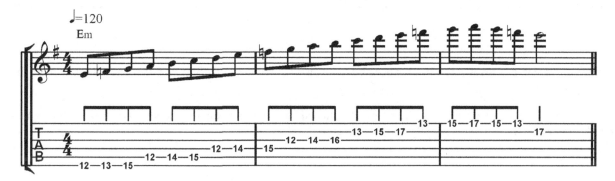

For our Phrygian phrase, I've really highlighted the characteristic interval between E and F (the root to flattened 2nd degree of the mode). **Example 3h**

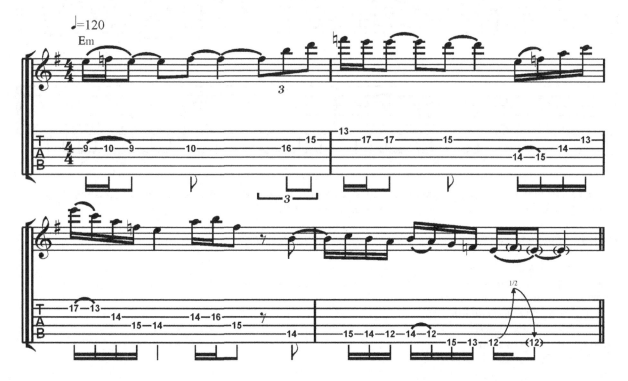

The final mode is E Locrian. When Locrian is harmonised, it forms a diminished triad rather than a minor chord, owing to its flattened fifth, hence why the accompanying chord is Edim. With all other modes the characteristic notes are always a semitone away from a note in the tonic chord, but Locrian is the exception because it is characterised by its flattened 5th, as well as the flattened 2nd.

Example 3i

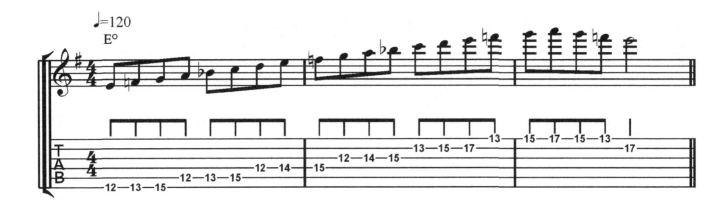

Locrian will rarely sound stable or resolved on its own because of its dissonant tonic chord, however, this line tries to explore the b5 before ending on the tonic.

The lick starts off by stating the tritone between the root and flattened fifth, before exploring some scalic legato playing and finishing off with a phrase based on the notes of the Em7b5 arpeggio (E, G, Bb, D)

Example 3j

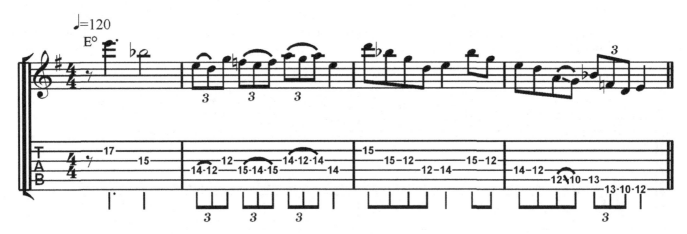

To really get a handle on how modes work, try playing each of the modes we've looked at in other fretboard positions. By playing each from the same root note, we can easily see how each mode differs.

Songs that make use of diatonic modes:

The Scorpions – *Sails of Charon* (Phrygian)
Ozzy Osbourne – *Crazy Train* (Aeolian)
Metallica – *Wherever I may Roam* (Phrygian)
Steve Vai – *For the Love of God* (Aeolian)
Machinehead – *Blood for Blood* (Locrian)
Steve Vai – *K'm Pe-Du-Wee* (Lydian)
Lamb of God – *Laid to Rest* chorus (Locrian)

Chapter Four: Legato

So far we've looked at ideas inspired by hard rock and developing melodic phrasing, but now I'd like to focus on the four most common modern rock guitar techniques and show how to go about developing idiomatic musical ideas using each one.

First up is legato. As a general musical term *Legato* means *smoothly*, but for guitarists this translates to using hammer-ons and pull-offs wherever possible. I've elected to start our technique study with legato for a good reason. The other three techniques all rely on having a developed sense of rhythm in the fretting hand before beginning to synchronise the picking hands. You will find that making a determined effort to improve your legato playing has a positive impact on your alternate picking as well!

I frequently see guitar students who are able to play fast legato scale runs, but on closer inspection they have little control or produce a weak tone. Most of the time the picking hand acts like an inbuilt metronome while the fretting hand holds down chord shapes, so it's unsurprising that the fretting hand requires special attention to reach the same level of rhythmic accuracy.

If you're new to legato, or would like some effective exercises to really hone your chops, be sure to check out *Complete Technique for Modern Guitar* also from Fundamental Changes. Practicing the licks I've compiled here will definitely improve your technique, although I'll be mostly looking at how the legato is applied in the context of real music rather than prescribing technique building exercises.

For the most fluid legato sound we can use a hammer-on instead of picking when moving to a lower string. This means that you only pick when changing to a higher string. This technique is sometimes called 'left hand tapping', or a 'hammer-on from nowhere'.

Between one extreme of applying hammer-ons to every note, and the other extreme of picking every note, we can combine both techniques in different amounts to produce a spectrum of textural possibilities.

Most of what we cover here will use the different positions of the major scale arranged with three notes per string as explained in the scale primer in Chapter Three.

Finally, muting the un-played strings is crucial, especially when playing with a high gain sound. As rule of thumb for modern rock lead guitar, mute the higher strings with the underside of the fretting fingers by keeping them flat to the fretboard, and mute the lower strings with the heel of the picking hand. The tip of your fretting hand fingers can also mute a lower string by overreaching the string that you're playing.

We start with some straightforward pentatonic sequences that develop the ones studied in Chapter One. However, we now we focus on using the legato technique and the smooth tone it produces. In the first example we are repeating a pattern on each string of the A minor pentatonic scale, using a hammer-on, pull-off and a final hammer-on.

Example 4a

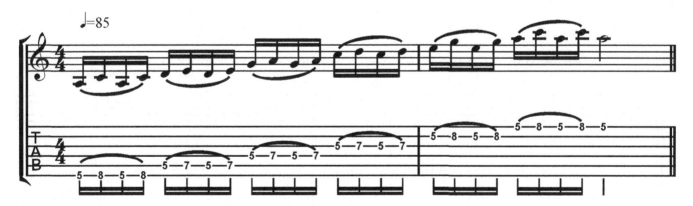

Our second example uses a three-note descending pattern played as a triplet rhythm. Get the first six notes sorted first before trying to digest the whole pattern. This way, the rest of the sequence will come much more easily. Likewise, isolate the first six notes of the ascending pattern in the second half of the example.

You can choose whether to use the third or the fourth finger for the notes at the 8th fret. Both approaches are valid so see which feels more natural to you.

Example 4b

Iron Maiden's guitarists can often be heard using rapid trills in many classic songs, (including *Phantom of the Opera* and *Aces High*). Start by trilling between adjacent notes in the scale then widen that interval to 3rds. This is a great way to develop both fretting hand stamina and speed while also learning scales along each string.

Example 4c

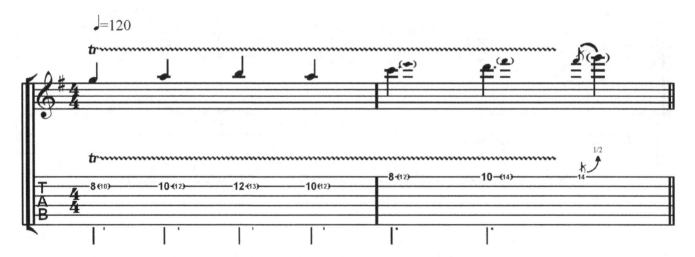

Here's a development on the previous idea in which the trill jumps up and down in octaves. This can be tricky at first, as the fretting hand index finger has to make a leap of faith across strings and positions. Let the picking hand follow across to mute the G string with its palm.

Example 4d

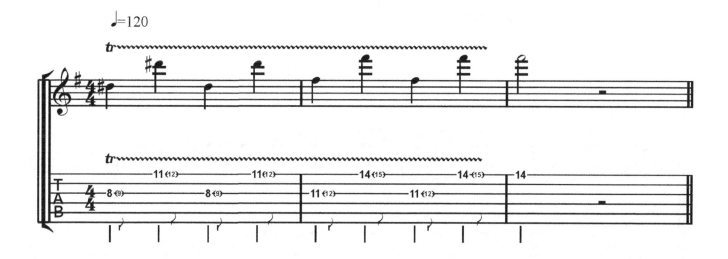

To warm us up for the three-notes-per-string licks coming up later in this chapter, here are two single string repeating licks that aim to get your technique honed before things get more complicated. The first example focuses on playing hammer-ons using the first, third and fourth fingers.

After picking the first note, the challenge is to hammer-on the remaining notes in an even triplet rhythm without rushing.

Example 4e

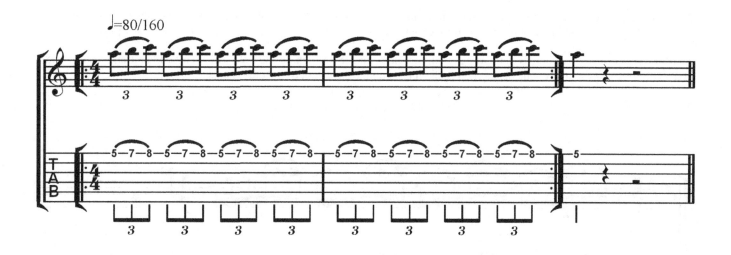

Once you have mastered the two hammer-ons, try pulling off from the 8th fret back to the 5th fret before hammering on again for the next group of three. This way, you can play the entire lick completely legato after the initial pick stroke and create the smoothest possible sound.

Now to reverse the direction of the previous example to get a pull-off workout instead! In this example we're using two pull-offs to descend along the E string. As I said in example 4e, the main difficulty when first getting to grips with this type of lick is the timing.

In most playing situations, the fretting hand holds down notes, while the rhythm is created by the picking hand. However, with legato playing, the job of both rhythm and pitch is being entrusted to the fretting hand.

I've changed the B to a Bb in this lick to give your fretting hand fingers another variation to practice. Use the index, middle and pinkie fingers to help you achieve the best hand position and build speed.

Example 4f

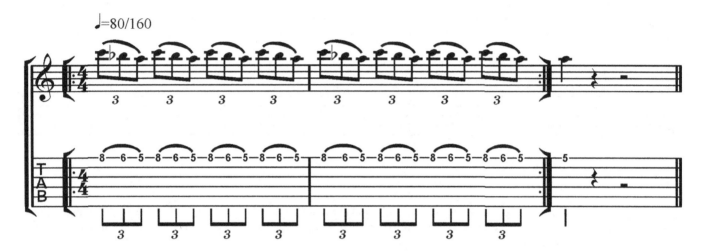

Playing both Examples 4e and 4f should feel like 'rolling' the three fingers onto or off the fretboard in order. We'll call these moves between the first to fourth fingers *half-rolls*, and we'll encounter a *full roll* later in the chapter.

With ascending and descending legato on one string both addressed, we can progress to applying this idea to two strings. In example 4g we have descending *half-rolls* on the E and B strings.

The only point to be aware of is that the index finger now needs to move between both strings, whereas in the previous examples the index finger could hold down the A note throughout. You may find it surprisingly unresponsive in its new job at first.

Don't be tempted to barre across both strings with the index finger throughout the lick. This is a bad habit and to be avoided. Barring both strings will allow them ring into each other and blur the sound of the other notes.

Example 4g

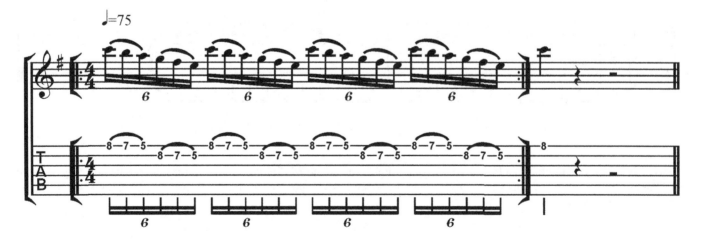

Here's a C major scale arranged with three notes on every string. Playing scales with three-note-per-string patterns help to give uniformity to runs and sequences across the strings.

It can be very tempting to play the following example as triplets (as in the last three examples), so to combat this impulse I've played them here as straight 1/16th notes. Listen to the audio and tap your foot with the metronome to hear the difference.

Try to accent the notes that fall on the beats with a more vigorous hammer-on/pull-off, or at least be aware of which notes fall on the beat so you can lock in to the tempo.

Example 4h

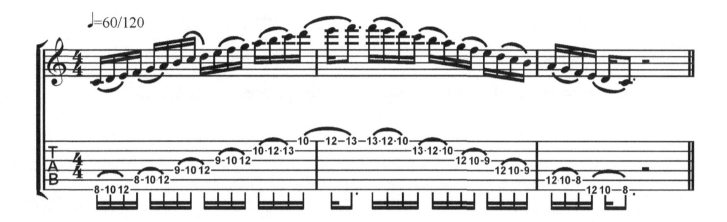

Everyone from Randy Rhoads and Eddie Van Halen to modern metal bands like Trivium has used the following ascending legato run. Simply repeat the half-roll fragment on each string across the neck.

It will be of great benefit to practice this lick using all seven major-scale shapes (covered in Chapter Three) so that you can learn to change position mid-shape and create longer ascending runs.

Example 4i

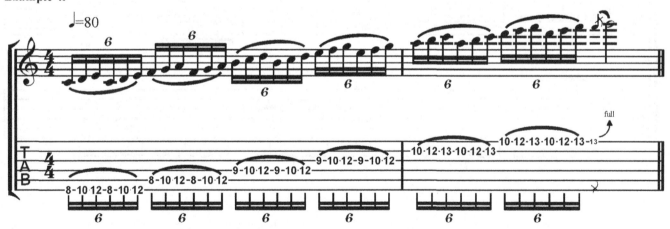

Here's another ascending idea using the 'half-roll' concept on each string.

This time we take advantage of the way three notes-per-string scale shapes repeat across the strings. After playing the lower four strings in order, we repeat the same shape starting on the D string an octave higher.

This is a great way to create a rapidly-ascending line over two and a half octaves, with the change of contour in the middle creating more interest than simply ascending the scale in a straight line.

Listen to the final lick in Randy Rhoads' solo on Crazy Train to hear the idea in context.

Example 4j

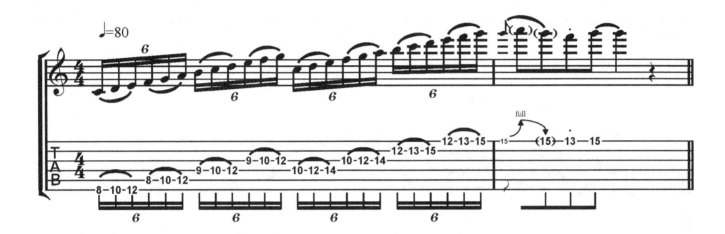

Moving to E minor now, we play a descending three-string pattern. Rhythmically we're performing this idea as sextuplets, but the groups of descending notes add up to nine, so the sequence becomes syncopated across the underlying beat.

Listen to the audio to get the hang of this feel and try not to over-think it. The rhythm will sort itself out as long as you are already confident playing example 4g.

Example 4k

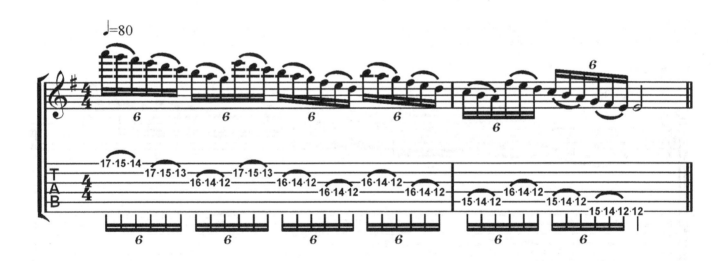

Find your own licks using half-roll legato moves, and experiment with different patterns across strings, and changing direction. The great thing about these scale shapes is that once you've learnt a run in one position it is quickly adaptable to any other three-notes-per-string shape.

In the next example, the legato scale fragment is played twice, each with a different ending phrase in D minor. It's important to practice linking new ideas into your existing material, so try jamming on the lick yourself and answering it with your own melodic pentatonic phrases. Always follow the picking directions closely and keep the fretting hand relaxed to help you get the best results. It can be tempting to push for speed early on but this will make your hand tense up and inhibit your playing in the long run.

Example 4l

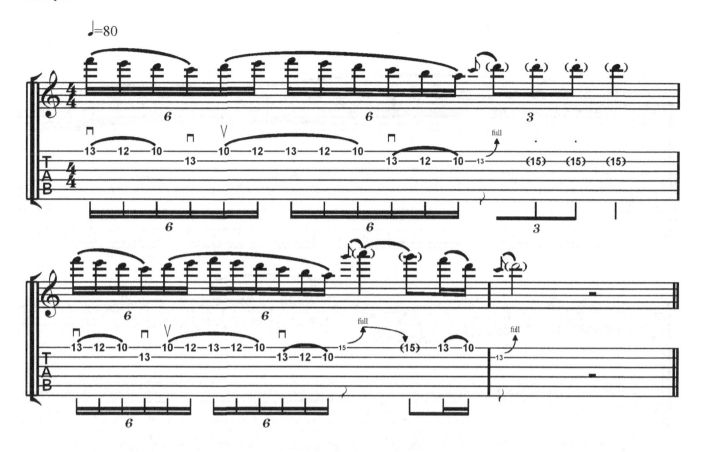

If you're having trouble getting used to the 'full roll' along the E string then try isolating the first six notes of the lick. The full roll is two half rolls tagged together, so we're 'rolling' from fourth finger to the first finger and back to the fourth again, or vice-versa.

Once you are comfortable with playing the pattern by picking the first note on each new string, try hammering-on to new strings when descending. The extra force needed to energise the string without picking can create unwanted noise from the other strings, so be sure to mute well (as described above).

Now for some longer legato phrases. The next lick covers a lot of ground, but it is simply a sequence of the two-beat phrase from example 4j across all the strings.

After the initial pick stroke, this descending sequence only requires one pick stroke per fragment if fretting hand taps are used to play the first note on the lower string of each pair. Pay attention to the timing before increasing the speed.

Example 4m

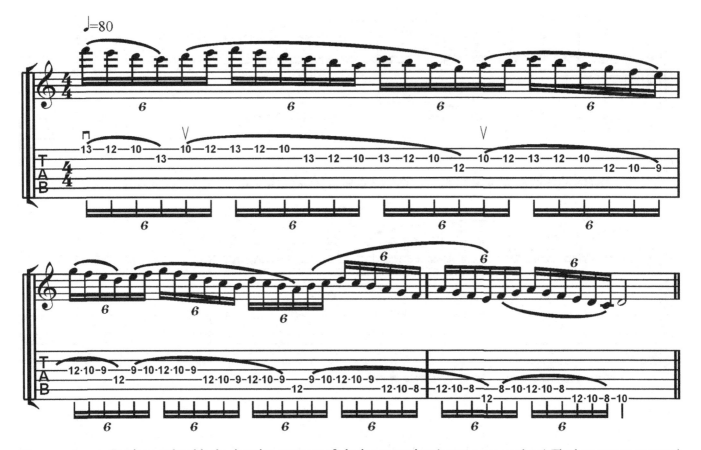

Now we move to B minor and tackle the daunting prospect of playing septuplets (seven notes per beat) The best way to approach this lick is to concentrate synchronising the first note on each new string with the click of the metronome and spacing the seven notes as evenly as possible in the space between!

Get used to rolling up and down each string's three-note shape, with practice it should soon feel natural.

Example 4n

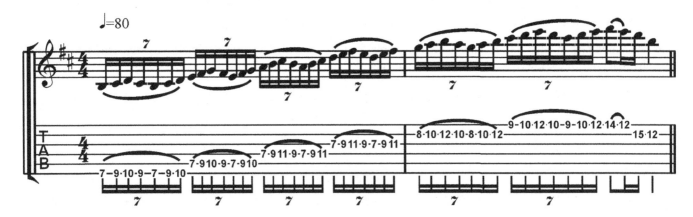

The following development of the previous example may prove more difficult; it requires strict control over the rhythmic evenness of the notes by fitting them into strict 1/16th-note rhythms. The benefit to your playing will be worth the initial effort.

Be aware that the pick strokes fall on different subdivisions of the beat.

Example 4o

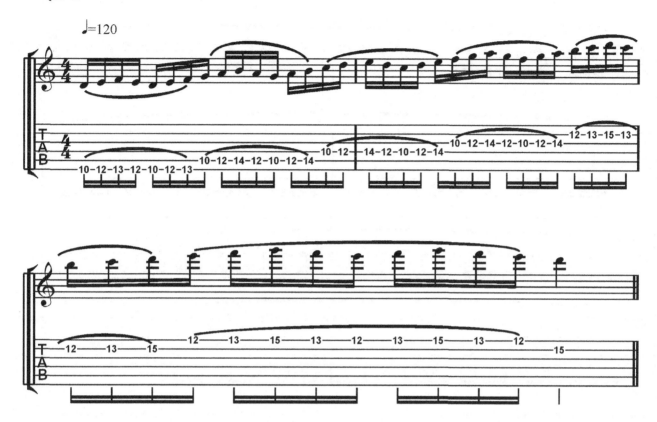

The next example returns to the three note 'half rolls' that we began with, but now the challenge is being able to jump between positions along one string quickly and accurately.

Each of the three-note cells should be played with fingers 1-2-4, or 1-3-4 depending on the spacing, and the index finger should move to start the next group in advance. Try to pick just as you slide, to avoid hearing the movement.

The hardest moment is at the end of beat two when we make a wide leap from the 5th to the 8th fret. Learning to execute position shifts in this way opens up new possibilities for playing longer runs and repetitive licks, creating a cloud of different cells that stutter excitedly around a target note.

Example 4p

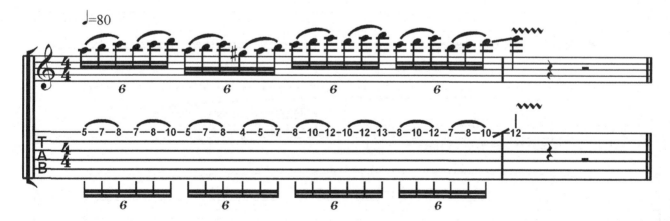

The next example is total legato! After the initial pick stroke, this whole line can be played with hammer-ons and pull-offs. As I said in example 4p, try to prepare for the position shifts in advance. The first finger should be moving up the fretboard in preparation for each shift.

Example 4q

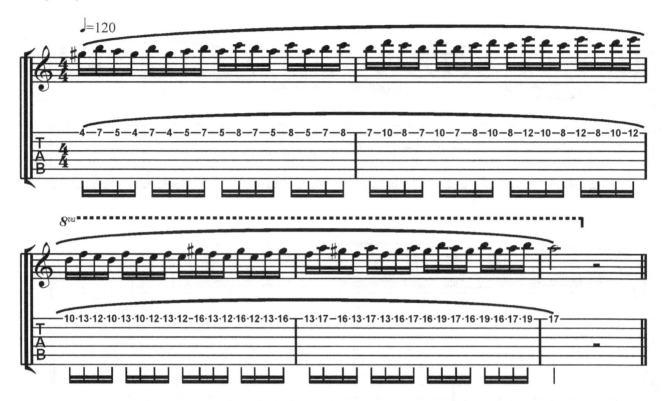

Example 4r is a descending version of the previous lick. The position shift is done with the pinkie and on the first position shift you should aim to contract the hand spacing to get the pinkie in place just as you finish playing beat two. Pay attention to navigating the leap from the G# to the F in bar two. It requires a tricky stretch. **Example 4r**

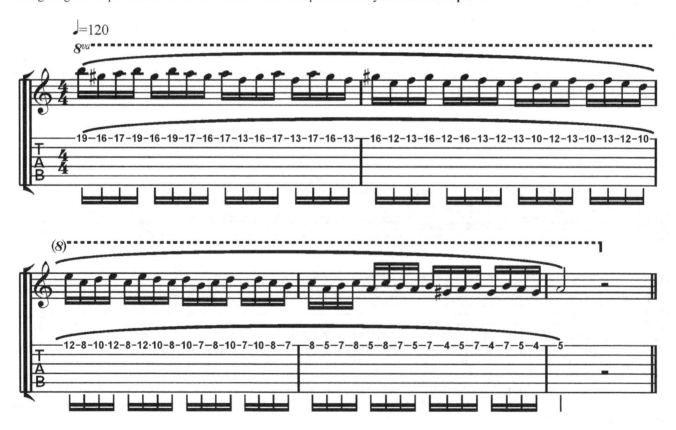

Most of these examples have used full rolls along the notes of each string, but this next, seemingly simple, sequential lick involves more alternation of the fingers. Practice the first six notes because later you'll find that the rest of the lick follows the same pattern due to the consistency of the three-notes-per-string shape. To mix things up we are using shape five of the E minor scale, which could also be seen as B Phrygian.

Example 4s

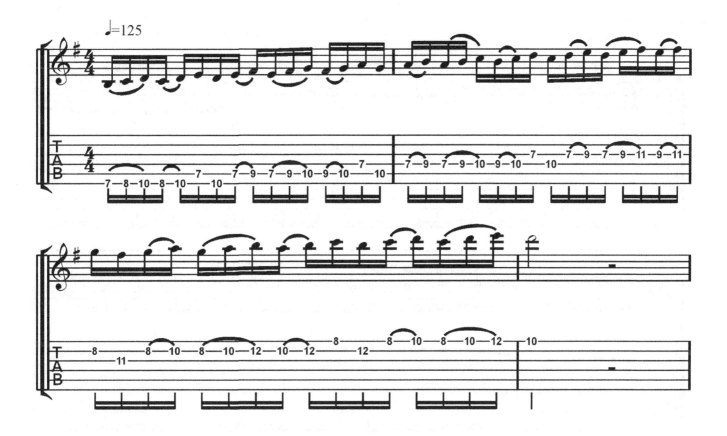

Finally, we introduce some slides to help us change position. Make sure to keep the first finger held down during the slide so that the string keeps ringing. Unlike when slides are used for expressive articulation, our goal here is to make the slide as quick as possible so there is minimal interruption between the two positions.

Example 4t

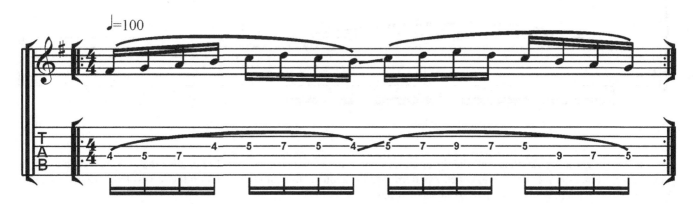

We can develop the previous scale fragment along the length of the neck. This following run moves through all seven scale positions before arriving an octave above the point where it began.

For the most legato sound possible, only pick when moving to the E string from the B string. Hammering onto the B string with the pinkie and sliding along the E string when changing position will take care of the other changes of string or position as you snake up the fretboard.

Example 4u

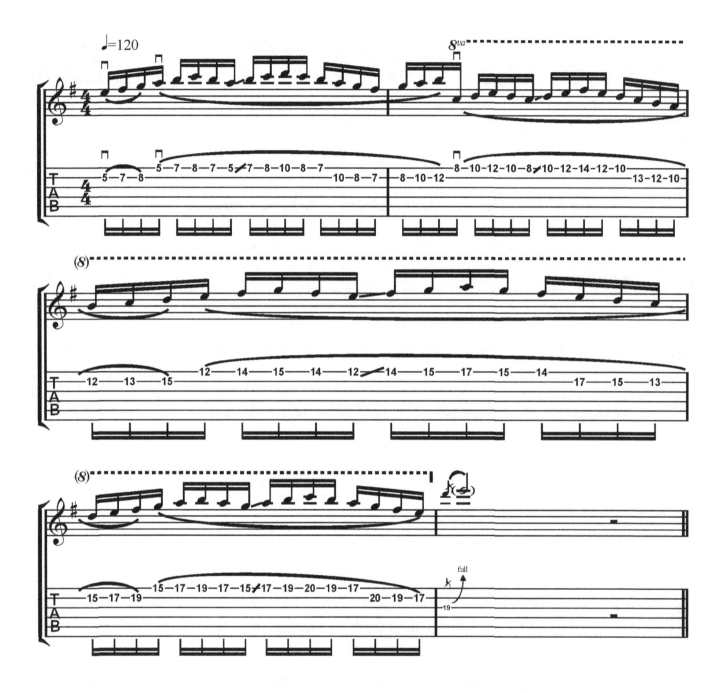

As you start to get more familiar with the different three-note-per-string shapes, you'll recognise many common patterns and relationships. For example, the previous lick's patterns are the same as the patterns found on the lowest two strings and follow the same order when played on any pair of adjacent strings.

By joining together short sections of different legato patterns, you can build up your own individual variations and combinations. Listen to any great legato metal guitar player and you'll hear that this is often how they construct their lines.

Chapter Five: Tapping Licks

After so much work on legato your fretting hand should be feeling pretty limbered up. Now we're going to develop our legato by adding the picking-hand fingers into the mix. Tapping first became popular with Eddie Van Halen and his instrumental showcase *'Eruption'* from Van Halen's self-titled debut record. However, it's worth noting that the technique existed before him when players like Allan Holdsworth and Frank Zappa experimented with tapping in the '70s, and Emmett Chapman's dedicated tapping instrument, The Chapman Stick was first conceived in 1969.

Using picking-hand fingers to fret notes opens up a world of different ideas that would otherwise require impossible stretches or position shifts; it also allows for faster and smoother execution of conventional scalic legato ideas.

Some modern players express reluctance to use tapping because of its connotations with the excesses of cheesy '80s hair-metal guitar playing. In my opinion these players do themselves a disservice. The creative options that tapping opens up are certainly worthy of investigation without regressing to indulgent 'widdling'. Any technique that brings a different texture to your playing is of value.

That said... we're going to begin in the style of Van Halen and his legion of imitators. Regardless of your direction, it's worth knowing how metal lead guitar style developed. These simpler licks will also help you to explore the more advanced ideas later on.

Some players (such as Van Halen and Paul Gilbert) use their first finger for tapping; however, it is common practice for modern players to use their second finger. This is the better option for two reasons: firstly, you are able to hold the pick normally while tapping which makes the transition back to conventional playing easier. Secondly, if you wish to use multiple fingers to tap, then the middle and ring fingers provide the best combination.

In the legato chapter, most licks were formed from scales where the distances between notes were small. By using two hands on the fretboard, we can spread out the distances between notes further and play wider intervals. Therefore this chapter's licks will involve more *arpeggios*.

Arpeggios are chords that are played one note at a time. They can be used in much the same way as scales if we view them as a pool of notes with which to create licks and runs.

If you're new to tapping this is a great place to start. Example 5a is a classic, Van Halen-style E major arpeggio that sounds impressive but is surprisingly easy to master.

Treat the tapping finger as you would any of the fretting hand digits and the pull off motion should be much the same. You've not talked about any pull off motion. Generating a strong tap might prove tough at first, as your finger will need time to develop the same callus as the fretting hand fingertips.

Example 5a

+ = Tap with right hand finger.

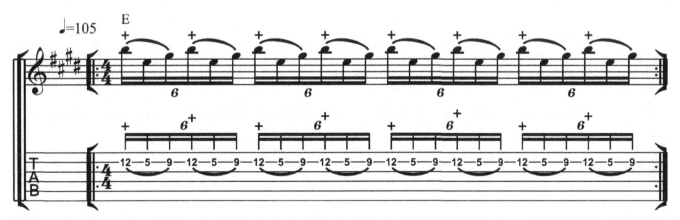

Here is the minor version of the same shape. Now that the chord is E minor, notice how the G# has been lowered to a G. Understanding how the individual notes in each arpeggio are laid out will help you enormously when it comes to arranging a sequence across different chords.

Example 5b

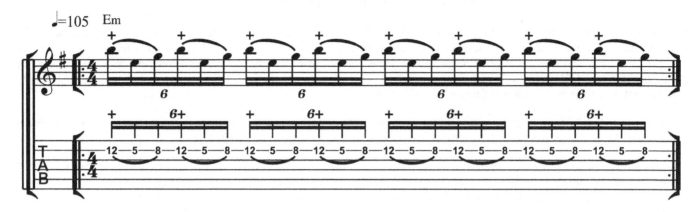

Once one arpeggio is comfortable, we can string several together to outline a chord progression. Be aware of how the shape changes between the chords.

Moving both hands along the fretboard independently can be a lot to think about, but notice how the fretting doesn't move in the first chord change, and the tapping hand doesn't move in the third one.

Many metal songs feature this type of structured arpeggio section, often before the main solo. Particularly famous examples include Van Halen's *Hot for Teacher*, Europe's *The Final Countdown,* and Ozzy Osbourne's *Crazy Train.*

Example 5c

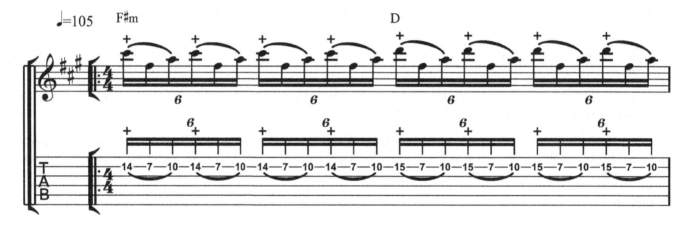

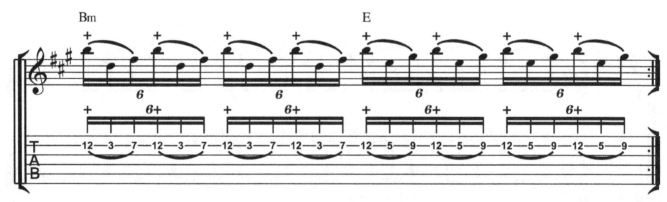

Here's an alternative pattern you can use in similar situations. It features a faster 'double tap' in the style of Randy Rhoads. To execute the two taps in quick succession, try using the wrist to generate the hammer-on rather than the tapping finger itself. Allow the hand to 'bounce' against the fretboard. Again, once this pattern is comfortable you should try to apply it over different chord progressions.

Example 5d

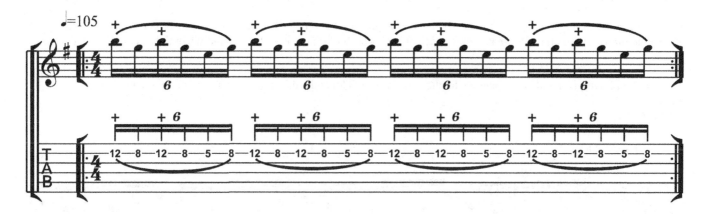

The more you apply these tapping ideas to different chords, the more they will feel natural and become a part of your expressive vocabulary. Players who sound most expressive when tapping are those who make no clear distinction between tapping and their other licks and can switch back and forth at will.

Here is another tapping section using the pattern from example 5d. The chords are drawn from the key of D minor and alternate between the top two strings. Once you start tapping on more than one string, you may find it helpful to have an anchor point on the side of the neck. You can use either the pinkie or the thumb.

Follow the fingerings closely to help make the string changes easier. Alternating between the third and fourth fingers of the fretting hand avoids any accidental pull-off to the open strings when changing string and helps to provide a smoother transition between arpeggios. **Example 5e**

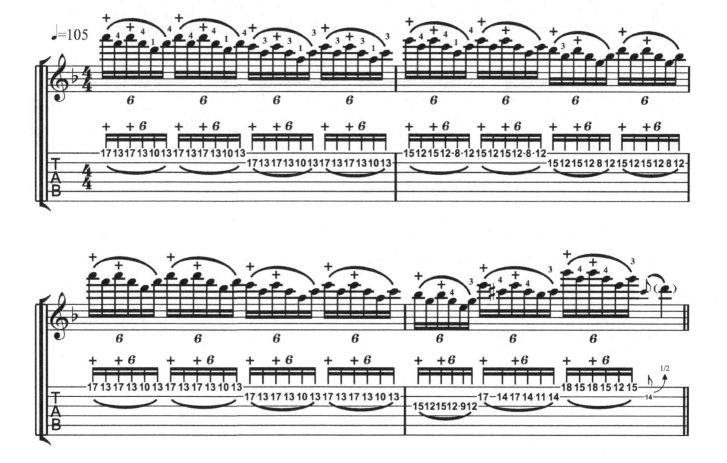

The final phrase of the lick features a diminished arpeggio that repeats across the top three strings. When both hands have to change position like this, it's usually better to watch the tapping hand, as the fretting hand is performing a familiar task.

Our penultimate example demonstrates a full octave arpeggio pattern that pulls off from the first finger to the open string. This technique limits you to arpeggios that contain open-string notes but has a great, 'full' sound when the key of the song allows for it.

Here, we're playing Dm and Gm arpeggios on the D string then Cm and a different voicing of Gm on the G string.

Example 5f

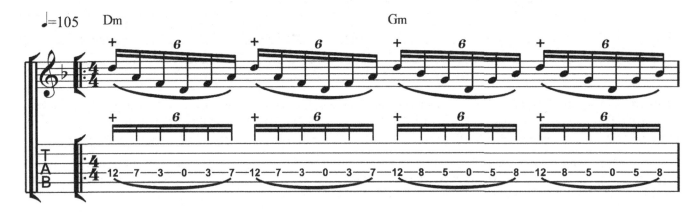

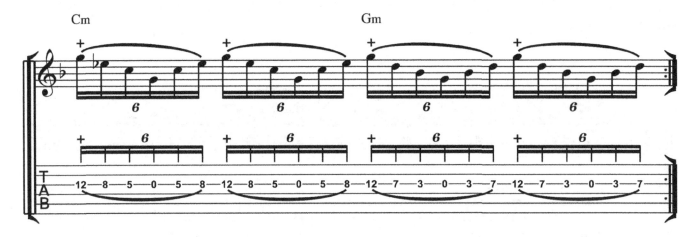

A interesting example of how this idea can be developed is in Joe Satriani's popular track *Satch Boogie* where Joe uses the open string as a pedal tone against a range of arpeggio type ideas whose unifying factor is the open string.

For a heavier example, Kerry King starts his solo in Slayer's *War Ensemble* with a similar idea on the low E string.

So far we've stuck to tapping on just one or two strings but next a six-note tapping lick moves across all six strings in a dramatic and exciting flurry of notes! Although we start off with A minor and E minor arpeggios, you'll find that as you get to the G and D strings that the remaining notes are drawn from the A minor pentatonic scale instead of sticking to one arpeggio.

To get the tapping finger used to crossing strings it will be helpful to break the lick up into smaller chunks of three beats before reassembling them to form the whole lick.

Example 5g

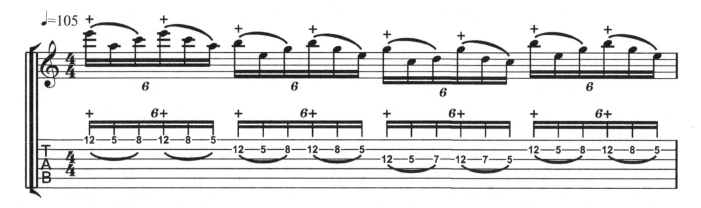

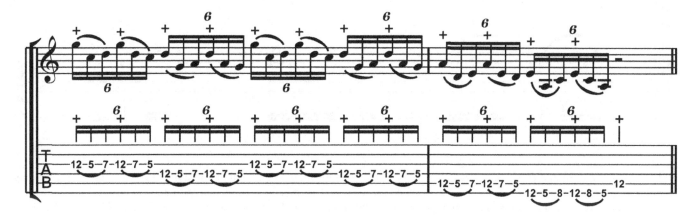

Once the interaction between the two hands becomes fluent and natural we can start to experiment with the articulation of tapped notes. Just like any other fretted notes, we can make taps more expressive with slides, bends and vibrato.

In the next example a stock blues lick is morphed into a more interesting intervallic lick by extending some of the string bends with tapped higher notes.

All of the bending motion should come from the fretting hand while the picking hand holds down the high note. Practice the sequence of motions slowly to master this lick. When confident, you'll be able to use this effect at will to provide climactic screaming bends to end your solos!

Visualise the minor pentatonic scale shape where you're tapping and remember that the pitch of the bend will be two frets higher (or one for a semitone bend). Zakk Wylde and TJ Helmerich have both used this technique, as has Synyster Gates of Avenged Sevenfold. **Example 5h**

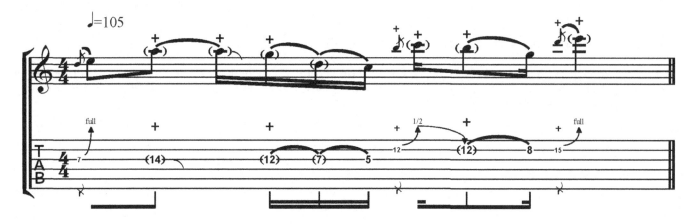

In the next lick we add extra interest to a tapped arpeggio by sliding up quickly from the tapped note. The slide is just to create an effect so don't worry about sliding to a specific fret. Our melodic ending phrase incorporates more articulated tapped notes like example 5f, first sustaining a tapped note at the 15th fret with vibrato, before tapping again and bending up from the 17th fret.

Again, all the vibrato and bending should come from the fretting hand behind the tapped note as it has more strength and leverage on the string.

Example 5i

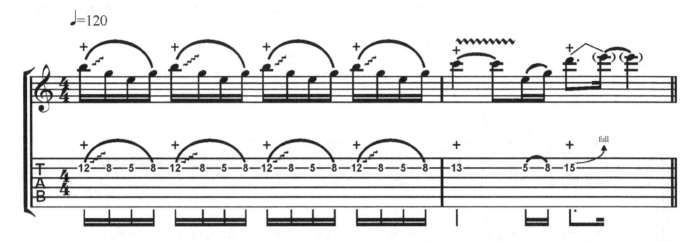

This novel method for achieving very fast and consistent trills was inspired by bass guitar shredder Billy Sheehan. Using tapping to take half of the workload away from the fretting hand means less strength and stamina is required to get an even and controlled sound. The trick is to make sure the two hands don't collide because they're both heading for the same fret!

Example 5j

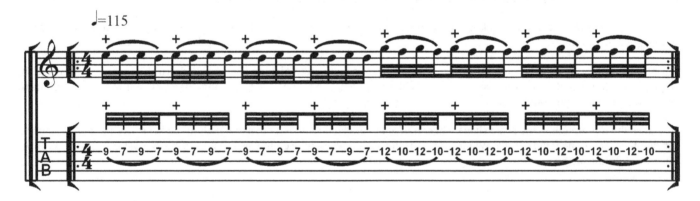

Starting from where the previous example left off, the following lick develops the idea into a long, flowing scalic run.

Make sure the first phrase feels easy before trying to race up the fretboard! Watch for the position shifts and lead with the tapping hand. A frightening example of Billy doing this in unison with guitarist Paul Gilbert is in the song *Addicted to that Rush* from Mr. Big's eponymous 1989 debut.

Example 5k

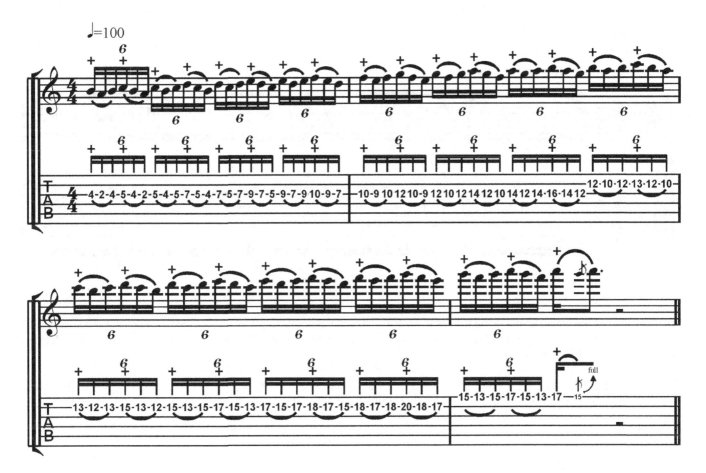

Now we'll address more scalic ideas that make use of tapping. The previous licks all delegated notes to the right hand to make the fretting hand's job easier. However, now we will use tapping to expand the vocabulary of the legato chapter by extending each position on the string into a four-note shape with the addition of a tap.

Example 5l

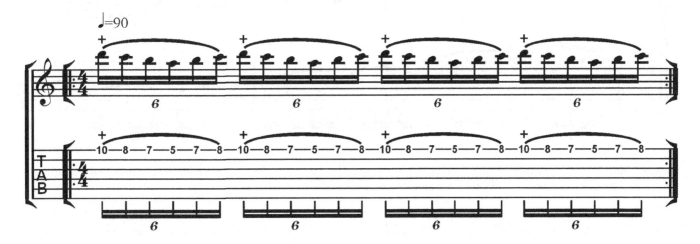

Though it is less common for guitarists to practice four-notes-per-string scales, experimenting with this technique will accelerate your learning of the fretboard layout by forcing you to constantly link together different scale positions.

In the previous example we remained in one scale position while borrowing tapped notes from the adjacent shape. This time we're limiting ourselves to one string and using slides to link the phrases together.

After completing the full roll of the four-note shape, we slide up to the next position within the B minor scale and begin again. The septuplet rhythm should sort itself out if you concentrate on syncing up the tapped notes to the beats.

Example 5m

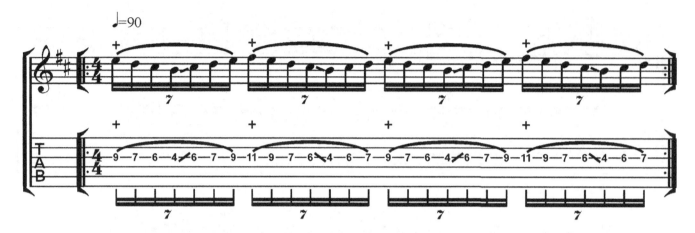

Here's a more advanced scalic run using the same principle. When playing the top E string, let the tip of the fretting hand's index finger touch and mute the B string. Repeat this position as you move across the strings. This helps to keep the notes clear and controlled when using distortion.

Again, repeating the same phrase across three octaves is a great way to get more mileage out of your ideas while repeating the same fingering for each. Just be careful of the position shift between octaves.

Example 5n

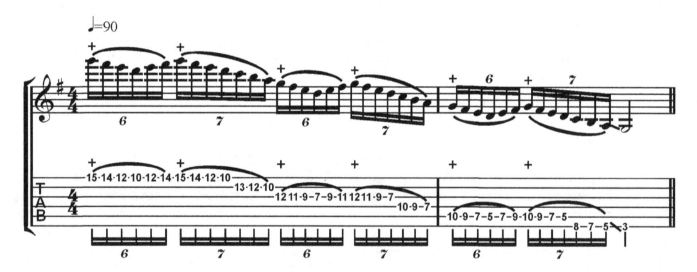

Inspired equally by Paul Gilbert and Eddie Van Halen, the next lick has a definite bluesy quality to it thanks to the hybrid scale shape that features a combination of chromatic and Dorian notes added to the pentatonic scale.

Try to make the hammer-ons to the new string with the pinkie strong and forceful; we're after consistency of volume between tapped, picked and legato notes. You may find this means hammering down on the fretboard from a greater height than normal.

Example 5o

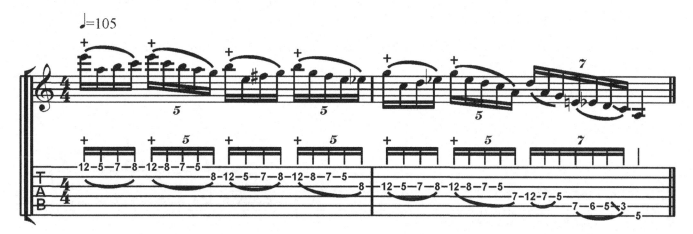

Winger/Dokken guitarist Reb Beach and fusion shredder Greg Howe both use tapping to play seamless legato lines using standard shapes. In the following licks we use a tap to play the notes that you would normally play with the pinkie in a three-notes-per-string shape.

To introduce this approach, here's a straightforward ascending scale run using B Aeolian. It can feel a little unnatural at first to lead with the fretting hand as almost all our examples so far have placed the tapped notes on the beat. Persevere though, as developing the independence to start with any finger on any beat will help your playing massively.

Example 5p

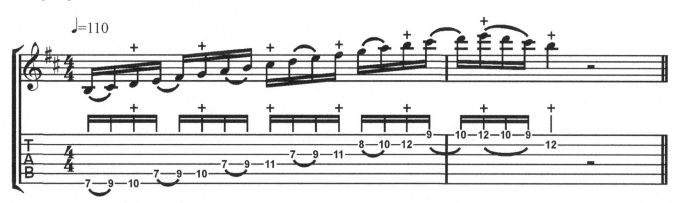

After having its workload reduced, the fretting hand can hammer-on with greater strength and speed.

Our first variation to this technique keeps things pretty uniform in both hands as the lick ascends using different two-string pairs.

Example 5q

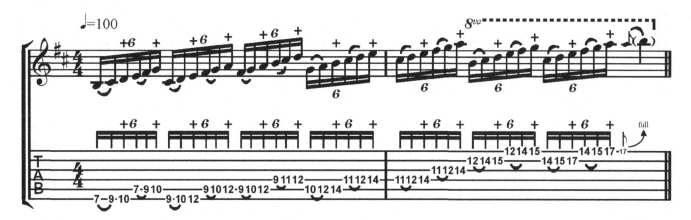

Our third lick using this tapping approach adds some slides by the fretting hand to move between positions, as well as adding some odd rhythms. The alternate quintuplet/sextuplet rhythmic groupings actually get easier once you speed up; just be aware the tapped note lands on beat 2, and is very slightly faster.

The effect of these ingredients is to make the lick more fluid compared to sticking rigidly to the underlying rhythm.

Although there may seem more to concentrate on, we are just repeating the same phrase in three different octaves. Seeing it that way should make it easier to visualise.

Example 5r

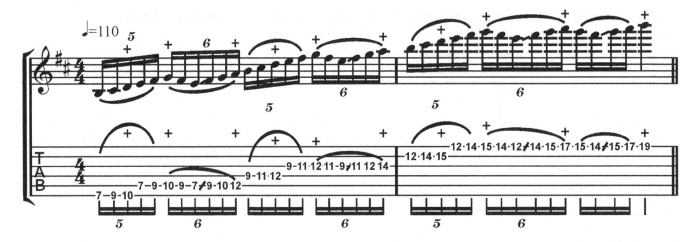

Finally, here is a quick tapping trick that delivers great bang for your buck! Instead of using a finger to tap, use the side of the pick to hammer as fast as possible. This produces a rapid trill between the 'tapped' notes and fretted notes.

This rather gung-ho technique does produce a pleasing balance of intensity with the ability to hear a melody. In our example, I'm fingering a melody with the fretting hand and then pick-tapping a suitable chord tone from an imagined chordal accompaniment.

Example 5s

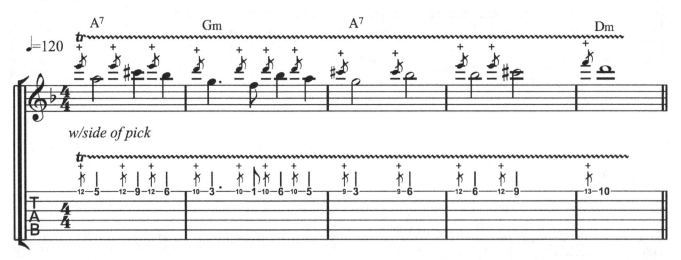

Recommended listening for tapping:

Van Halen – *Eruption*
Bon Jovi – *You Give Love a Bad Name*
Joe Satriani – *Surfing with the Alien*
Metallica – *One*
Buckethead – *Electronic Slight of Hand*

136

Chapter Six: Alternate Picking

A confident picking technique is beneficial whether you're playing rhythm or lead guitar. It'll help to create a strong sound and consistent timing. Picking all, or the majority of the notes in a phrase provides a more percussive and aggressive feel compared to the legato approach we've explored in previous chapters.

If you watch players with particularly developed alternate picking abilities, there are as many hand positions and ways of holding the pick as there are players. Whether they rest fingers on the guitar body or to grip the pick with one finger or two, the common factor among these guitarists is that the picking motion comes from the wrist rather than by moving the thumb or fingers individually.

Experiment with how you're touching the strings to discover new tonal options. Try striking the string with the pick at different angles. Picking with the pick flat against the string produces a strong solid tone, while angling the thumb forward to slice through with the edge produces a thinner tone. I recommend adopting a 45-degree angle with the pick to balance good tone with the lower resistance of the pick's edge.

Using a thicker pick is common among players with strong picking techniques. A less flexible pick avoids the delayed attack caused when a thin pick is bent back by the string. Popular picks for playing metal guitar are usually about 2mm thick and have a pointed tip.

Once you have a grasp of the mechanics of picking, you'll find that the main hurdle in your development is syncing the hands up perfectly. If you've worked on the legato examples that focussed on timing, then coordinating the hands should happen more quickly as you've already started to instil rhythmic accuracy.

To help anchor both hands to your internal sense of rhythm, make sure to accent the notes on the beat with a stronger pick stroke. In this first short example the notes marked with arrowheads should be played with a harder pick stroke to make them stand out.

As the speed increases, these accented notes will act as markers to help you feel the overall pulse rather than having to count each note individually.

This tremolo picked lick isolates the high E string, and demonstrates the idea of accenting the notes on the beat to help stay in time. Keep the picking hand relaxed and use a wider arc when picking the accents.

Example 6a

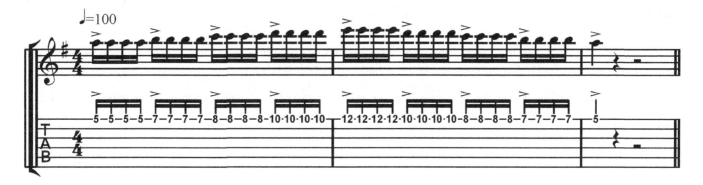

Even if you're a confident metal rhythm player with a strong picking technique, you may find it challenging to pick evenly on the thinner strings. Try to be lighter with your attack by striking the string with less of the pick.

As with any 'technical' playing, be sure to warm up slowly. The goal should be clean and relaxed execution rather trying to push for speed.

You will find that picking makes the position shifts in our first lick easier on the fretting hand. Aim for as light a touch as possible but without the note buzzing. If you have trouble syncing the hands, accenting the start of every group gives the hands a regular reference point to match up to.

Example 6b

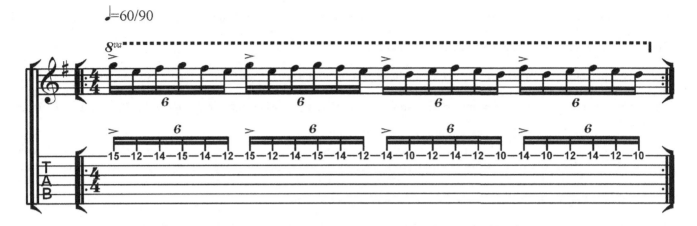

This Yngwie Malmsteen-influenced single string passage is a great workout for developing the third and fourth fingers. Developing your speed with these ideas allows you to isolate the picking motion without having to contend with string crossing, helping you to work on a consistent attack and economy of motion without unnecessary complications.

Example 6c

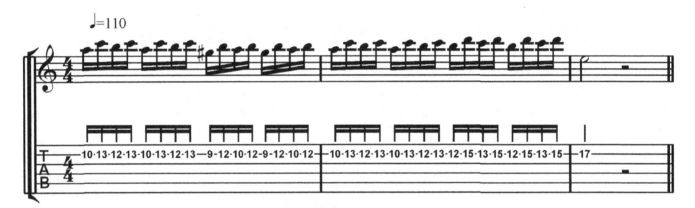

Our first single-string picking lick is derived by starting from each finger in turn. The resultant melodic pattern delivers a great independence workout for the fingers and is nicely unpredictable for the listener.

The lick repeats the same four notes from E minor, but you could also move the whole bar up through the scale if you wish.

Example 6d

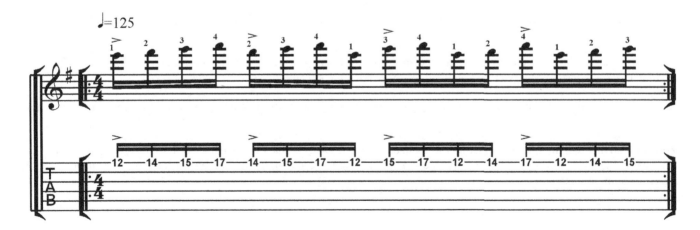

While the pentatonic fingering of this lick should be very familiar to you, the two-notes-per-string picking-pattern may be demanding at first. To help make the tone and wrist movement consistent, keep moving the picking hand across the bridge as you change strings so that each new string is in the same relative position to the pick.

Fast, alternate-picked pentatonic sequences feature prominently in the playing styles of Zakk Wylde, Gary Moore and Alexi Laiho (Children of Bodom), and give an aggressive, bluesy injection into your solo.

To enhance the percussive effect of picking every note, it's common practice to palm mute with the heel of the picking hand, particularly on the lower strings where the notes can be less defined. To get the most consistent tone across the strings, be sure to move the picking hand across the strings so the pick meets each string at the same angle.

Example 6e

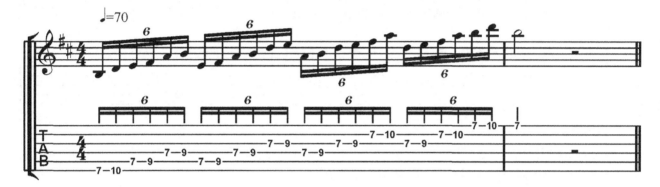

Fast scale runs are particularly effective for building exciting transitions into new sections or to ascend to a prominent climax on a high note. It is important to practice ending a run cleanly with a quality vibrato, or string bend. While you should aim to nail all the notes, the last note is probably the most crucial moment in the run as this one leaves a lasting impression.

Most of the next lick can be played with the first and third fingers, these being the strongest finger combination. However, be aware of how the pattern changes. You may find it better to use the pinkie on the fourth shape and the middle finger on the fifth.

Example 6f

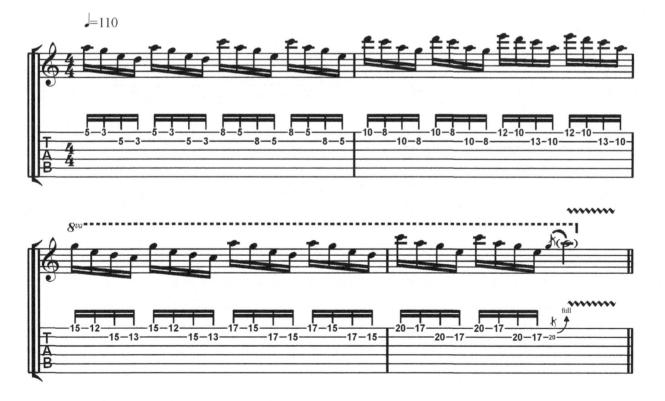

Combining 'standard' licks with less predictable rhythms is a great way to keep your solos sounding fresh. In the following example we play a descending pentatonic sequence in groups of five notes. Note that the beat is still being subdivided into straight 1/16th notes so the phrasing of the fives moves across the pulse of the music, forming what is known as a *cross rhythm*.

Break the lick down slowly and observe how the patterns relate to each other before increasing the metronome speed.

Example 6g

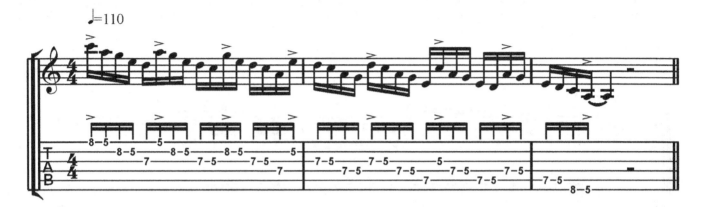

There are two possibilities when changing strings using alternate picking; *outside* or *inside* pick strokes. The following two bars demonstrate the differences clearly.

The first uses *outside* picking, and you'll notice the pick hooks around the outside of the new string, whereas bar two keeps the pick 'inside' the strings.

Most players find inside picking more awkward as the pick can feel 'trapped' between the strings making the hand tense up. However, both should be practiced equally if you wish to develop a dexterous picking technique.

Example 6h

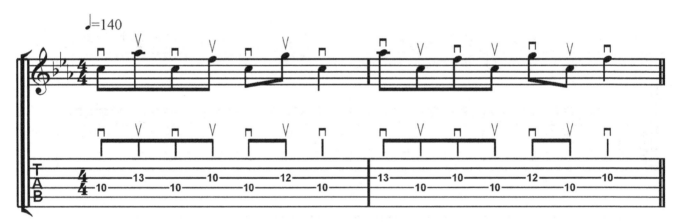

The following alternate picking lick is an important building block that can be used to create longer runs. Accenting the upstroke on the G string will help to get all your upstrokes stronger. Players who have a mastery of three-notes-per-string scale runs like Paul Gilbert and John Petrucci frequently draw on cells like this in both their rhythm and lead playing.

For extra benefit, try starting with an upstroke as well.

Example 6i

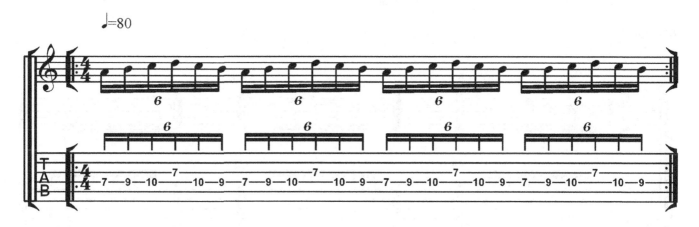

Now we move the fragment in example 6h across the strings to create a longer ascending run. As you pick on the higher strings, you may find you have to pick with a lighter touch to avoid snagging the string unexpectedly as the higher strings offer less resistance to the pick than the lower strings.

Remember to make the final bend clear and in tune, as this is the climax of the run.

Example 6j

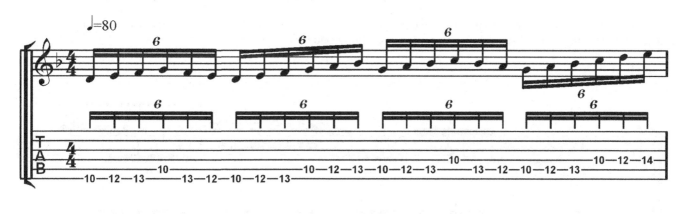

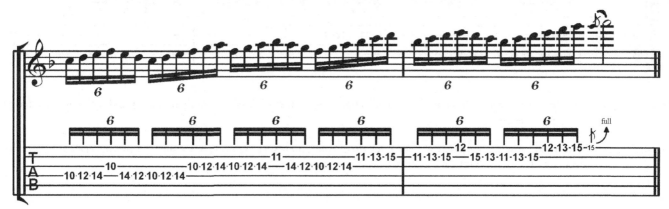

To create individual picking runs, it's important to work on a range of picking fragments until they feel easy. You can then link them together in different combinations while moving through different positions of a scale.

In the example below we have three separate fragments which you could apply across any three-notes-per-string scales you know, in the same way that we did in example 6j to the fragment from 6i.

Example 6k

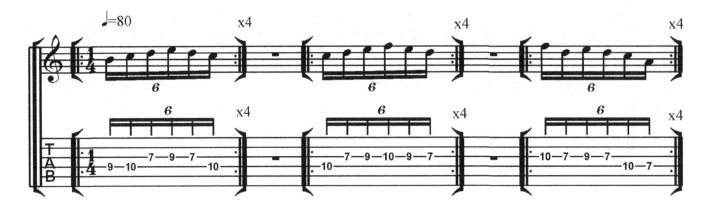

I suggest finding fragments that you like, practicing them in different positions, and then using them to create your own lines. This way you'll be developing original licks rather than just copying my examples note for note.

Steve Morse (Dixie Dregs/Deep Purple) is well known for his formidable picking. He adds chromatic passing notes to his solos to give a jazzy tinge to his shredding rock solos. John Petrucci acknowledges Steve's influence on his own style.

In the next, Morse-inspired lick, use the first three fingers and be careful to make the position shifts tidy when the index finger replaces the ring finger on the same fret (e.g. at the start of the second beat).

Example 6l

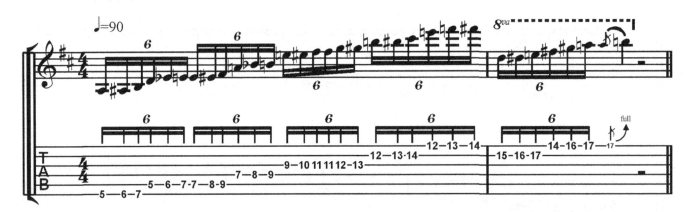

Now for a full roll across two strings. You may find that the picking element is easier here than in the previous examples due to there being fewer string changes.

If you've already worked through the scale runs in the legato chapter, and were rigorous in ironing out timing inaccuracies, then you'll find synchronising the hands a lot easier and speed will quickly develop.

Example 6m

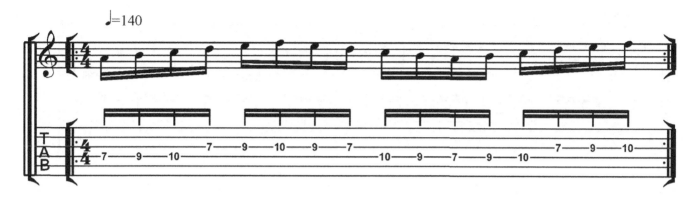

The previous full roll is now moved through several scale positions to cover more ground in less time. Learning the seven positions of the diatonic modes is crucial to being able to play these lines without premeditating them.

Example 6n

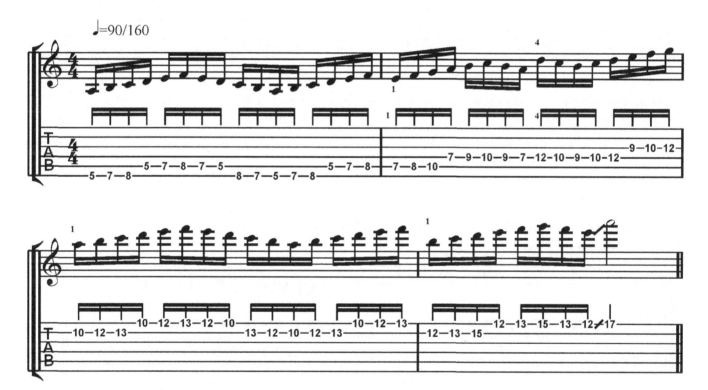

The eight-note pattern is now reversed and is used to descend in a similar fashion. This time all string changes are achieved with inside picking. Start to palm mute a little as you move to the lower strings; this helps make the notes more defined and allow the melodic contour to come through.

Here we're exploring the G Harmonic minor scale to give things a neoclassical tinge.

Example 6o

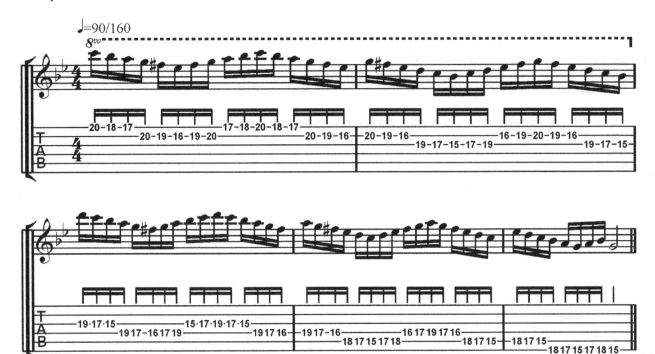

Here's another alternative fragment with which to create your lines. The full roll along each string adds up to seven notes, so playing them as 1/16th notes produces a slightly disorientating cross rhythm that works particularly well at higher speeds.

These uneven phrase lengths highlight the importance of being comfortable with both types of string crossing, as the direction of the pick strokes changes every time due to the seven-note phrase length.

Example 6p

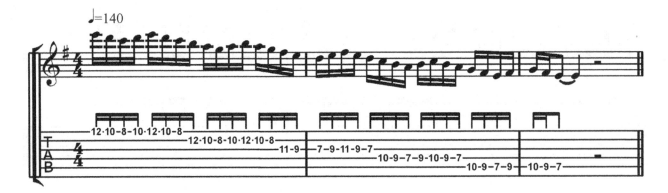

Recommended listening for examples of alternate picking:

Deep Purple – *Fireball*
Yngwie Malmsteen – *I'll see the Light Tonight*
Europe – *Halfway to Heaven*
Michael Angelo Batio – *No Boundaries*
Death – *Secret Face*
Dream Theater – *Erotomania*
Racer X – *Superheroes*

Chapter Seven: Sweep Picking

This is our final chapter on "technique-centric" vocabulary. I've left sweep picking until last because it requires a good sense of timing in the fretting hand, perfect synchronisation, and a good grasp of alternate picking. Having focussed on each of these elements individually, you should now be well equipped to tackle some sweeping and economy picking licks.

Like tapping, sweep picking enables us to play much wider intervals at speed. Whereas tapping allows for large intervals along the length of a string, sweep picking is used when we arrange notes with only one-note-per-string.

Just like tapping is associated with Eddie Van Halen, the poster boy for sweep picking chops from hell is undoubtedly Yngwie Malmsteen, though many other players were starting to use similar ideas at the time. (There is footage of 'country gentleman' Chet Atkins busting out some shred worthy sweep-arpeggios during a TV appearance with Jerry Reed back in 1975!)

Most of our licks so far have been composed from scales and playing adjacent notes in order. However, like the tapping chapter, many of our sweep picking licks will use arpeggios. An arpeggio is just the posh name for playing the notes of a chord separately. By playing an arpeggio we are able to give the same flavour as playing a chord but in a melodic format. Due to the wider intervals involved in an arpeggio they can be more exciting to the ear.

The fleet-fingered sweep arpeggios used by players like Yngwie Malmsteen, Jason Becker and more recently Jeff Loomis can easily start to sound prosaic, and as expressive as a retro video game sound effect if used too often. We will study more modern ideas that combine sweep picking with alternate picking to produce a dexterous and flexible technique known as *economy picking*.

The ability to effortlessly combine scalic and intervallic ideas into your licks can produce a wealth of fresh musical ideas. Most jazz players use some form of economy picking as jazz lines typically employ a variety of scales and arpeggios. The ideas we'll examine draw on the jazz-fusion influence of players like Frank Gambale and Allan Holdsworth who are both cited as inspirations by many rock and metal players.

The sweep picking technique is similar to the classical rest stroke but produced with a pick rather than the thumb. To perform a downward sweep, you should start by picking 'through' the low E string so that the pick comes to rest on the A string. Continue through the strings one at a time, coming to rest on each string until you come out on the other side of the high E string. After getting the hang of this, try to repeat the same thing but in a continuous single movement slowly across all the strings, pushing the pick across the strings in a slow controlled strum.

Once you have a handle on the basic idea the primary concern is to train the picking hand to perform it in time. Sweep picking must be practiced at a very slow speed because your picking hand and fretting hand need to synchronise perfectly.

This first short Am7 arpeggio is a simple way to develop your downward sweep pick. We'll use it as a building block to develop larger licks and arpeggio passages later, but you could use it straight away in your playing to integrate sweep picking into your expressive toolbox. For example, it could be used as an embellishment to melodies or held bends, in a similar fashion to the slides and scale runs shown in chapter two.

Example 7a

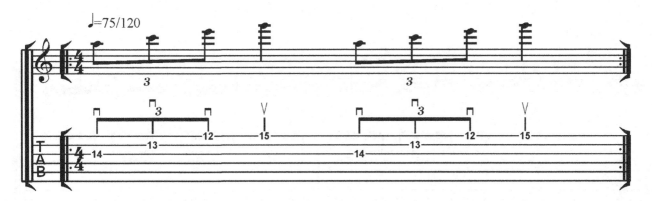

The next of our arpeggio-based patterns uses the downward sweep motion from the previous example, coupled with a single upstroke and a pull off to form each four-note grouping. Take this very slowly to at first, as it is initially difficult to keep relaxed when trying to do such a short sweep.

Example 7b

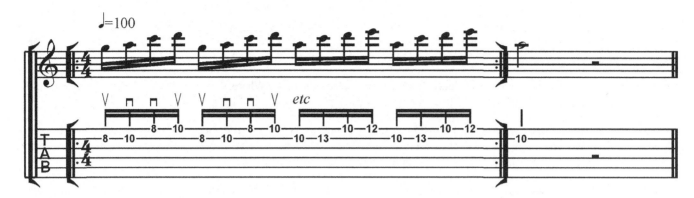

This next pentatonic fragment illustrates the economy of motion that sweep picking allows. Compare this with the movement the pick would make if you were to alternate pick it.

Follow the picking directions, and after the initial upstroke just repeat down and up sweeps across the two strings. This economy of motion means there is great potential for playing this idea with speed once you are comfortable with it.

Example 7c

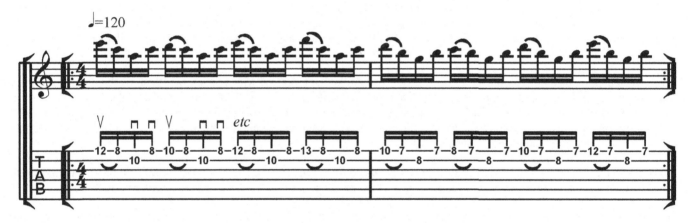

In the following example, it's good practice to play all the notes according to the picking directions as it gives a uniformity of tone but you could also use a pull-off between the first two notes. The trouble may be in 'hooking back' to down-pick the high E string after finishing the upwards sweep on the G string. This will have to be practiced slowly to avoid accidentally catching the B string.

Example 7d

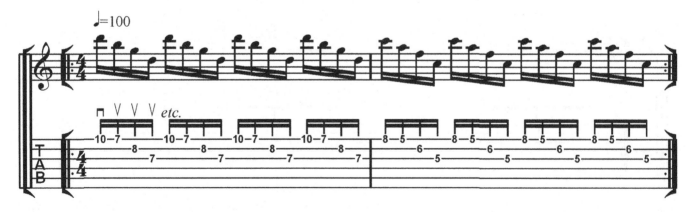

Once up and down sweep picking strokes are starting to make sense, try linking them together to perform a complete arpeggio pattern like the one in example 7e. The first two beats are an A minor arpeggio, and beats three and four complete the G major shape from the previous example.

Example 7e

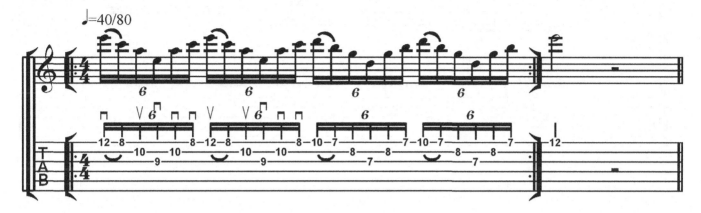

The next lick is a melodic development on a single minor arpeggio. Starting on D minor we then alter the top note of each pattern to create a melodic line. You could also try this approach with the G major shape from the previous examples and use your ear to tell you where to move the top note.

Example 7f

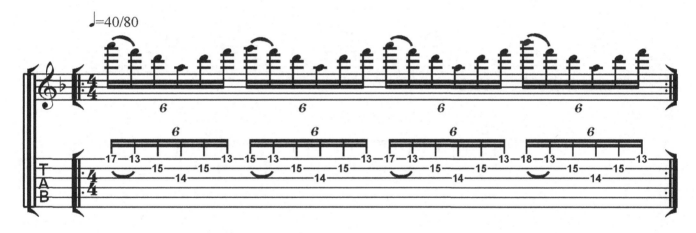

The next example shows three different arpeggio shapes. However, on closer inspection they are all using the same three notes. These are known as inversions and it's important to familiarise yourself with them so that you can freely navigate up and down the neck.

Here we have an A major arpeggio in all three inversions. Try to visualise the familiar open chord shapes from which they're drawn: 'E' shape, 'C' shape, and 'A' shape. This will help you locate shapes for different triads all over the fretboard using existing knowledge.

It's worth noticing which note of the chord each shape starts from. The first starts on the 3rd (C#), the second on the 5th (E), and the last starts on the root (A).

Example 7g

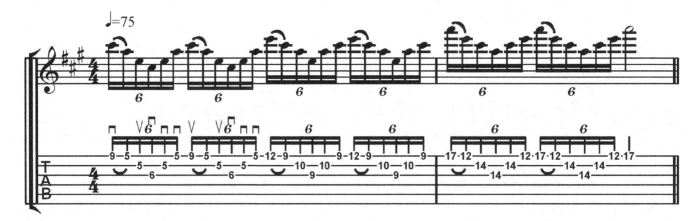

The next example shows the minor versions of the same shapes. By comparing the two sets of arpeggios you should be able to identify the root, 3rd, and 5th in each inversion, which is useful when attaching melodic phrases to 'sign off' from these licks.

The first minor shape can be challenging to begin with because of the 'barre roll' with the first finger. Barre all the notes at the fifth fret with the first finger, but to stop the notes ringing into each other the finger has to be rolled from the tip to the pad so that only one string is left ringing at a time.

A very small amount of palm muting over the G string can also help if you're struggling here.

Example 7h

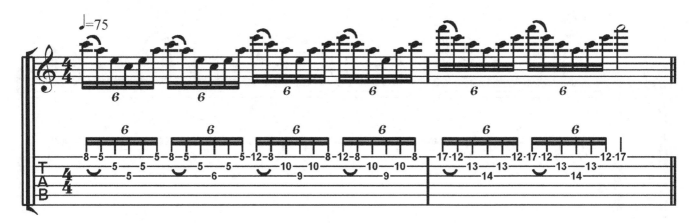

Now we're going to string together a run of different arpeggios. The best place to start here is to sequentially play through each arpeggio in one key. As an example here we have all the triads found in C major, played in order using the 'E' shape from examples 7e and 7f. Triads are a three-note chord or arpeggio. It would be of real benefit to work out permutations of this idea using other inversions, sweep shapes, or in different keys before moving on to examples 7h-7j.

Example 7i

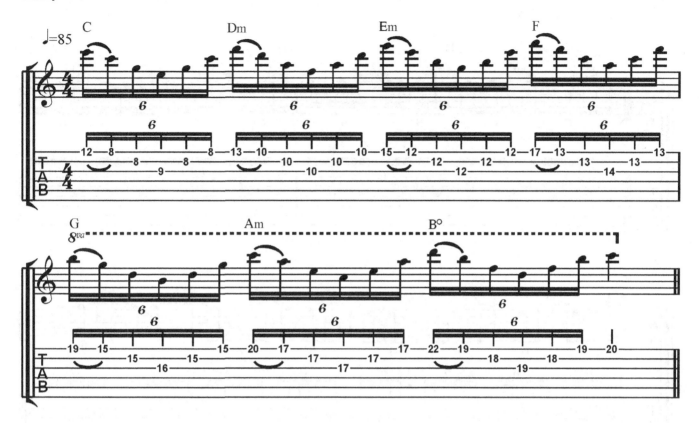

Voice Leading is when we change between chords by moving each note to the closest available note in the next chord. Good voice leading allows us to move between chords more smoothly and produce a more musical sound than just shifting the same shape up and down the neck. Fluency in different arpeggio inversions allows us to do just that. By knowing several shapes for each chord we will always be able to visualise the closest arpeggio to move to.

Follow the chord symbols given in the example and identify the root notes in each shape. Then experiment by writing your own etudes over different chord progressions to start to take ownership of this concept.

There are plenty of great examples of these arpeggio passages used in different contexts. Particular favourites of mine are Yngwie Malmsteen's *Demon Driver*, and Michael Angelo Batio's *Rainforest*.

Example 7j

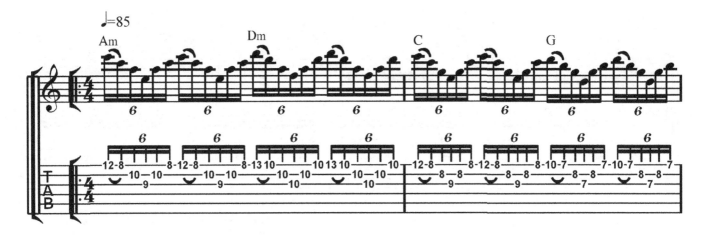

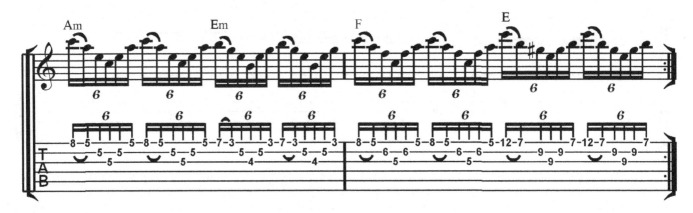

After having been faced with all those major and minor inversions, there's thankfully only one *diminished* shape to learn, as each inversion is identical. The additional note on the G string involves a little legato so be sure to not rush through the shape.

Be careful with the transition from the second bar into the third bar, as well as with the adapted arpeggio shape at the end that loops back to the beginning.

Mick Thompson is fond of these shapes. You can hear him using them to achieve the frenetic and chromatic soloing style that he employs on several Slipknot tracks.

Example 7k

Diminished chords can function in a similar way to dominant 7 chords because they share several common tones. A diminished arpeggio starting on G#, B, D or F contains most of the notes of an E7b9 chord. When played preceding an A minor, these notes will give the same sense of harmonic resolution as playing E7b9 - Am.

We can therefore use the diminished shape as a convenient tool to provide a *cadence* into any chord. The result is a sense of continual modulation through different keys because every chord is being *tonicised* (preceded by a dominant 7 chord), bringing a classical flavour to the lick.

Each shape is only played once in this arpeggio sequence. Take it slowly and think ahead to keep up with the quickly changing harmony.

Example 7l

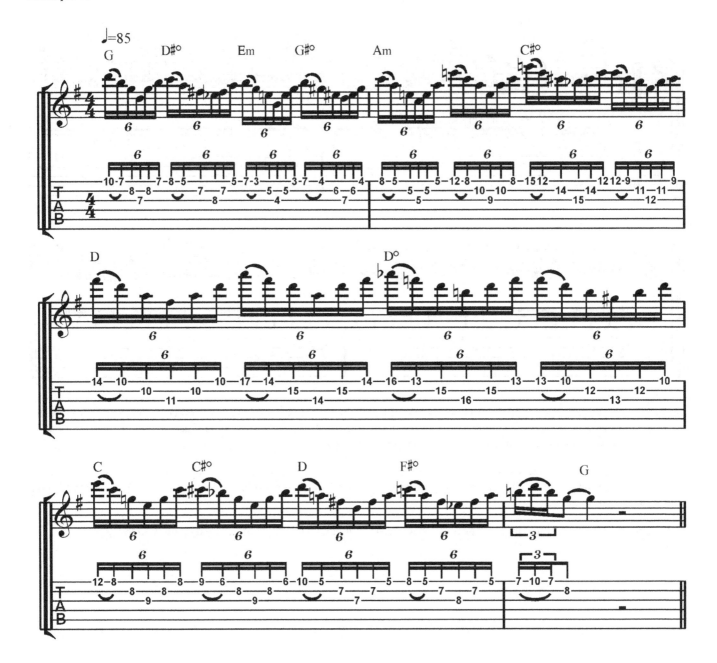

Once three-string shapes are starting to feel comfortable, have a try at the following five string shapes. Here I've shown you the A shape major and minor arpeggios. You should be able to picture the shape of the A and Am barre chords more clearly now, and this will help to identify the root notes.

It's easy to let the legato at the top and bottom of each shape rush or lag, but starting with slow metronome practice will build evenness into your muscle memory.

The major shape can be particularly difficult due to the three string 'barre roll' with the second finger. Ensure you get clear separation before speeding up, otherwise the result will be more like a mushy distorted chord rather than a crisp, cleanly-articulated arpeggio.

If you're struggling, use the picking hand palm to cut off the previous notes when ascending.

Example 7m

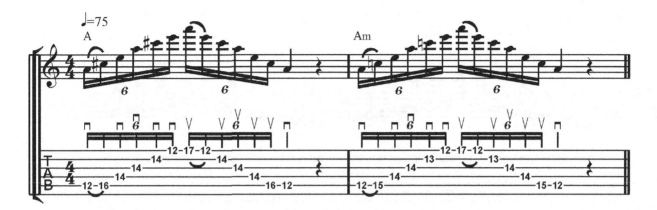

Once both of these arpeggio shapes are sounding fluid and relaxed, you're ready to approach a longer progression by shifting them around the neck to outline each chord. Practice the position shifts slowly and think carefully about the fingerings to change between shapes to get the join as seamless as possible.

As well as the two shapes from example 7k, I've included some 'E shape' and 'C shape' arpeggios. Take them slowly as well to make them comfortable.

These five-string shapes help the guitar to emulate the long cascading arpeggios that are common to classical piano playing. This following example may sound daunting at first, but once you can play one five string arpeggio cleanly then you can soon link several together.To keep things quiet, flatten the fretting fingers over the strings and use the fingertip to mute the string below. The picking hand palm can also help to mute the low E string throughout.

Example 7n

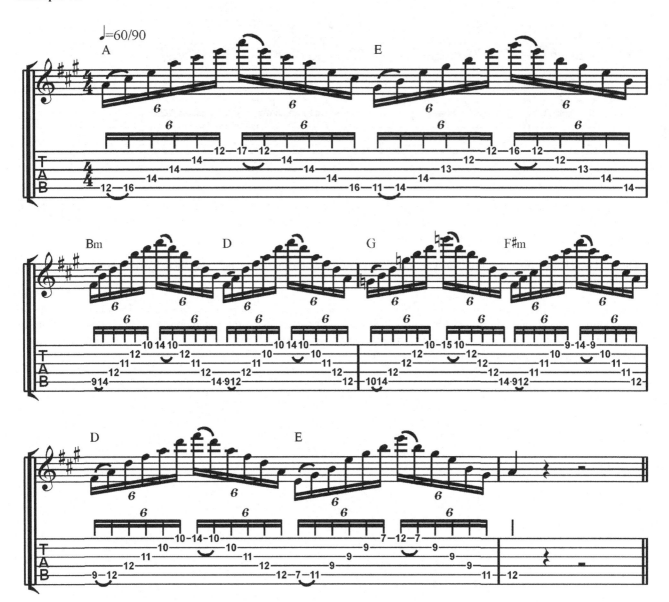

To really get to grips with this style of lead playing, compose your own sweep picking studies using the different arpeggio shapes we've looked at. Start by writing a chord progression with which to work. You could pick one from a song or just create one from scratch.

Pick an arpeggio of the first chord in a comfortable position on the neck, and then locate the different shapes of the next chord in the progression. By combining the A, C and E shapes, there's always going to be an arpeggio shape close by that you can link with, to ensure the smooth voice leading we discussed earlier.

Recommended listening for sweep picking licks:

Yngwie Malmsteen – *Blitzkrieg*
Metallica – *Leper Messiah*
Jason Becker – *Altitudes*
Children of Bodom – *Kissing the Shadows*
Outworld - *Riders*

Chapter Eight: The Whammy Bar

In this chapter we'll cover the essential licks and tricks using the whammy bar in metal, but I'd also like to show you how the whammy bar can produce a range of very musical articulations that are not possible using conventional string bending or vibrato.

Used creatively, these whammy-bar 'tricks' can sound exciting and link phrases together. I like to think of them as the guitar equivalent of a vocalist adding 'woahs' and 'yeahs' between lines of lyrics.

The bar can be used expressively by adding subtle and unique inflections to a melody. Many players use it to smooth the movement between notes to invoke the sound of slide guitar or of ethnic instruments that do not have frets. Guitarist Jeff Beck has an awe-inspiring degree of control of the whammy bar, and uses it to get a sound reminiscent of slide playing.

Let's start by using the whammy bar to provide a subtle vibrato to a melodic phrase. When we apply normal finger vibrato, the pitch of the note can only go up. However, if we choose to use the whammy bar for vibrato, the pitch can be taken up or down from the starting point.

Be careful not to overdo the vibrato as a modest movement of the bar can alter the pitch dramatically. Excessive movement makes the vibrato sound over-the-top and unnatural. The aim of this example is to harness some control and subtlety before we get into sound effects.

Example 8a

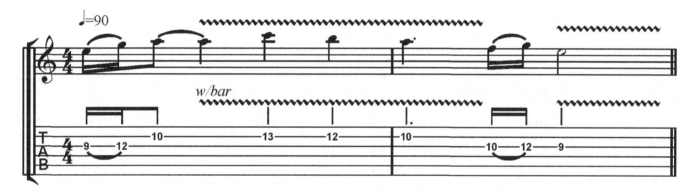

Adding vibrato to multiple pitches is easy with the use of the bar, especially when the fretting hand has much to deal with. In the next example we're manipulating doublestop bends, but we can also use this technique to bring a shimmer of vibrato to full chords while playing rhythm guitar. Have a listen to the start of Dream Theater's tune, *Pull Me Under* for a nice example of this.

Example 8b

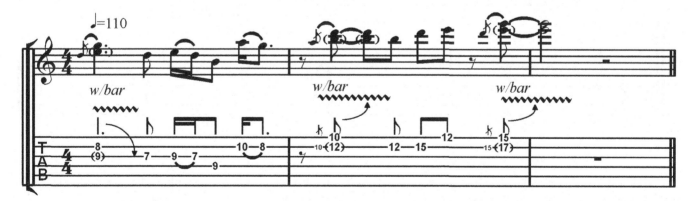

When picking and whammy bar use are combined, you may have to experiment with how to hold the bar. Some players like to tighten the bar into the bridge so it stays in a fixed position, but this can mean it gets in the way when playing normally.

I prefer to rest my second and third fingers *over* the bar to keep it within reach. This is normally easier on floating bridges as less pressure is needed to depress the bar than on Strat-style bridges.

Example 8c uses a technique known as scooping. *Scooping* into each of the notes slightly blurs the definition of each pitch to produce an inflection inspired by ethnic instruments. To really nail this, depress the bar slightly before picking the note, and release it as the note sounds.

Example 8c

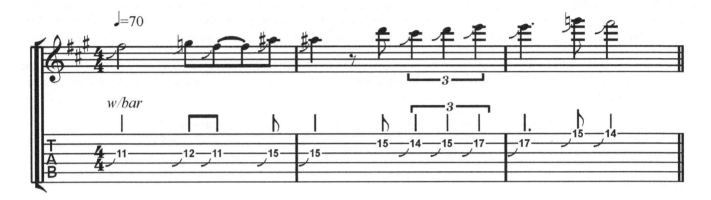

The next idea is similar to Example 8c, but instead of depressing the pitch, we pre-bend before descending to the target pitch.

For the best results you may wish to rotate the bar 180 degrees so it is pointing away from the neck. In this position the physical technique is the same as for the scoops although the pitch change is in the opposite direction.

With the picking hand operating the bar in this position it is impossible to pick the notes, so fretting hand hammer-ons are used. To avoid any open strings ringing out, the best approach is to mute all the strings with the first finger (in a barre position) while the remaining three fingers hammer-on. A bit of quick movement round the fretboard is needed to make up for the lack of the index finger, but this is the cleanest option.

Example 8d

Gargling is the result of making the bridge vibrate freely on its axis. It is an effect only possible with a floating bridge as the bridge needs to move across both sides of the at rest position, like a pendulum.

The bar can be in either the normal position or 180 degrees out, as in Example 8d. Either way, you will need it to be tight enough to stay in position without being held.

The bar is 'flicked' by sliding your finger off the end of the bar as you pull on it. The sound should be like an impossibly fast vibrato. How well the gargle works is affected by the firmness of the bridge. Having the guitar set up with light gauge strings and only two back springs will help reduce the movement in the bridge, making it more inclined to gargle.

Example 8e

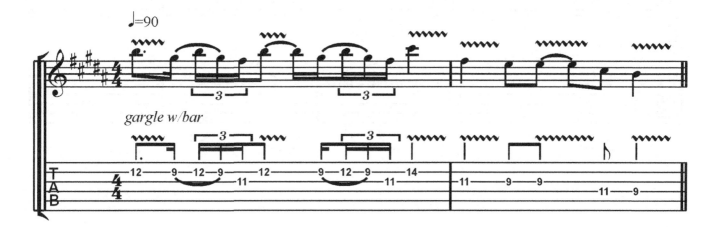

A held note can be re-articulated by dipping and releasing the bar after picking the note normally. This method can also give the impression of playing repeated notes in a 'legato' style.

Example 8f

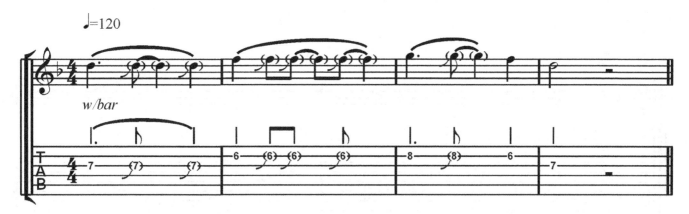

Some floating tremolos can bend notes up by a perfect fourth depending on string gauge (and your courage in risking string breakage!). However, as a starting point we will just brave a semitone bend up. Using the bar to reach definite pitches rather than just raising or lowering pitch arbitrarily is a great way to train the ear.

You need to pay close attention to the intonation to avoid creating a bad Theremin impression! Play the notes in the brackets first to get your ear tuned into the target pitch. You may find it helpful to sing the melody at the same time. Listen to the audio example to hear this in action.

Example 8g

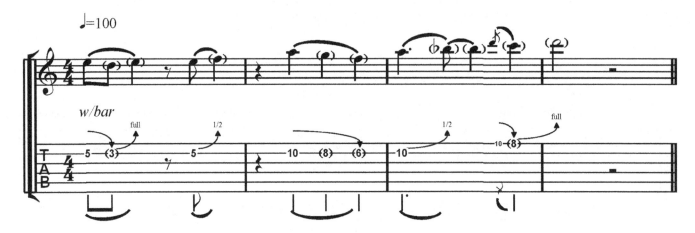

Now for some obligatory, over-the-top whammy bar tricks!

Reach over with your fretting hand to grab the whammy bar and start with the bar depressed, though not to the point of slackening off the strings. Next, play a pinch harmonic in the usual way with the picking hand and release the bar gradually. Be sure to deaden the lower strings with the picking hand palm to keep the harmonics clean and distinct.

The recognisable 'elephant' sound-effect used by King Crimson, Steve Vai, DragonForce and many others combines this idea with a volume swell at the start to mask the initial attack. This is most easily achieved with a volume pedal. These sounds are difficult to illustrate with conventional notation, so listen to the audio and match the contour of the pitch.

Example 8h

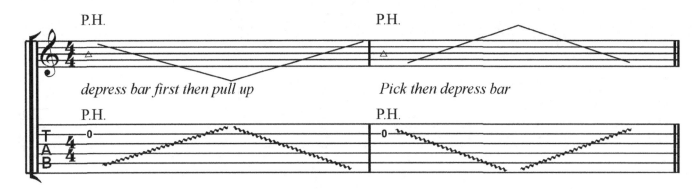

In the next example we start with a silent tremolo dive bomb, but as the bar gets fully depressed; activate the G string with the first finger of the fretting hand. The action is best described as a pull-off from nowhere as the note you're 'pulling off' from shouldn't be audible.

As you release the string, flatten the pad of your first finger against the G string over a natural harmonic node point. This may take a few tries to get clean and consistent. Experiment with different harmonics, particularly those between the fourth fret and the nut that are often too difficult to bring out as normal harmonics.

To hear a very musical application of this technique, listen to Swedish virtuoso Mattias Eklundh who combines cleanly executed hammered & touch harmonics with the whammy bar as a way of articulating melodies!

Example 8i

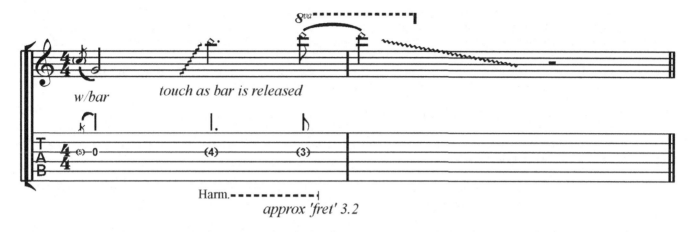

Now we will combine some of the ideas we've studied in this chapter into an expressive, musical phrase. Take the whole example piece by piece, memorising the movements slowly, particularly those moments that juggle the bar with picking. At first you may find it helpful to first play the notes without any whammy bar to learn the melody.

Spending time incorporating just one idea into your playing, such as scoops, and making it feel comfortable, rather than taking a 'kitchen-sink' approach. Introducing lots of new ideas at once will give only a superficial understanding. Too much fancy articulation can make a phrase sound cluttered.

Example 8j

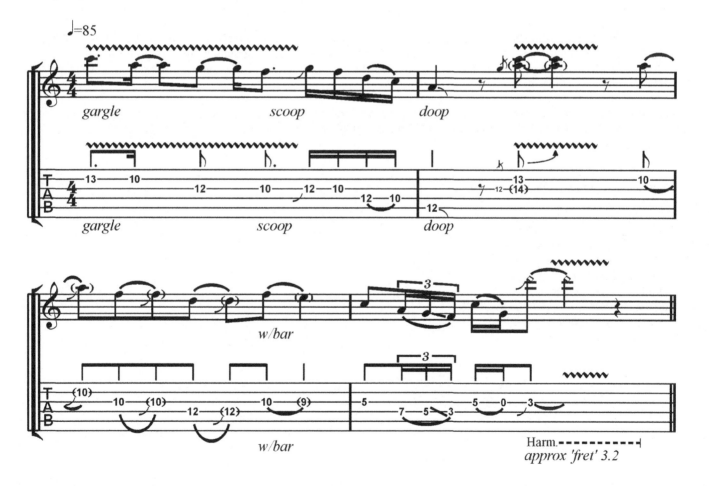

Setting up Your Guitar's Bridge

Going back the '60s and to Jimi Hendrix and his much-abused Fender Stratocasters, heavy use of the whammy bar can cause severe tuning problems. Usually the problem is not that the string is being stretched but that when returning to tension, it is pulled from the machine head. To overcome this, the locking top nut and bridge tuners of the Floyd Rose design were invented.

Here are some quick tips to help your guitar perform best when using the whammy bar, whether you're using a Strat-style guitar, or one with a floating bridge, having a good setup with make a world of difference.

If you are using a Strat-style guitar, then you can try the following tips to alleviate common problems.

Firstly, use a sharp pencil to rub soft pencil lead/graphite into the nut slots (specially made nut lubricants are available too). This stops the string sticking when being moved across the nut.

Secondly, invest in a set of locking machine heads. Since fitting a locking top nut is out of the question without fine tuners at the bridge, locking machine heads are often the best option, and work by pinning the string in the eyelet of the tuning post.

If you find the action of the whammy bar quite stiff, it can be worth loosening the back spring screws slightly, but loosen them too much and the bridge plate starts to 'float' away from the body causing intonation and action problems.

If you are using a guitar equipped with a good quality *floating* tremolo, such as a Floyd-Rose, then ensuring the guitar is well set up should solve any tuning instabilities, even when performing the more extreme whammy bar stunts. The key is to make sure the bridge is balanced between the tension in the springs and the tension in the strings. It can be a lengthy process to get the guitar set up well because much adjusting and retuning is required to hone-in on the right balance.

My top tip for doing this is to start with the springs at fairly low tension, and wedge a block of wood (a few coins taped together work great too!) between the bridge block and the cavity wall. Whatever you use, it is *crucial* that your woodblock is exactly the right shape to wedge the bridge at the balanced position parallel to the body of the guitar.

As you tension the strings the block will be gripped between the two surfaces, effectively fixing the bridge in place. In this state you are free to tune the strings up to pitch accurately without the bridge reacting (assuming the springs are still loose enough). With the guitar in tune, start tightening the back springs slowly – a quarter turn on each – until the woodblock falls out or can be removed with minimal resistance.

Some further adjustment may be needed as the guitar settles into its new strings but this process should get you to the right ballpark without the tediously repetitive process which most guitarists experience.

Recommended Listening for whammy bar use:

Deep Purple – *Black Night*
Van Halen – *Ain't Talkin' 'Bout Love*
Joe Satriani – *The Extremist*
Motley Crue – *Kickstart My Heart*
Steve Vai – *Bad Horsie*
Metallica – *Enter Sandman*
Matthias 'IA' Eklund – *Smoke on the Water*
Velvet Revolver – *Sucker Train Blues*
Symphony X - *Nevermore*

Chapter Nine: Building a Solo

I've dedicated the final portion of this book to four solo studies that are stylistic of different subgenres of heavy metal. After spending time looking at different techniques and stylistic ideas in isolation, we're now going to address how to put them together to make a cohesive musical statement. Each of these longer examples illustrate my suggestions on how to write a well-balanced metal solo using the ideas covered in this book.

Though each solo contains different ideas, generally speaking they all build from simple, slower ideas towards faster ones. Building intensity is a great basic framework to have in mind when you're crafting solos. Try to consider how natural the flow is between licks, and whether the energy builds in a gradual way.

Of course, every song is different, and depending on its place in the song and the dynamics of the sections before and after, a solo may need to follow a different dynamic trajectory. For a great example, listen to James Hetfield's solo in Metallica's *Nothing Else Matters*. After building the song's dynamic to a climax in the preceding chorus, the guitar takes over at a loud volume opening with a bold musical statement but by the end the solo dies away to leave the song at a quiet level before finishing with a sparsely accompanied verse.

Try to come up with your own solos over each of the following rhythm parts. I have included longer backing tracks for each solo for you to jam over as well as a separate chord chart for each one; this is to help you nail the chord tones when playing melodically as we saw in chapter three.

Solo 1 – Early '70s

The first solo is in the guitar-friendly key of E minor and is played over a classic heavy metal backing riff in the vein of bands like Black Sabbath. We're using a blues based soloing style but with the more aggressive tone and vibrato of the heavy metal pioneers.

A feature of this style that distinguishes it from the blues is the 'quantising' of the phrasing. In contrast to the way blues players frequently play behind the beat to get a lazy feel, this solo should be played very in time and on top of the beat to match the forward motion in the rhythm section.

The guitar tone of this period was all about fuzz pedals and valve amp overdrive, rather than the more modern distortion we've been using in a lot of the examples. Typical amps were made by Marshall and Orange.

Figure 1 shows the rhythm guitar part for the first solo study. There are two distinct sections to this example. The A section has a spacious riff, which opens up the possibility of question and answer phrases in the gaps before moving on to the B section.

We use two-string power chords throughout, but tonal contrast comes from allowing the power chords to ring out fully in the A section before palm muting in the B section to keep them in the background of the texture.

Example 9a (Backing)

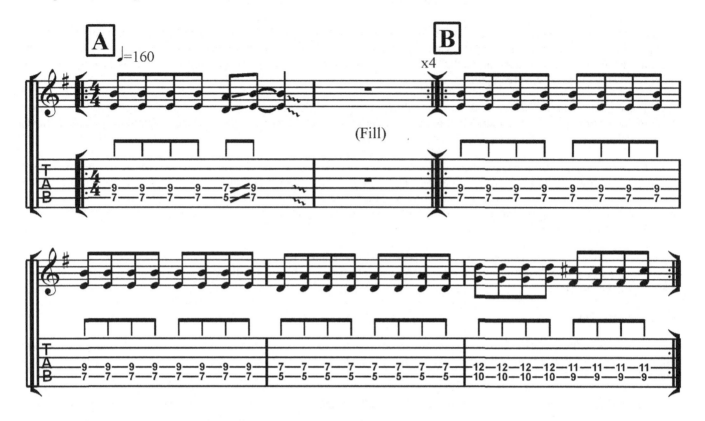

The solo sticks to the minor pentatonic scale throughout, moving freely between several different positions as we build up from melodic 1/8th note phrases to busier licks.

Example 9a

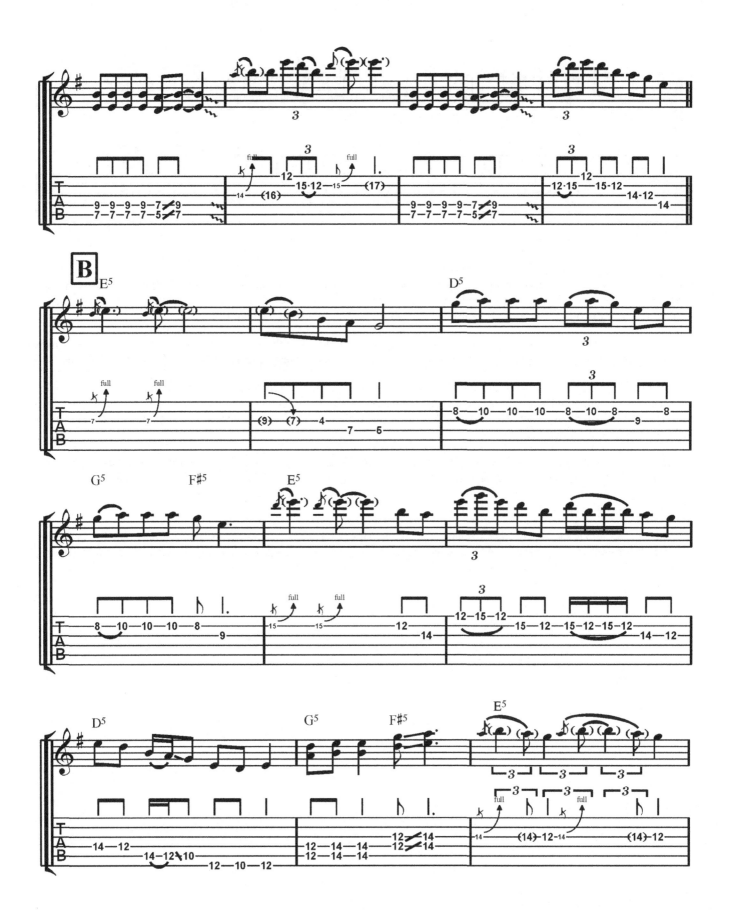

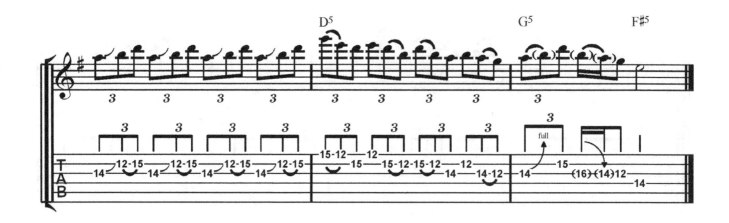

Bars 1-8: I've included the accompaniment riff in the solo transcription to show clearly how the question and answer phrases function. You are welcome to try to play both parts at the same time, but be careful with the swift position shifts to make smooth transitions. To start with, focus on playing just the lead fills before trying to combine both parts.

Bands with only one guitar player commonly employ compositional ideas like this to give the impression of a bigger ensemble. Not being supported by a rhythm guitarist when soloing in a live context can leave the overall texture sounding quite thin.

Bars 9-12: Now we're into the main solo, and I've started with a straightforward melodic pentatonic phrase. Although these licks seem simple, it's important to make sure your string bends are confident and in tune. The vocabulary of early heavy metal was rooted in the blues-rock of Cream, Hendrix and the Yardbirds. Be sure to keep driving forward by not allowing the phrasing to swing or fall behind the beat.

Bar 13-16: The next four bar chunk re-states the repeated string bends from bar 9 before taking things up a gear with a faster triplet phrase into a slippery descending pentatonic scale. Use fingers one and three to play the whole phrase, as this is the strongest combination to handle the legato in bar 10. Doublestop pentatonic licks like in bar 16 help to thicken up lead guitar parts in absence of guitar or keyboard accompaniment.

Bar 17-20: The solo is rounded off by a sustained passage of triplets across bars 18 and 19. You can choose whether to alternate pick all of these notes or use pull offs. Alternate picking will give you the most aggressive tone but can become two dimensional if overused. Finally the solo signs off with a common melodic bend to land on the tonic, E.

Solo 2 – Pop/Glam Metal

Our second study moves forward into the late '70s and early '80s. It takes inspiration from the more melodic pop-influenced metal of Van Halen and (later) Bon Jovi, Europe, and many others. Glam metal had a much more upbeat style which helped it enter the mainstream, while the more abrasive thrash subgenre remained largely underground, arguably up until Metallica's 'Black album' in 1991.

Most of the content we have looked at has been in a minor key or mode, but here is an example in the bright sounding key of F major, using just the I IV and V chords.

Example 9b (Backing)

The solo uses the F major, and major pentatonic scales. To help give the solo some structure and connect with the accompaniment we're aiming to end each of the phrases with notes from the underlying chord.

There's also some typically '80s tapping towards the end of the solo, and a short sweep picking phrase, as both techniques were starting to enter the vocabulary in the early '80s.

Example 9b

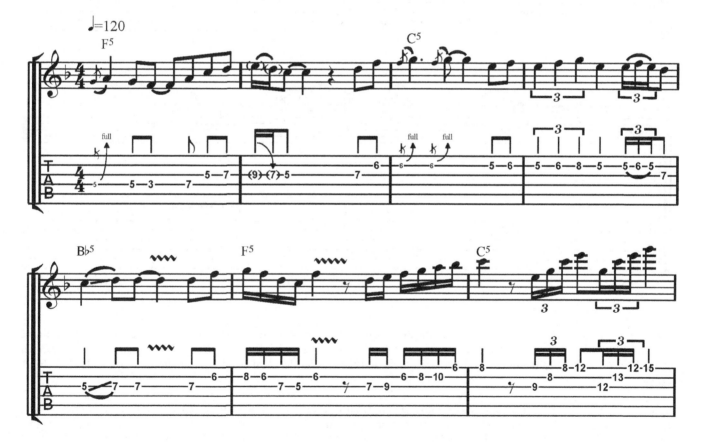

Bars 1-4: This style is all about upbeat catchy melodies with more than an ounce of rock 'n roll swagger! Bring this phrase to life with subtle slides into certain notes and slow, controlled vibrato. Use the bridge humbucker to give it the necessary bite. The phrase in bar 4 leading to the next chord is more lyrical and focuses on the third (E) before landing on D, the third of the Bb chord.

Bars 5-8: After the singable 1/8th note based introduction, we use scale runs to push into the change to F and C chords. In bar 7 there is a short example of sweep picking. Use a downward pick stroke to play each of the arpeggios and catch the last note of each group with an upstroke. Notice how we land on C as the backing reaches C major, and each of the following sweeps target the other notes in the chord (E and G).

Be sure to stay relaxed when sweep picking and practice slowly to avoid the notes becoming a poorly defined rake across the strings.

Bars 9-12: Here's the tapping lick. Over these three bars we use three different tapping patterns, so try to isolate each bar in turn before linking them up into one seamless phrase.

In Bar 9, the picking hand taps the 13th fret then immediately performs a rapid slide up the fretboard before pulling off to the 10th fret. Don't worry about sliding to a specific fret number; the important thing is to get the sound effect of the slide. Take care in bar 10 as the tapped note changes twice as often as the fretting hand.

We finish the run with a scalic idea into a tapped bend. To execute this, we tap as usual at the 15th fret, but then use the fretting hand behind it to bend the tapped pitch up to an E. The vibrato should also come from the fretting hand rather than the tapping finger. Use the neck pickup to give the smoothest tone when playing this kind of tapping or legato lick.

Bars 13-16: After the barrage of tapping, we bring things to a close with some soaring unison bends. Switch back to the bridge humbucker to let the bends scream as much as possible. The melodic phrase in bar 15 could benefit from slower bends to wring out the most expression before rising to end on a singing C note.

Solo 3 – 'NWOBHM'

Our next solo study harks back to the glory days of the New Wave of British Heavy Metal. Inspired by mid '80s Iron Maiden and Judas Priest. The backing track uses an AABA form to give a sense of structure and development. The majority of the solo employs a typical 'gallop' feel in the rhythm guitar part. Accent the power chords at the start of each bar while keeping the picked notes in between tightly muted. The A section is contrasted by the half-time feel of the B section in bars 9-12, where the chords are allowed to ring.

Example 9c (Backing)

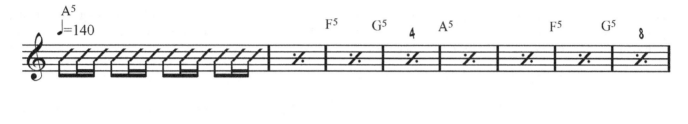

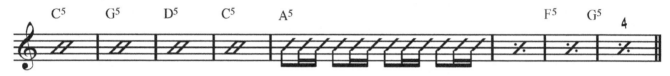

Although the A minor pentatonic scale or Aeolian mode would work fine over the whole progression, it is always worth keeping the notes of each chord in mind so you can make your phrases target the most appropriate chord tones.

The solo features a lot of bluesy phrasing littered with bends and some subtle whammy bar manipulation balanced with melodic phrases drawn from the A natural minor scale. At the climatic points we see a combination of past pentatonic ideas and legato trills.

As this track shows, you can make your solo feel like an integral, thought-out part of the song by composing a developing accompaniment part. In bar 9, the tempo moves to half time and the lead guitar reacts by phrasing appropriately before picking up the pace again for the final four bars.

Example 9c

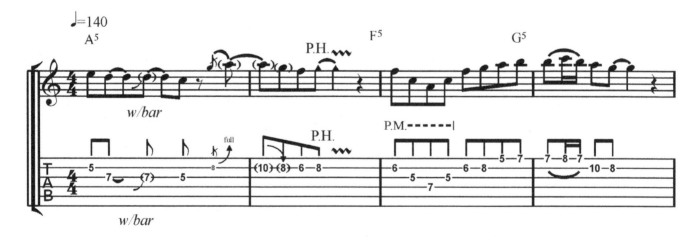

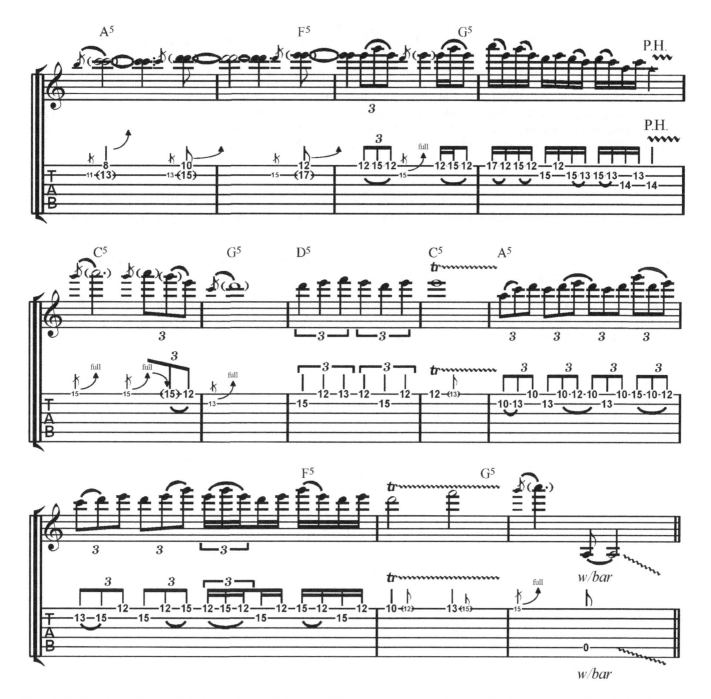

Bars 1-4: Opening with a straightforward melody is a good idea as it gives you plenty of headroom to grow into during the solo but as with any 'rule', there are plenty of instances where the opposite is true and coming out 'all guns blazing' can also be very effective in other songs.

However, the simplicity of the first idea allows us to bring it to life by using interesting articulation. Here we have a quick scoop on the whammy bar to play the second D, a bend up to the A, and finally a pinched harmonic on the final note. Notice how the melody in bar 3 is based around an F major arpeggio (C shape) before targeting the B and G from the G major chord in bar 4.

Moving with the harmony is especially important when playing melodic material; it makes the solo sound more 'composed'.

Bars 5-8: Make the most of these unison bends by adding some vibrato and using a strong attack to get that really aggressive sound.

As well as following the harmony we can mirror the rhythmic feel. In this piece, most of the chords anticipate the downbeat by occurring on beat '4 &' to give a sense of forward momentum.

Stepping up a gear, the next two-bar phrase starts as a typical blues lick, before stretching out of the box shape to play a fast descending phrase, mostly achieved with pull-offs, before finishing with another pinch harmonic and wide vibrato.

Bars 9-12: This is the 'bridge section' of the solo. The drums play in half time and the chords all land right on the beat instead of the previous anticipation giving them a grandiose and triumphant feel. To enhance this feel, the melody uses held bends and a half-time triplet phrase. The presence of the F over the D5 chord hints at the A natural minor scale, and the final trill, combined with the chord changes moving in fifths all give a neoclassical flavour to this section.

Bars 13-16: Typically, a good solo should build before the final chorus comes crashing back in! This usually means developing from slower melodic phrases towards faster licks. To stay true to the style I've remained mostly pentatonic for the triplet licks (though with a little stretch thrown in on bar 13).

The series of trills from different notes are very characteristic of Iron Maiden's Dave Murray and serve to balance the intensity of lots of notes with a recognisably melodic dimension.

The final bar may take a little time to learn to execute cleanly as cutting off the bend, grabbing the whammy bar, and dive-bombing all happens very quickly, so commit the motions to memory slowly. It is helpful to delegate 'picking' the A string to the fretting hand, whilst using a quick pull-off to the open string.

Solo 4 – Thrash Metal

I've begun by notated the riff over which we'll be soloing. It's a typical '80s thrash metal riff featuring fast, precise alternate picking and sliding power chords. Keep the open Es palm muted so that the notes are short and percussive to make the intricate rhythm clear. Allow the power chords to ring out fully by lifting the palm off the strings.

Example 9d (Backing)

Our final solo takes inspiration from the early thrash metal bands. This track employs a lot of faster ideas with a couple of different techniques, so take your time and work through them carefully to achieve a polished performance. You'll notice that many phrases are repeating licks using pentatonic shapes, so by now they should feel quite familiar.

Early thrash metal was greatly influenced by hardcore punk, which was all about speed and high-energy performances. The big names of this genre are Dave Mustaine, Kirk Hammett and Gary Holt.

Example 9d

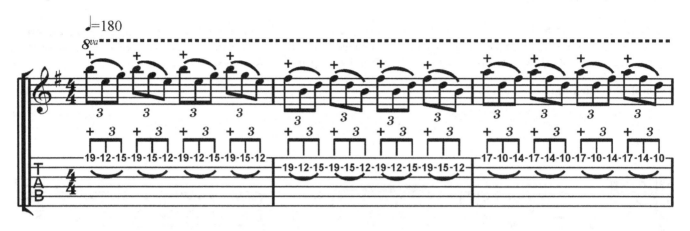

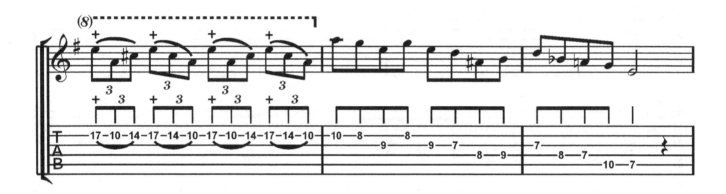

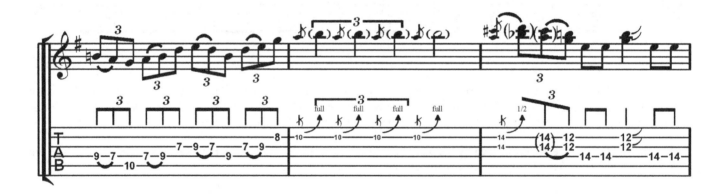

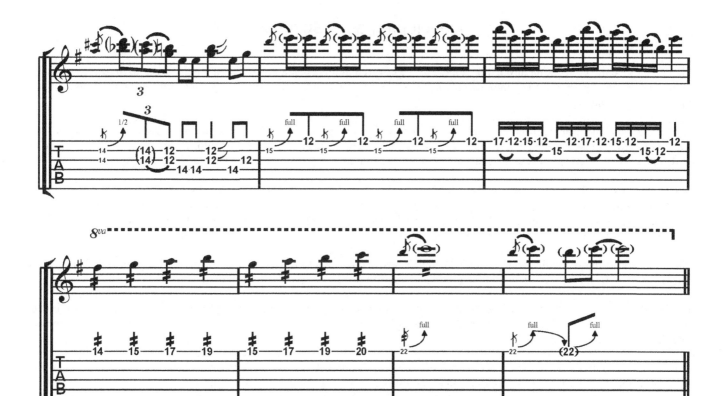

Bars 1-4: Bursting straight out of the gates with furious tapped arpeggios, this solo shows you don't always have to 'start slow and build up' when soloing. After working through the licks we explored in the tapping chapter, this section should be very approachable. However, make sure you know what both hands are doing when shifting position between shapes.

The chord progression we're outlining is Em-Am-D-G. The backing riff is a pedal tone on E but it is possible to superimpose any chords found in the key of E minor without sounding 'incorrect', so long as they are resolved confidently.

Bars 5-8: To resolve the momentum of the frenetic tapping introduction we have a short descending blues scale phrase. However, this is thrash metal and the energy immediately steps up again with an ascending pentatonic sequence into some string bends.

This four-bar chunk shows how players like Kirk Hammett managed to carry bluesiness into such an extreme musical style. At the end of the phrase, make sure to really dig into the bends with the pick to get the aggressive sound we're aiming for.

Bars 9-12: More steroid injected blues licks here with a double string bend. The added crunch of two notes played with distortion makes doublestops particularly responsive to a wah effect, so if you have a wah pedal you could use it here to provide another gear change for second half of the solo.

The pentatonic lick in bar 12 is very fast indeed and it will probably take time to develop the necessary stamina to play it comfortably. You could opt for alternate picking, or use a short sweep pick when moving from the B string to the E to keep the picking hand more relaxed.

Bars 13-16: The home stretch, and its time to pick like hell! We're playing a melodic rising scale using E Aeolian but the tremolo picking gives this last phrase a climactic intensity. Practice picking four, even 1/16th notes on each pitch to develop a sense of control and accuracy, but don't be afraid to cut loose when performing and just pick as fast as possible. As long as the fretting hand is moving from note to note in time, the tremolo is all about texture.

In bar 15, bend up slowly over the course of the bar to the high E while continuing to tremolo pick, then drop down to bend up again in the final bar and add plenty of slow, wide vibrato to make it sing.

Developing as a Guitarist

I hope you've enjoyed working through the topics we've covered in this book and feel like it's helped you to improve as a metal guitar player. To close our journey into learning metal lead guitar I'd like to offer some suggestions on ways you could continue to develop your playing.

One of the most under-appreciated and under-developed skills amongst modern rock guitar players is a strong aural ability. The ear should always take the lead in any musical learning, but when music can be quantified into 'boxes' of specific technique or scale maps it can easily degenerate into playing by numbers with no aural awareness of what we're actually *saying*.

In Chapter Two we discussed some ways in which we can connect the ear to the fretboard by singing along with what we play. I would urge you to transcribe guitar parts from songs you want to learn. A great exercise can be to try to work a song out by ear and then check it against the sheet music afterwards, particularly on a more complicated section of music. The more time you put in trying to work things out by ear before falling back on to using the written music, the more benefit you'll get out of the process.

Although *transcribing* literally means writing the music down, this is not the most important aspect of the approach. We're most interested in understanding the sound of the music and then finding those sounds on the guitar.

Finally, I encourage you to take the licks found in this book and create your own versions of them. This could involve mixing up the order of the notes, or playing in a different position or key. Use the extended versions of the demo solo backing tracks to help practice these licks in a musical context.

If you would like to develop your metal rhythm playing too, then check out my book *Heavy Metal Rhythm Guitar* that covers loads of different musical aspects, from technique and timing, to style and creative riff writing.

Also, look out for volume two of Heavy Metal Lead Guitar where we'll be delving into further technical possibilities, as well as dissecting the defining points of different subgenres' styles, with a load of fresh licks and full solo studies.

Until then, take care and happy shredding!

Rob Thorpe

Progressive Metal Guitar

An Advanced Guide to Modern Heavy Metal Guitar

Published by **www.fundamental-changes.com**

Copyright © 2016 Rob Thorpe

The moral right of this author has been asserted.

www.fundamental-changes.com

Engineered and mixed by Declan Pearson of Colossus Audioworks

Introduction

Welcome to Progressive Metal Guitar, the third volume of my series on playing Metal guitar!

This book gives advanced guitarists a greater stylistic understanding of the genre as a whole, and offers fresh ideas to help you break out of a creative rut to reinvigorate your playing.

If you've been following the series, we've seen how metal emerged from electric blues and hard rock in the '60s and '70s, and became increasingly diverse and technically challenging. We've explored the style from both a rhythm and lead standpoint by analysing how each idea is constructed on a musical level, while at the same time honing your technique.

In this third volume we're going to expand on what we've already learnt, looking at specific stylistic choices as well as how these techniques can be employed in more unusual and creative ways.

After discussing the advanced use of specific guitar techniques, I'll address compositional tools like harmony and arranging for multiple guitars, beginning with classic harmony guitar from Iron Maiden and Judas Priest. I'll then get in-depth with rhythmic riff writing by focussing on the modern cross-rhythmic style used by bands such as Meshuggah, Periphery, Tesseract and others.

From the '90s onwards, the metal and progressive rock genres increasingly overlapped. The more 'art-music' and complex approach to writing music (a defining feature of prog rock), has affected a greater proportion of metal music. After being hinted at in the songs of Iron Maiden and Fates Warning, the progressive metal sub-genre exploded with bands like Queensrÿche, Dream Theater and Symphony X. These musicians mixed the longer song structures and concept album approach of progressive rock with the increased technical level of the shred-metal movement. This created a style that was at once heavy and technical while including depth and creativity in songwriting.

In the '90s Thrash metal developed into death metal, taking the traits of aggression, dissonance and speed to their logical conclusion, with vocals becoming more guttural. The lyrics also took a more cerebral turn, exploring gruesomely vivid imagery with clinical objectivity, as well as dystopian futures, science fiction and robotics. This subject-matter related well to the direction of the music which started to feel increasingly mechanised and inhuman.

Certain bands within the genre introduced the unlikely influence of jazz fusion in the early '90s. Death's later records, as well as the work of Atheist, Watchtower and especially Cynic showcased an intricate and dynamic way in which these two styles could be melded successfully.

Use of advanced harmony and rhythm not found in other forms of popular music but instead recalling classical music of the 20th century has become more common. Comparing the music of composers such as Stravinsky, Béla Bartok, Prokofiev and Schoenberg to the more experimental metal of Spastic Ink, Buckethead, Fantomas and Meshuggah suggests some influence.

I hope you enjoy working through this book and find much of interest to use in your own music. As always, most benefit will come from taking these ideas as a starting point and applying them creatively to form your own unique voice.

Thank you and good luck!

Rob Thorpe

Chapter One: Neoclassical Phrasing

We will begin by exploring the characteristic ideas from neoclassical metal, popularised in the '80s by guitarists like Yngwie Malmsteen, Jason Becker, Vinnie Moore, Tony MacAlpine and others. As rock guitar became a more formally studied craft at schools like G.I.T, Berklee and the Musician's Institute, the technical bar was continually raised. In these environments, it made sense that guitarists would look to classical music, the archetype of formally taught music, for inspiration.

Neoclassical 'shred' metal is closely associated with the Shrapnel record label, the owner of which, Mike Varney, discovered and promoted guitarists who were on the cutting edge of rock technique.

As you might expect, emulating these players is a daunting task. Very precise technique is needed to achieve such speed and clean execution. To play these licks we'll be using the techniques we learnt in *Heavy Metal Lead Guitar*. However, it's not all about shredding; you can draw inspiration from the style and apply it at whatever speed you like, without having to retreat to a hermitage to spend years with a metronome!

The 'classical' element mainly draws on the Baroque period of music, as exemplified by the instrumental works by J.S. Bach, Vivaldi and Handel. This involved lots of scale runs, patterns and sequencing, pedal point and arpeggios which we'll apply to the guitar.

At the end of the book is a transcription of Paganini's Caprice No. 16, originally written for solo violin but arranged for electric guitar. This piece is a goldmine of interesting arpeggio-based licks and will be a great workout for your technique.

I'd like to quickly address the theory we'll be working with so that you can digest the musical information and get writing your own neoclassical licks right off the bat.

Harmonic Minor

Harmonic Minor is a scale very similar to Natural Minor (or Aeolian mode) with which you should already be familiar. The difference is that the 7th note of Harmonic Minor is sharpened by a semitone. This sharp note has several knock-on effects to the way the scale can be used.

Firstly, chord V of Harmonic Minor, is a dominant 7 chord rather than the minor chord found in Natural Minor. This allows for the very dramatic-sounding V7- i progression, common in classical music but not often heard in hard rock before the Neoclassical movement.

Secondly, Harmonic Minor's raised 7th creates three pairs of semitones (2-b3, 5-b6 and #7-R). These can be exploited melodically to add tension and excitement, as each pair contains a note in the tonic chord and an approach note.

Finally, the Harmonic Minor scale contains both a Diminished 7th chord, and an Augmented triad. Major modes don't contain these dark and dramatic sounds. The Diminished 7th chord and Augmented triad are symmetrical, meaning that they are formed by stacking intervals of the same distance. This means that once you know one Diminished or Augmented shape you can move anything you play with them up or down by the intervals used to build them.

We'll focus more on that in Chapter Eight.

Arpeggios

An arpeggio is simply a chord played one note at a time. In Metal lead guitar playing, this translates as using the notes of a chord melodically, and not letting the notes ring into each other. Much of western classical music has concerned itself with harmony, chord progressions, and cadences. Arpeggios are commonly used because they enable us to spell out chord progressions while playing a melody.

We will look at some different arpeggio ideas in the Chapter Seven, but the best place to start is to use one arpeggio per chord to give your solo a strong connection to the rest of the music (rather than just wailing regardless of the harmony). Arpeggios are frequently played with sweep picking or tapping, which help us to perform wide intervals easily.

Sequencing

In the first book of this series, *Heavy Metal Rhythm Guitar*, I looked at how sequences can develop to be quite complex and mathematical; but for the neoclassical lead style we will be sticking to moving a scale fragment up and down within a key, just like baroque composers such as Bach. Our ears are adept at identifying patterns in music and quickly latch on to sequences. The use of sequences helps to make fast playing more comprehensible to the listener.

Pedal Point

A pedal is where one note or motif alternates with a changing note or motif. The static part is often the lowest part and is known as the pedal, from its origins on the church organ. Bach was principally a church organist who wrote many works for the organ including the famous Toccata & Fugue in D minor. Pedal point helps maintain energy in faster playing as the ear will naturally pick out the moving part as separate from the pedal.

To kick things off here's a simple sextuplet scale pattern. In this chapter we're more concerned about the note choice and phrasing than specific techniques so feel free to use either legato or picking. Either way be sure to make the timing even.

Example 1a

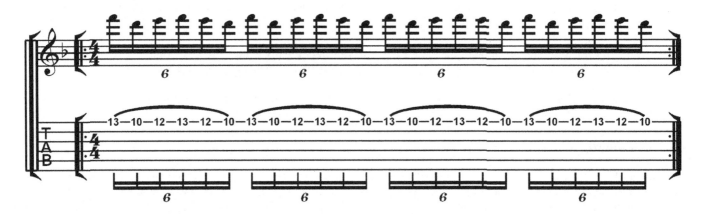

Next we apply the basic motif to the A Natural Minor scale. If the wider spacing of the lower strings proves difficult, practice each string's pattern in isolation before trying to move from string to string.

Example 1b

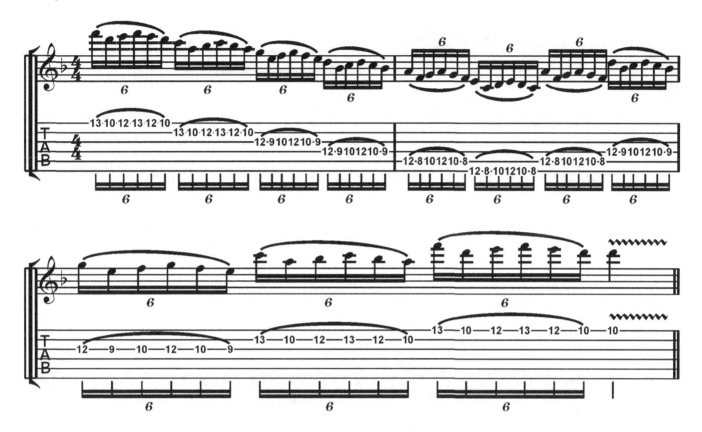

The following baroque-inspired Yngwie lick involves groups of four notes sequenced through the A Harmonic Minor scale. We're taking this at a fairly pedestrian pace, but listen to any of Yngwie's recordings to hear the potential of these single string lick.

The main challenge is the position shifts with the index finger. Practice each position slowly and accent the first note of every four with a harder pick stroke to help keep the hands in sync. Also watch out for the wider Harmonic Minor stretches at the start.

Example 1c

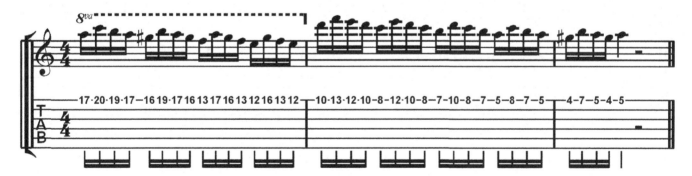

Next we have the ascending version of the same lick. This one is a little more difficult because the position shifts are made with the pinkie, but the same approach should be taken as before and with regular practice they will like second nature.

Example 1d

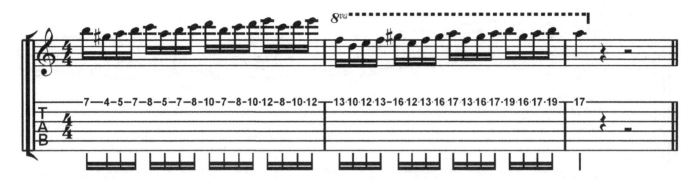

This time our four-note sequence traverses the strings. Groups of ascending four notes are moved up through the E Harmonic Minor scale, however to mix things up, I've displaced the rhythm so that the groups of four start on the final 1/16th note of each beat to make the lick sound little less predictable.

I've opted for legato here to keep things varied but you can try picking too. Always practice a lick with a range of techniques so you can choose how to articulate it, and not become limited to 'painting in just one colour'.

Example 1e

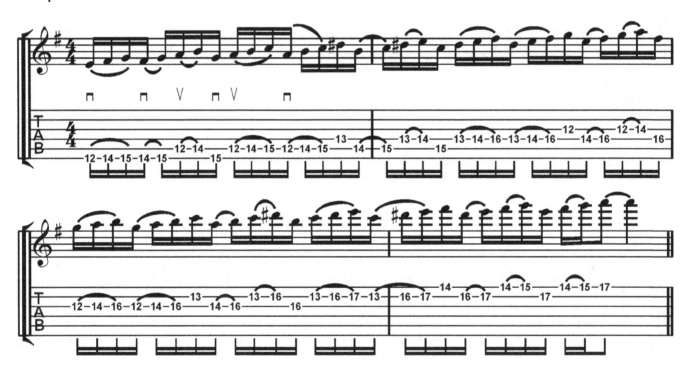

In our final sequential lick, we play ascending steps while the line gradually descends

Example 1f

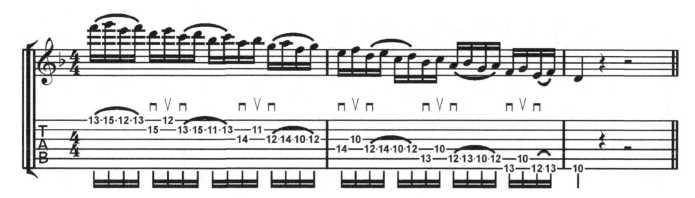

Try experimenting with sequencing ideas of your own by taking different motifs or lengths of scale fragment; then vary the direction of the sequence, making note of ones that you particularly like. It can be helpful to use notation or sequencing software to help with this so you can be objective about listening to new licks, before attempting to get them under your fingers.

Pedal Point

Our first pedal point lick illustrates the 'pedal' concept very clearly. The fretting hand plays the E Harmonic Minor scale along the length of the string. 'Pulling off' to the open E provides the pedal. Follow the suggested fingering for the fastest and most fluid results.

This type of lick is easier than it sounds, as the open string is doing half the work for you. Learning scales along the fretboard is an often-neglected skill but one that really opens up the fretboard for you.

Example 1g

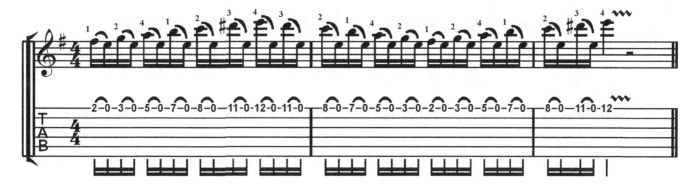

Here's another common neoclassical lick that uses the same idea, but this time the pedal is the highest note rather than the lowest. Getting the correct fingering can be tough at first due to the weaker 3rd and 4th fingers, so be patient and try to keep them relaxed.

Example 1h

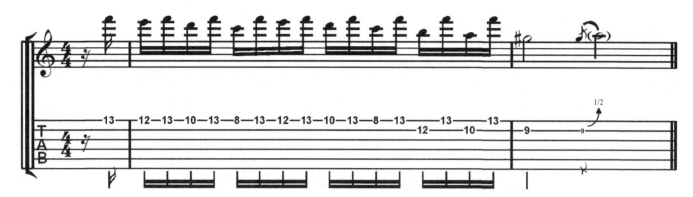

An alternative way to play example 1h would be to use the picking hand to tap the high pedal note, while the fretting hand takes care of the melody part. This can open up more interesting lines rather than just descending the scale.

In the following example, the fretting hand plays a descending sequence of three notes against the pedal. Tapping ensures a completely legato articulation, which may, or may not, be the sound you're looking for...

Example 1i

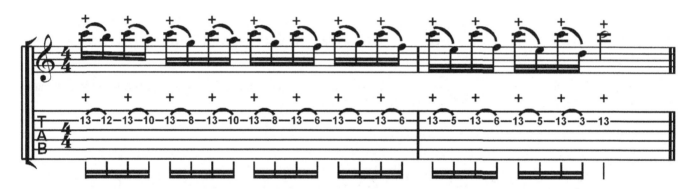

If example 1i proved unsatisfyingly slippery, the following pedal point idea reaches for a less common guitar technique in metal: hybrid picking, to deliver a bit more bite!

To play the following example, hold the pick normally and use down-strokes to play the lower notes. Use the middle finger of the picking hand to pluck the high B notes (12th fret).

In the notation I've indicated upstrokes when all the notes are on one string as this is how I played it. Many players however, would pluck with the middle finger throughout, try both and see which you prefer.

For an added classical influence, I've used the Melodic Minor when ascending scale with the major 6th and 7th (G#, A#) intervals and reverting to the Natural Minor intervals b6 and b7 (G and A) when descending.

Example 1j

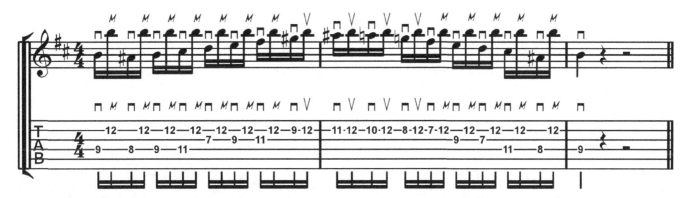

The final two pedal point ideas substitute the pedal tone for a three-note motif. The first is inspired by Vinnie Moore and uses alternate picking. Be careful of the wider stretches on the highest notes, if they prove difficult it will help to keep the thumb lower on the back of the fretboard and angle the guitar neck a little higher.

Example 1k

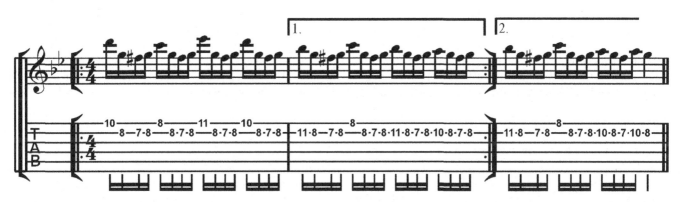

To conclude our collection of pedal point licks, we'll revisit the tapping of example 1i. This time, however, the tapping hand provides the moving part while the fretting hand repeats the pedal motif. To really nail the tapped bend on the last note, hold the D# (16th fret) with your tapping finger and apply the bend/vibrato from behind with the fretting hand as if you were fretting the note as normal.

Once you're comfortable with this lick, try moving the scale fragment *and* the tapping hand along the string to create some very interesting intervallic phrases.

Example 1l

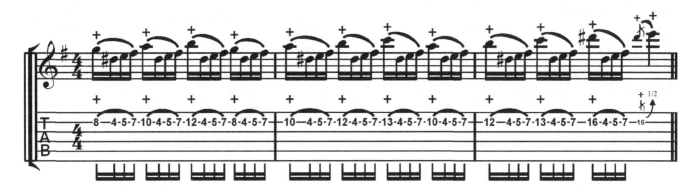

Arpeggios

To break up these long streams of notes, here's a more melodic phrase demonstrating the use of arpeggios to outline a chord progression. Try to identify the familiar open position chord shapes behind these fragments.

To create a cohesive structure, the same melodic contour is used over each chord while the notes themselves change to fit the harmony.

Example 1m

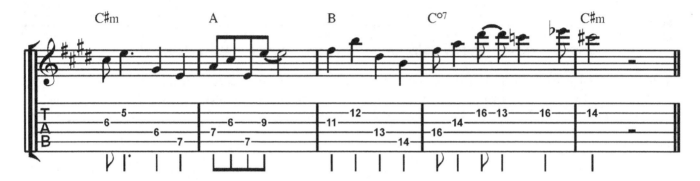

An important chord progression in western music is the circle of 5ths. This sequence of chords gives us our system of key centres and forms the foundation of classical music's functional harmony. The basic principle is to move chords in intervals of a 5th, each chord being the dominant of the next one. After twelve movements the cycle will return to the starting chord.

For example:

C G D A E B F# C# G# D# A# E# C (note: E# = F)

When ascending a 5th, the musical result is an increase in tension as you move through the keys in a constant cycle of I-V progressions or *imperfect cadences*. Descending in 5ths (or ascending in 4ths) gives a sense of continual resolution, as we're going V-I, V-I repeatedly in a long chain of *perfect cadences*.

The following example outlines descending circle of 5ths progression with arpeggios. The arpeggio shape used is built on the common open D chord shape with the root on the B string.

Example 1n

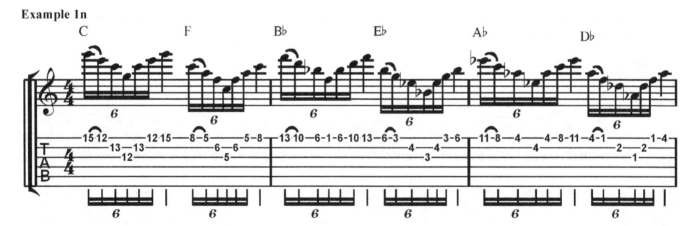

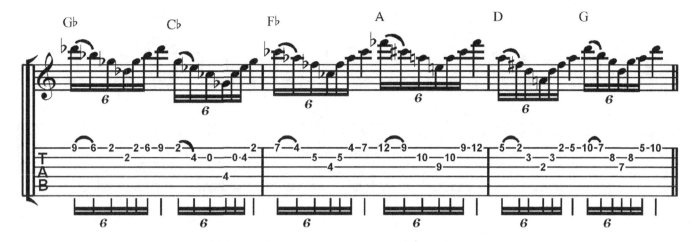

In the previous example I moved one arpeggio shape all over the neck to illustrate the progression clearly, but to get the most flowing melodic line we should start each arpeggio to on the closest note in the next chord. Rearranging the notes of a chord in different orders is known as the different *inversions* of a chord, which I covered in Heavy Metal Lead Guitar.

The next example plays the same circle of 4ths but uses all three inversions to keep the line as smooth as possible with no sudden wide leaps between chord changes. The progression is referred to as a circle because after twelve changes you should arrive back at the chord you started on, in this case C major.

Example 1o

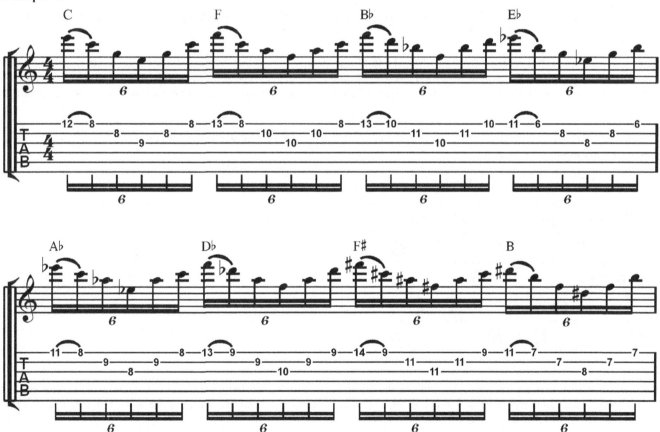

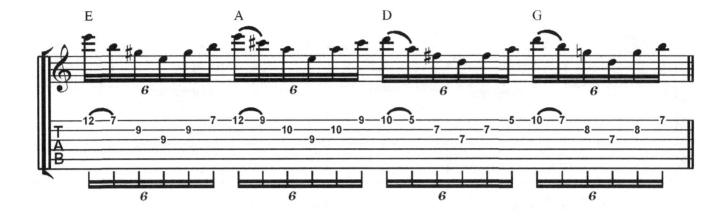

To get really familiar with this chord sequence and the different arpeggio shapes, try playing this example starting on different chords and with each of the three inversions. Remember to always look for the closest inversion of the next chord.

Using Diminished Chords

The strongest harmonic resolution is the perfect cadence (moving from chord V to chord I). The effect of which can be heightened by the tweaking of notes in the V chord to make it even more dissonant, and make the tonic more consonant by comparison. Without wading too far into the murky waters of chord theory, one of the notes we could add is the b9, or second degree of the scale, measured from the V's root.

In the key of D minor, the V chord is A7, which can be 'extended' to include a 9th (stacking another 3rd above the 7th). In minor keys this is a flattened ninth (Bb).

The V chord (now A7b9) contains A C# E G Bb. The final four notes (C# E G Bb) create a Diminished 7th chord. Because of this, Dim7 chords can act much in the same way as a V7 because they share most of the same notes. For example, you will often see the chord Bb dim7 used as a substitute for an A7 chord. By playing a Bb dim7 chord over an A bass note we create an A7b9 chord.

Compare the following pair of chord diagrams and you'll see that the only difference is the Bb in the Diminished arpeggio has replaced the A in the A7 diagram.

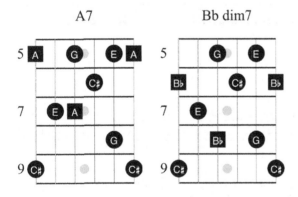

Diminished chords contain a flattened 5th and double flattened 7th which gives them a dark and dissonant sound compared to minor chords. They are often used as a source of tension before resolving to the minor scale or arpeggio. The lick signs off at the end of the bar by returning to the safety of a D minor phrase.

Example 1o

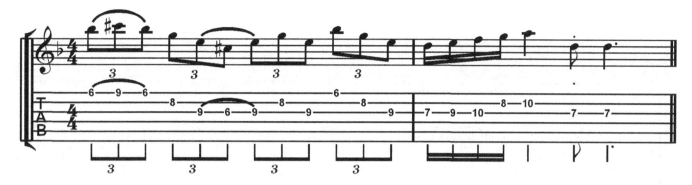

In the next example, we use the symmetry of Diminished chords to move a lick up the neck. Each note in a Diminished chord is a minor 3rd (three frets) apart, so it is common to move the same idea around the neck in three-fret intervals. After three *inversions* of the pattern the line finishes with an E Harmonic Minor run.

Example 1p

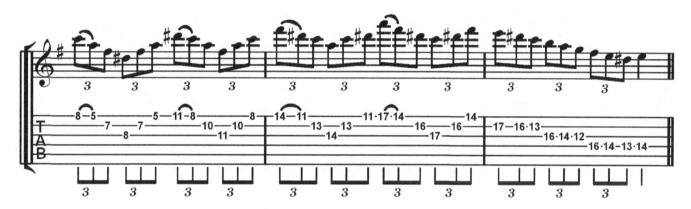

Next, the Diminished arpeggios are used in conjunction with the major and minor triad shapes we studied in book two. Pay special attention to the position shifts and try to 'hear' the chord changes go by as you play through the example.

Example 1q

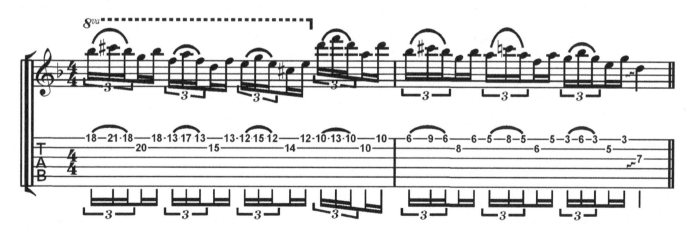

We couldn't visit neoclassical metal playing without looking at a frenzy of crazy arpeggios in the style of Paul Gilbert's work with Racer X. This lick is demanding, but playing two notes on each string feels more like a stretched out Pentatonic line, so the general approach should be familiar.

This line follows the written chord changes and uses Diminished arpeggios to resolve into the different chords. Warm up with smaller stretches and take this very slowly at first - don't strain yourself!

Example 1r

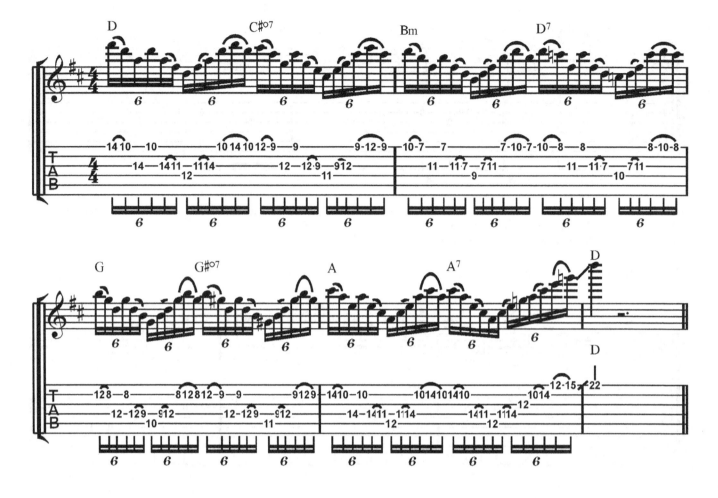

At the end of this book we'll go back to the classical source with a transcription of a piece of music originally written for violin. Among violin virtuoso Nicolo Paganini's (1782-1840) best known compositions are a set of twenty-four caprices. We'll be looking at the 16th caprice, in G minor. I've arranged the original violin part onto the guitar fretboard in the most playable way possible.

The piece makes use of all the techniques we'll develop over the next four chapters. The smaller size and 5ths tuning of the violin also means several of the phrases force us to deal with unnatural position shifts.

Recommended listening for neoclassical metal and baroque influences:

J.S. Bach – 15 Two Part Inventions
Handel – Flute Sonatas
Vivaldi – The Four Seasons
Scarlatti – *Sonata K. 1 in D minor*
Paganini -5th Caprice (from the 24 Caprices)
Deep Purple – Highway Star
Ozzy Osbourne (w/Randy Rhoads) – Over the Mountain
Yngwie Malmsteen – Black Star
Racer X - Scarified
Cacophony – Speed Metal Symphony
Jason Becker – Altitudes
Symphony X – Eve of Seduction
Adagio – Fire Forever
Sonata Arctica – What Did You Do in the War, Dad?
Time Requiem – Optical Illusion

Chapter Two: Legato

This chapter teaches you to use legato playing to navigate the fretboard with great fluency. We look at linking up the positions in different ways before exploring ideas using wider stretches in four note-per-string and string skipping ideas.

One of the biggest challenges with any legato technique is keeping unwanted string noise to a minimum. Be strict with yourself when practicing: Pay attention to reducing unwanted noise, and also play with only a mildly overdriven sound. It's very tempting to use more gain and distortion to help the intended notes sustain but this also increases the volume of unwanted noise too.

It's become popular to dampen the strings at the nut with a hair band or other soft material, which makes your playing sound cleaner, but I would recommend always practicing without one to be as critical as possible, as you probably won't have the mute onstage mid-song. This means you're not using a crutch to mask weaknesses in your technique.

Our first lick features lots of 4th intervals which gives it a modern fusion flavour. The fingering pattern should feel consistent with Pentatonic rock licks but the wide stretches along each string add an extra level of difficulty. Playing 4ths in one position means we get a repeated note when changing between strings. The different tone of each string makes it musical, resulting in a stuttering melodic contour.

The second half of the lick changes position to avoid the repeated notes and the position shifts can become unwieldy as the speed increases. Train the index finger to change position while the pinkie is fretting, so that the hand moves up the fretboard in a more dynamic way.

Example 2a

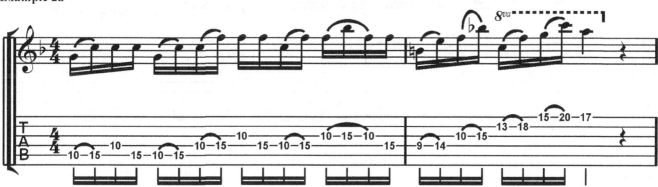

This next single-string idea features slides to jump between positions. The jumps are quite wide here as we're skipping up and down the neck. The quintuplets should arrange themselves quite easily so long as you concentrate on performing the shifts on the beats.

Example 2b

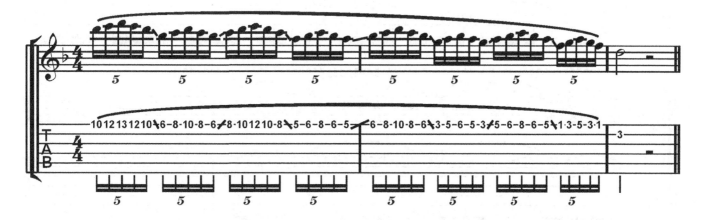

The next four examples demonstrate that small fragments can be combined to create long passages that span the fretboard. Using a twelve-note fragment, we descend through the different positions of F# minor along the neck. Practice the position shifts slowly at first. Concentrate on moving your pinkie towards the new position while the first fragment is being completed. This may sound like a lot of multitasking but it will stop you having to jump abruptly between shapes.

Take it slowly at first and note where the position shifts occur, and the fingering used to achieve them.

Example 2c

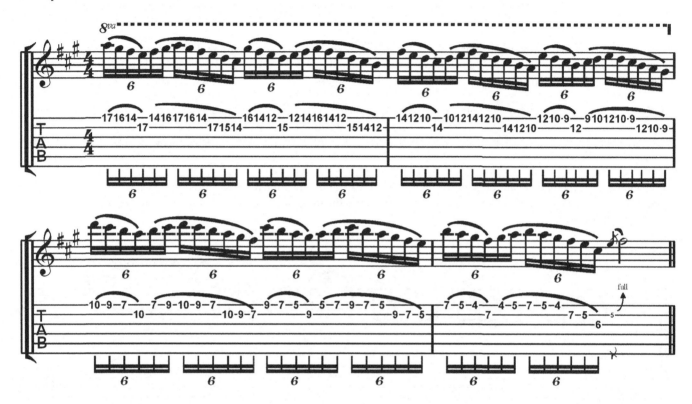

The next fragment-based legato lick uses a consistent eight-note pattern with a slight variation at the end. Once the basic building block is practiced, focussing on the starting note of each group will help to stop all that movement getting out of control. **Example 2d**

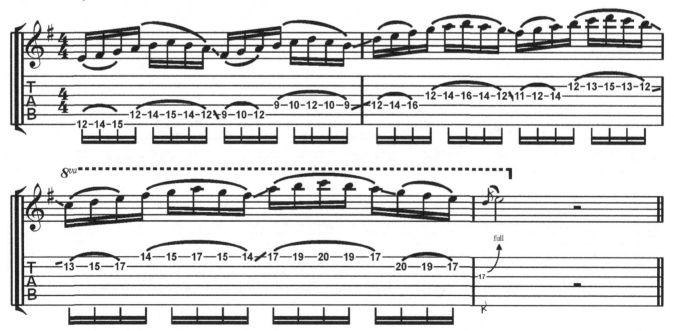

The melodic line in example 2e is deceptively varied, so work through it in small chunks to memorise the whole passage accurately.

Example 2e

Our second, longer legato run involves string skipping as an added hurdle. Continuous stepwise motion can be a little monotonous and skipping strings can help to break this up by adding ear-catching wide intervallic leaps into the scalic phrases. Brett Garsed's, and the great Shawn Lane's playing both exhibit this approach.

Example 2f

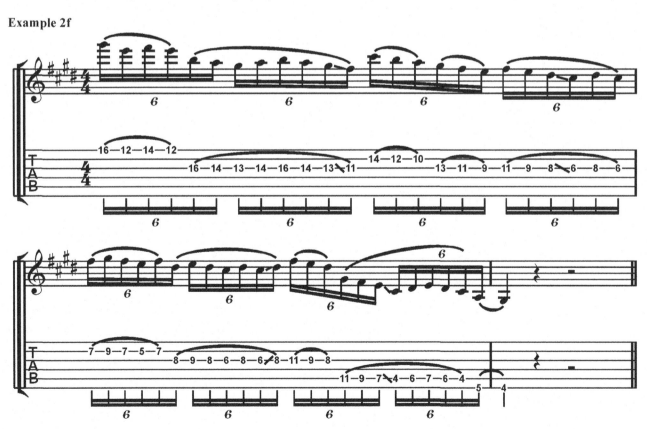

The following Diminished lick comes with a health warning! The wide stretches will take a good level of dexterity and stamina to maintain, so make sure you're warmed up before playing and stop if you feel any stress in the wrist or fingers. Keeping the thumb low on the back of the neck and angling the neck more vertically will both help with the wide stretches.

Notice how we resolve the dissonance of the Diminished arpeggio onto a Dm arpeggio spread out along the D string and end on notes from D Harmonic Minor.

Be careful when sliding to the final note (A) at the 22nd fret. It can be helpful to bunch the other fingers up behind it and slide the whole hand as one rather than just the pinkie. Don't forget to add some suitably ostentatious vibrato!

Example 2g

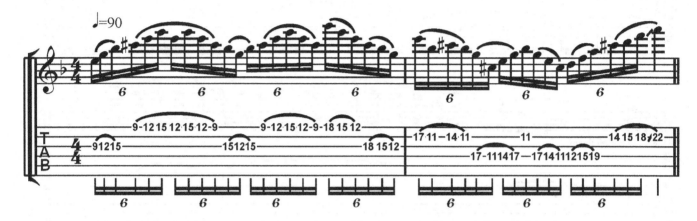

Recommended listening for examples of great legato:

Joe Satriani – *Crystal Planet*
Symphony X – *Savage Curtain*
Sikth – *Scent of the Obscene*
John Petrucci – *Curve*
James Murphy – *Epoch*
Opeth – *Heir Apparent*

Chapter Three: Tapping

In Heavy Metal Lead Guitar, many of the tapping licks we explored were based around arpeggios in the style of Van Halen and Randy Rhoads. In this chapter we're going to look at more scalic lines. Tapping as an extension of legato technique allows for the smoothest possible sound by fitting more notes on each string.

We'll return to arpeggio tapping towards the end of the chapter but with a more contemporary slant, focussing on the string skipping tapped arpeggios of players as diverse as Greg Howe, Guthrie Govan and Michael Romeo of Symphony X.

It's usual to phrase tapping licks with the tapped note on the beat. However, it's important to break away from these limiting muscle memory associations. To be most liberated, we want to be able to place any note on the beat so that the technique enhances the music instead of dictating it. At first this may be confusing for the hands so take each lick slowly to get the interaction between the hands as even as possible.

Both Van Halen and Paul Gilbert use their index finger for tapping, however, it's now common practice for modern players to use their middle finger. This is the better option for two reasons: Firstly, you are able to keep hold of the pick as normal so making the transition back to regular playing is easier. Secondly, if you wished to use multiple fingers to tap (such as example 4h), then the middle and ring fingers provide the strongest combination.

After exploring some advanced lead applications of tapping, I have included several riffs that incorporate the technique. In modern metal and instrumental rock, textural and pattern-driven compositions have blurred the division between 'rhythm' and 'lead' vocabulary. Death, Limp Bizkit and Funeral for a Friend often use tapping to create riffs in this way.

Progressive bands like Sikth and more recently Scale the Summit have used tapping to create intervallic riffs that would be impossible without the two handed approach.

Our first line is played as straight 1/16th notes, and the taps do not fall on beat one of each group. This can feel uncomfortable, but breaking the dependence on a physical reference point for rhythm will improve your ear and sense of pulse.

Start slowly, and make sure you know which notes fall on the beats so you can keep in time. A great way to practice this rhythmic freedom is to break the lick up into small chunks and, with a metronome, practice stopping on different beats. This will show you if you're really staying in time throughout the lick, or just cramming notes together between two beats.

Use the fretting hand add the vibrato from behind the tapping finger on the final note. **Example 3a**

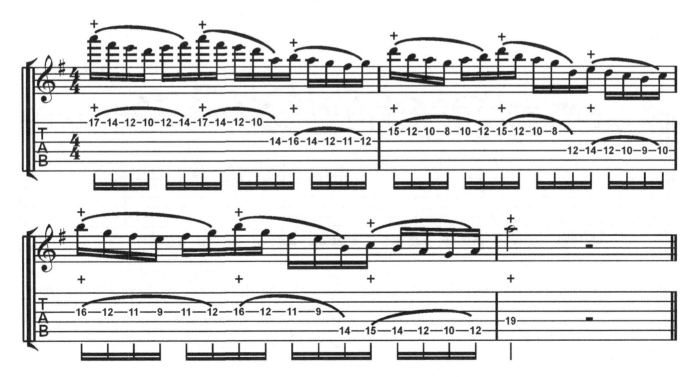

The main challenge is hammering-on to a new string with the first finger of the fretting hand. This poses two problems: Firstly the first finger is actually surprisingly weak for most people because normally it never needs to hammer-on, and secondly, the force of the hammer-on often causes unwanted string noise.

Unfortunately, the index finger is rather overworked as it must simultaneously play the desired note *and* mute the other five strings. To tackle this, experiment with how you hammer-on so the first finger not only lands on the desired pitch, but also mutes the adjacent lower string with its tip and the higher strings with the side of the finger. To consistently get all three things right may take some time, but once you've mastered it, the knock-on effect will pay dividends for your playing in general.

Our next lick spans three octaves of a B7 arpeggio and focuses on hammering-on from nowhere with the fretting hand. The basic triad is in the fretting hand with the tapping hand adding the b7 (A).

Example 3b

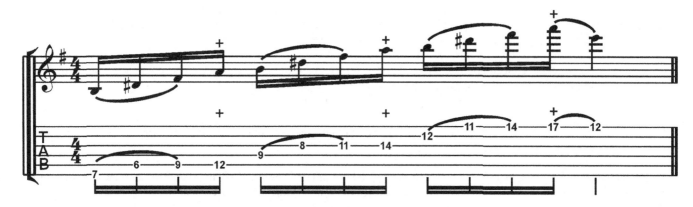

Building on the previous idea, the following lick combines the B7 with a Cmaj7 arpeggio found right next door. Focus on the first note of each four-note grouping to keep track of where you are and initially practice the fretted part before adding the tapping.

The combination of the two arpeggios gives a strong B Phrygian Dominant flavour, just as you would get by strumming the two chords one after another.

Example 3c

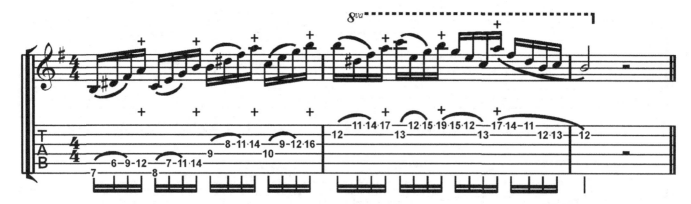

In the following example we lay out the notes of an Em7 arpeggio in one position, based around the 'A shape' Em barre chord.

Michael Romeo of Symphony X has a masterful command of this type of lick; incorporating them musically into his highly technical neoclassical soloing style.

Example 3d

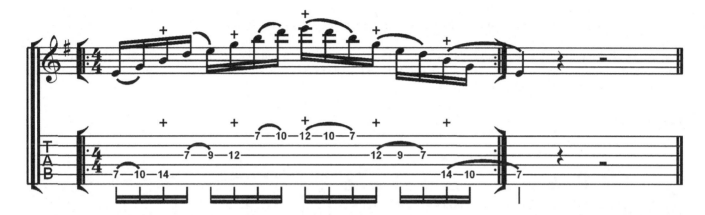

Here's the same shape, but this time using sequences of four notes. To get this idea clean will require serious muting and strong hammer-ons, otherwise the notes will disappear in a muddy mess of distortion and open strings. Remember to keep fretting hand fingers flat against the strings to mute them, playing with the pad of the finger rather than the tip.

Example 3e

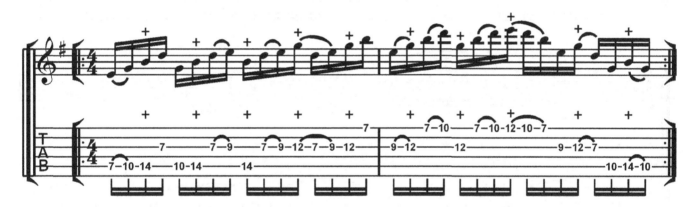

The same Em7 arpeggio can be played with all four chord tones on one string and repeated in octaves. This is easier to visualise when improvising, particularly in less familiar keys. Keep the thumb low on the back of the neck to make the five fret stretch more manageable and, as always, be vigilant against unwanted noise.

Example 3f

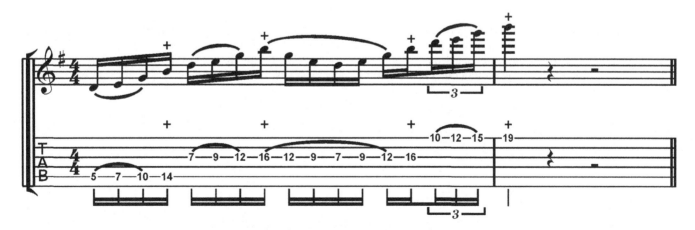

Here's a descending pattern in the same fashion as example 3f but this time in D minor. The stretch for the fretting hand may be a little awkward because of the bunching up of the index and middle fingers. Guitar wizard Guthrie Govan quite often employs phrases like this to achieve a wonderfully fluid saxophone-inspired articulation. Listen out for a preposterous example at the start of the solo on his track Fives that combines several different arpeggios into one phrase.

Notice how we've relocated three octaves of the same arpeggio onto the E, D and high E strings. Although a wider string skip is needed, the fretting hand avoids the lateral movement found in the previous lick. This should make moving backwards and forwards between each string more fluid.

Example 3g

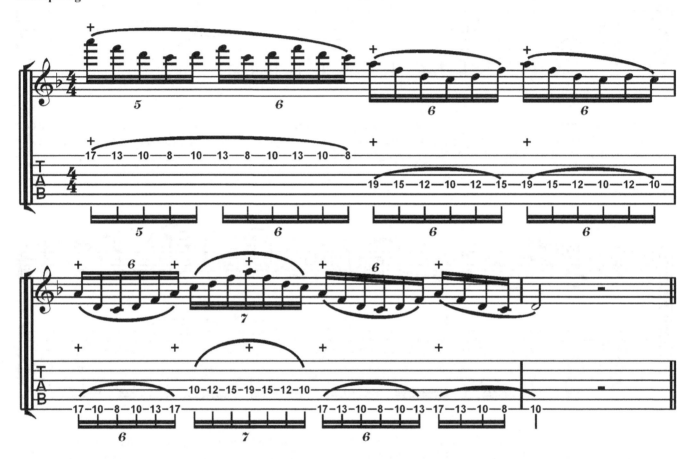

Let's explore this concept even further by tapping using two fingers on the picking hand to give five notes on one string. If you've not used more than one finger on the picking hand to tap with before, then don't panic, the ring finger operates in exactly the same way as the middle finger, although a subtle pull off is needed from the ring finger after tapping to give the third tapped note sufficient volume.

Practice the first four notes in isolation to get a feel for hammering-on and pulling-off between the tapping fingers.

The fact that there are three consecutive tapped notes allows a sufficient time for the fretting hand to change string. I prefer to pull off upwards into the palm but pulling off either upwards or downwards is equally valid if the results are comfortable and sound good.

Example 3h

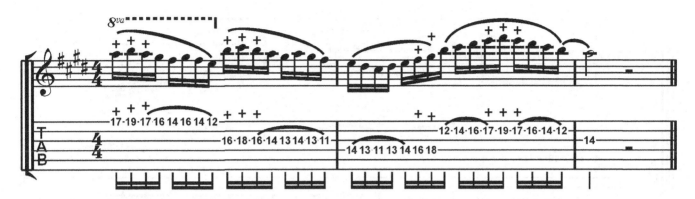

As with the previous lick, example 3i uses two tapping fingers to help the fretting hand. In the spirit of Van Halen (and later Greg Howe), we're using tapping to share the work of each hand in what is otherwise a quite conventional sounding blues lick.

You'll have to hammer-on with the fretting hand for the F#m arpeggio on beat one, so be on guard against unwanted noise. Lift each finger as the next one comes down, while once again using the tips of each finger to mute the adjacent lower string.

The lasting appeal of Van Halen is that despite using flashy technical ideas, at the core he is still in touch with The Bluesy vocabulary inherited from hard rock. Listening to, and learning some of his solos will help you to integrate these two aspects successfully.

Example 3i

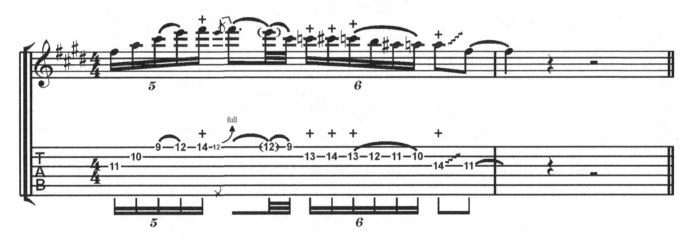

For the next example we're using the Whole Tone scale which lends the lick a tense 'Augmented' sound, ideal for dark and dramatic moments. Although the Wholetone 'fits' over Augmented triads and V7b5/#5 chords, try using it over other chords to create an 'outside' sound on an otherwise diatonic solo. If your ears like the results, go for it!

Notice how this lick momentarily moves outside of the E Whole Tone scale as we move chromatically up the top E string. Also, the final two tapped notes start with the ring finger (unlike our other examples). Be sure to get things dialled in slowly and accurately.

Example 3j

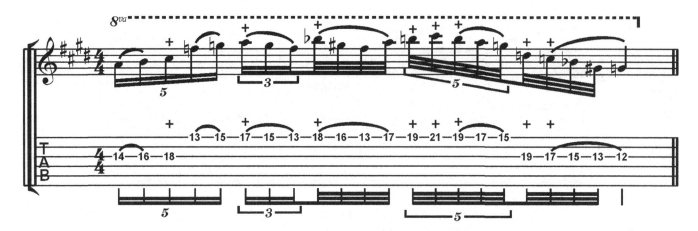

Sliding tapped notes is an interesting alternative to using two tapping fingers to extend a melody.

The following example demonstrates both of these characteristics by sliding a tone on the G string then sliding a major 3rd on the E string.

Example 3k

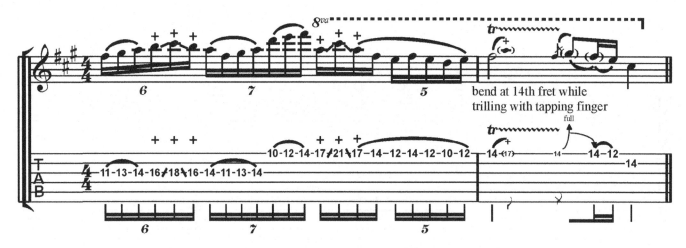

As with example 3j, try to ignore how complex the rhythmic groupings appear on paper, but observe which notes land on the beats.

Use the audio as a guide, and then just go for it! The way the notes float over the pulse enhance the legato feel, but it's important to keep a sense of time so that you can land on the beat whenever you choose… just as an acrobat controls their landing after somersaulting through the air!

Rhythm Tapping

The rest of this chapter explores riffs (rather than licks) that feature tapping. Tapping can provide high-pitched accents that would otherwise be impossible. It also allows wide interval patterns at higher tempos, and helps achieve a flowing, piano-like texture. Rhythm parts need to tightly lock in with the drums, so be prepared to practice your legato/tapping playing to the same rhythmic precision you would demand when picking.

Picking becomes problematic when several picking hand fingers get involved, so we become reliant on fretting hand hammer-ons. You'll find that with this amount of fretting hand hammer-ons, muting the unwanted strings becomes a serious challenge. Take each section slowly; making sure your technique is watertight by flattening the fretting-hand fingers and using the picking hand palm to mute unwanted noise.

We'll start off with a fairly straight forward riff that follows closely from our lead work. This has a distinctly classical sound to it, thanks to the use of pedal point. Be careful with the position shift of both hands at the start of bar four. Practice the fretting hand until it is fluent before adding the tapping.

Example 31

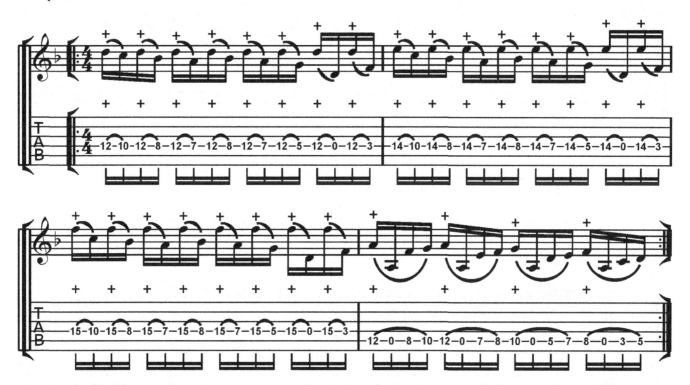

Tapping and picking don't have to be mutually exclusive! Here we augment a tight, thrashy triplet riff from Annihilator or Lamb of God with a descending tapping run. Work through the final bar in isolation before combining it with the riff. It has three, four-note groupings which fall across the main pulse, so count it out slowly before raising the tempo.

The movement of the picking hand between palm muting at the bridge and tapping at the fourteenth fret needs to be carefully rehearsed so that the rhythm and pick attack aren't compromised. It's a bit of a juggling act so use the legato at the end of bar three to cover the picking hand's leap.

Example 3m

The next riff uses tapping to add extensions to a G power chord. Here we alternate between the Bb (b3) and A (9th), but you should go on to experiment with adding other notes with tapped notes.

After a strong Gm(add9) tonality in bar 1, the second half answers with a tenser G Dorian #11 phrase, a mode of D Harmonic Minor, (also known as the Romanian Minor scale)

Example 3n

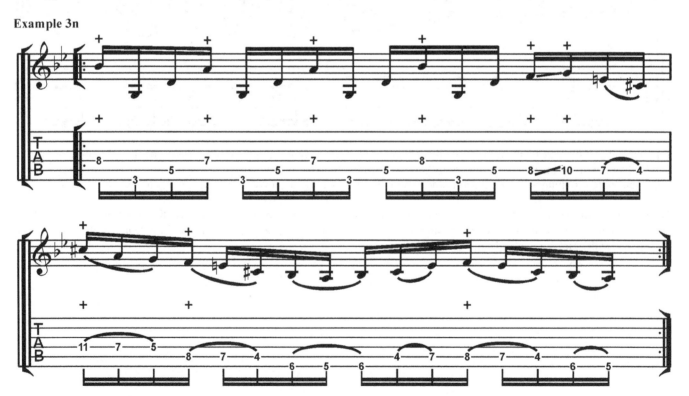

Keeping a power chord in the fretting hand remains a common theme, but now the fretting hand is leading rhythmically.

Listen to the audio to absorb the odd rhythm until you hands can tap the rhythm in each part. Many of these ideas feel like drumming between the hands, so learning to coordinate the two hands in different ways is the best starting point.

In this example, I've actually brought the thumb into play to gently pluck the open E string in bars two and four. This is marked with the symbol 'p' in the notation.

The softer attack of the thumb blends closely with the tone of the tapped notes. Also the first tapped chord in bar four is most easily played with a combination of index and ring fingers.

Example 3o

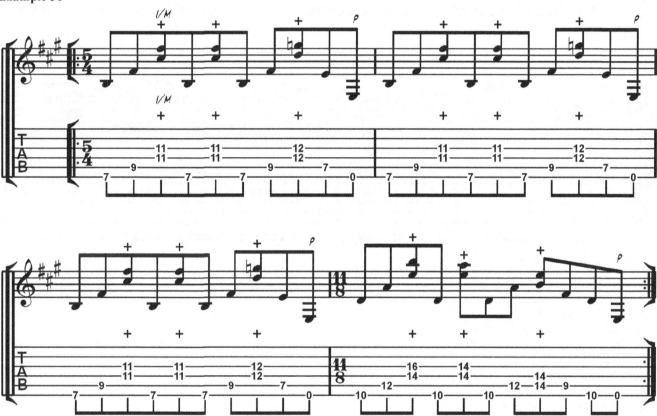

All of the previous examples used a constant stream of even notes, but the final tapping riff adds more rhythmic interest. This increases the difficulty as the notes can no longer be lined up evenly. Be sure that the hammer-ons are locking in tightly with the 1/16th note pulse.

We outline a chord progression of D, D/C, Bm and G, although several passing scale notes are included on each chord. Bars one and two employ sliding taps, while bars three and four use two tapping fingers to play notes on adjacent strings. Practice this movement in isolation to avoid letting the two notes ring into each other. I used the middle and index, as in example 3h, so the pick can be kept in its usual grip ready to return to a normal playing position.

Example 3p

Recommended listening for tapping techniques:

Meshuggah – *Future Breed Machine*
Sikth - *Skies of the Millennium Night*
Animals as Leaders – *Cafo*
Periphery – *Zyglrox*
Scale the Summit – *Dunes*
Chon - *Knot*
Protest the Hero – *Bloodmeat*
Steve Vai – *Building the Church*
The Fine Constant – *The Resurgent*

Chapter Four: Alternate Picking

A strong picking technique is essential to great metal playing, and most of your time will be spent 'locking in' with the drums and bass as a member of the rhythm section. Locking in with the rhythm section requires a very high degree of precision and this accuracy will carry over into your lead playing to give your licks polish and crispness.

As we all know, the best way to achieve accuracy is with a metronome or a drum loop. Practice one lick slowly until it feels like it can't go wrong, and then start gradually raising the tempo to build your speed while remaining relaxed. Keep your foot tapping on the beats and sync up your hands by accenting the notes that land on each beat.

Once you're feeling confident with the three-note-per-string runs we worked on in Heavy Metal Lead Guitar, it's time to step up a gear. In this chapter we're going to be looking at alternate picking licks that make more demands of your technique. The speed at which you play any of the licks is of course up to you, so we'll be raising the bar in terms of rhythm and string crossing, rather than just shredding harder!

Keep the heel of the picking hand in contact with the bridge, and move it across the strings as you change string with the pick. Having this consistency will give an even attack and help you to avoid losing control when skipping strings by having a constant point of contact.

To start with, we've got a couple of picking runs that demonstrate how we could develop some diatonic fragments. After practicing different patterns and clusters of notes we can stitch them together to form longer runs full of twists and turns.

Example 5a switches from a sequence of four notes to three notes, then into a straight scale with a quick legato turn at the end. Split the line into short two-beat sections and make sure they feel easy before you combine them into the full run.

Try playing this idea descending, then combine other sequences to build your own phrases.

Example 4a

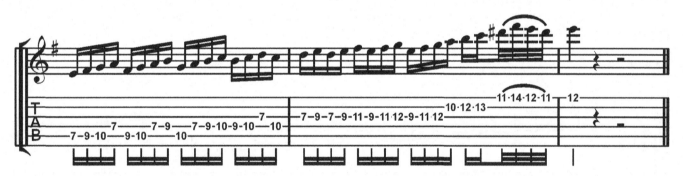

The second example maintains stepwise motion throughout the line, but changes direction at different times to keep the contour of the lick less predictable. Practicing the different permutations of each two string cell will enable you to improvise runs like this with ease, because you're assembling small building blocks, each of which have been carefully rehearsed.

Example 4b

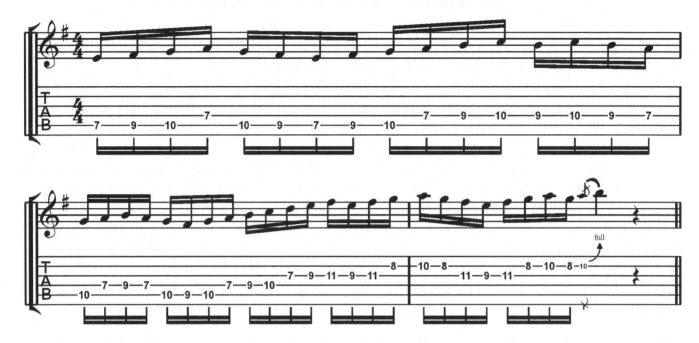

Michael Angelo Batio is one of the fastest shredders, and his picking prowess is in no doubt despite using an unconventional hand position. This demanding string-skipping lick is his style and will test your control, but the leaps in pitch make for an exciting pattern that covers a large range.

Moving the picking wrist as you change strings is even more important when you skip strings. Start slowly to check your pick crosses over the skipped string with minimal clearance. The pick should not be noticeably 'lifted' out from the strings but rather the skip is an extension of the last pick stroke.

Example 4c

Now we've skipped one string at a time, let's skip two! Each melodic cell in the next example is repeated an octave below each time. The change of position and jump between strings may feel unwieldy to start with, but focussing on the destination fret rather than your hand should help build accuracy.

Practice the picking of this lick before worrying about the notes: Alternate pick eight strokes on each string using just one pitch so the picking hand learns its role.

Example 4d

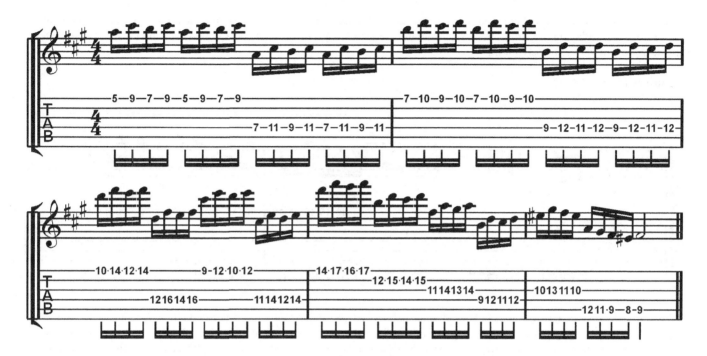

Tremolo picking is playing a single note repeatedly at high speed, and is usually added as an effect to a slower melody without worrying about the actual subdivisions of the pick strokes. However, it's quite common for players to include sections of tremolo picking in particularly intense picking licks.

After ascending through a scalic phrase in the next example, the highest notes of each contour are tremolo picked. Repeating these notes helps to reinforce their melodic importance.

Keep in mind that while tremolo gives a sense of speed and frantic energy, the picking hand should remain loose and relaxed so that the rest of the scalic playing will be accurate.

Example 4e

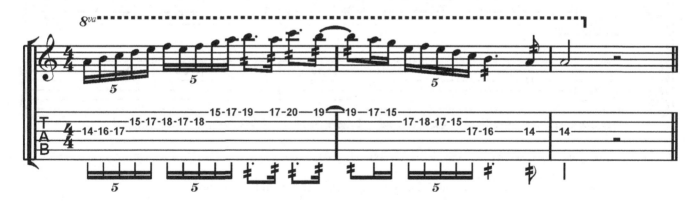

In the legato chapter, learnt about either sticking religiously to the rhythmic pulse of the music, or floating over the time and cramming in notes so that the target note lands on the beat. It's worth developing the same freedom with picking, though the challenge is increased by having to keep both hands synchronised.

One way to work on this is to practice moving between different groupings of notes is shown in the next example.

Here we start in 1/16th notes before putting on a burst of speed to play two beats of sextuplets, ending with a mixture of 1/16th notes and 1/8th note triplets. Accenting the notes on the beat is again here your friend. Listen carefully to the audio to help gauge how much speeding up/slowing down is needed for each grouping.

Keep your foot tapping throughout, and with a good sense of time, you'll know when to drop back into rhythm at the end of runs of this type. Playing to a drum loop or metronome while you experiment with speeding up and slowing down will develop this illusive, but very expressive skill.

Example 4f

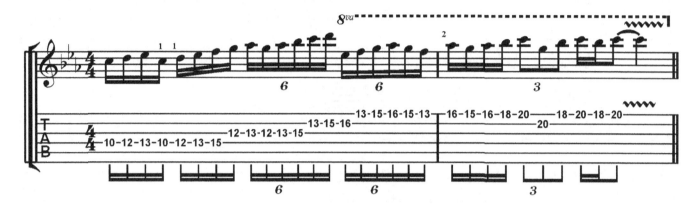

Now to touch on some intervallic licks after all that scale-based vocabulary. Obviously with lots of wider intervals in quick succession, there's going to be more jumping between strings. This first example involves lots of 5ths which provide a very angular yet consonant sound. First the line ascends by double picking each note in a line of 5ths before shifting a fifth motif up and down within the scale.

Here Steve Vai's influence is clear. Furthermore, Vai's use of 5ths licks likely comes from his time with Frank Zappa, so go back to the source!

Follow the fingering I've recommended to avoid getting tripped-up during the position shifts.

Example 4g

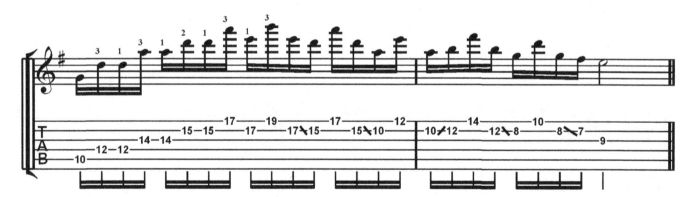

You could also experiment by converting this lick to a version based on 4ths.

For some interesting intervallic licks check out John Petrucci's earlier work with Dream Theater.

In the following three examples we'll explore the possibilities of playing wider interval licks. Example 4h uses diatonic 6ths. Like 3rds, 6ths are sweet-sounding and harmonically strong, but the wider leaps make them more interesting.

There are lots of different patterns to explore with each of the different intervals. Finding a pattern you like, and then applying it to another interval is a great way of modifying licks to suit your taste. Explore the other intervals - 4ths, and 7ths – and note the flavour of each.

For more useful patterns, check out the Fundamental Changes book: **Guitar Fretboard Fluency**

Example 4h

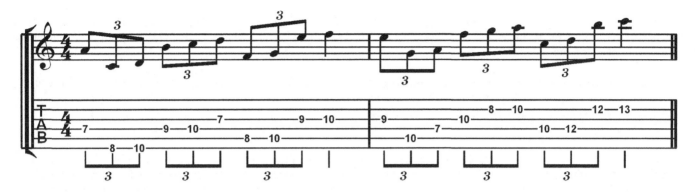

The next intervallic lick uses octaves. Whereas other intervals have a distinctive musical flavour, the octave has a different effect. By moving the same note up an octave, we make it more prominent in the overall musical texture.

Simple lines can sound modern and individual if we move certain notes up by an octave. This technique is known as *octave displacement*. For example, this line of adjacent notes in the D minor scale, would be quite boring, but with octave displacement it takes on an entirely new sound.

Example 4i

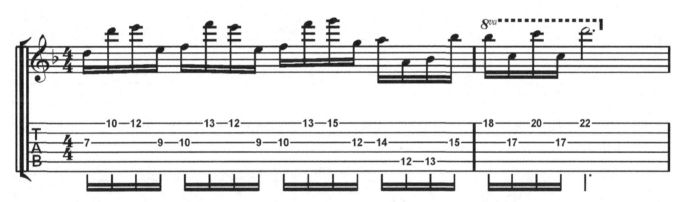

It might be tempting to use hybrid picking for this example, but alternate picking provides consistency of tone, plus it makes for a great exercise.

To me these erratic licks have a quality almost like a synthesizer's arpeggiator mode, where unconventional patterns are created that you wouldn't readily choose on guitar. I've deliberately avoided sticking to any one interval or sequential pattern for more than a few notes so as to make the most of the line's quirky and unpredictable appeal.

Example 4j

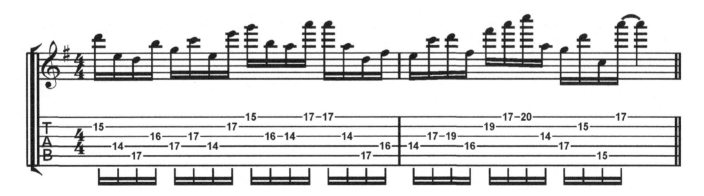

Odd Rhythmic Groupings

We have seen that longer runs are usually constructed from lots of connected cells that can be practiced individually. In the final portion of our chapter on alternate picking we're going to expand on that idea by using more creative groups of notes that break away from being rhythmically predictable.

The idea is to come up with cells that last an odd number of notes. When the pattern is cycled, a different note will be accented on the beat on each repetition. Rather than stringing several different fragments together, the constantly changing relationship between your lick and the underlying pulse is what maintains the interest, while retaining the consistency of each cell throughout.

When playing these ideas in a real musical situation, you must be aware of the main pulse of the music. As you become more adept at feeling different cross-rhythms, you'll more able to independently feel the underlying pulse, but begin by working out beforehand the beat of the bar your licks will end on. That way you'll immediately be able to fit back into normal time again reliably.

The first lick illustrates this idea by using a six-note pattern played in straight 1/16th notes. Here, focus on rhythm by accenting the start of each six with a louder pick to highlight the cross-rhythm.

Example 4k

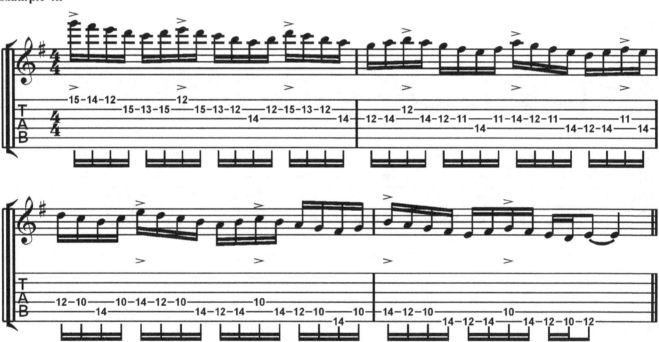

The following run uses less predictable groups of five. As you accent the start of each cell you'll notice that they fall on both down- and up-strokes. This is great practice for your picking control and teaches you that you don't need to play down-strokes on strong beat. This is beneficial when playing in odd time signatures.

Example 4l

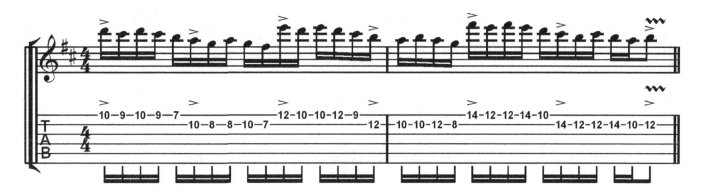

Example 4m uses a repeating fragment that lasts for eleven notes! This can be difficult to hear clearly, so work through the full line slowly. It can be helpful to play each fragment individually at first, and leave a short pause between them, before putting the whole line together using a metronome.

Example 4m

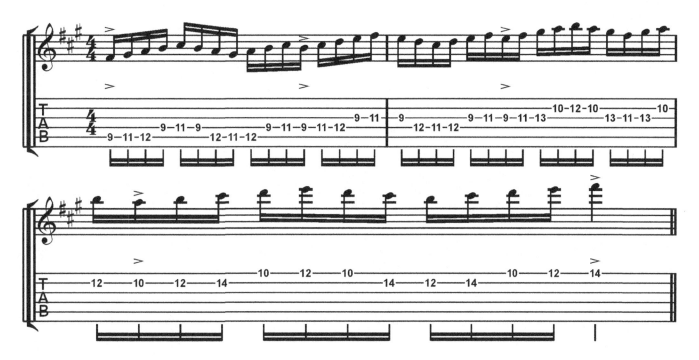

The last example in this chapter turns this concept on its head by superimposing a common phrase over an odd rhythmic grouping. This example has three layers of rhythm going on so hold onto your hats!

The main beat is subdivided into septuplets (seven notes per beat). Across these groups of seven, the melodic contour is divided into groups of four.

Physically this lick should hopefully be quite familiar as the sequence is a common one. To approach the rhythm, First, get comfortable with septuplets separately by ascending a scale or by picking seven notes on each string in turn.

Once the feel of the septuplets is confident, apply the four note sequence to them in small bursts. Start by playing just the first group of seven and landing on the following beat.

Seven notes per beat is quite fast so this type of lick is limited to songs with slower tempos. Later, in your own practice try applying similar ideas to other groupings such as triplets or quintuplets, which would work at faster tempos.

Example 4n

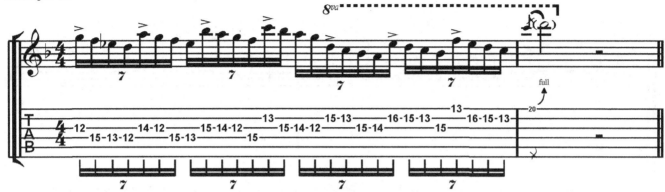

Recommended listening for examples of advanced alternate picking:

Dream Theater – *The Glass Prison*
Avenged Sevenfold – *Bat Country*
Cynic – *I'm But a Wave To...*
Disperse – *Profane the Ground*
The Contortionist - *Thrive*
Haken – *1985*

Chapter Five: Economy/Sweep Picking

I've left sweep picking until last because it requires a good sense of timing in the fretting hand, perfect synchronisation, and a grounding in alternate picking. Having discussed each of these elements in the previous chapters, you should now be well equipped to tackle some advanced licks.

Like tapping, sweep picking enables us to play much wider intervallic- and arpeggio-based lines at high speed. Whereas tapping achieves this by spacing intervals along the length of a string, sweep picking is used when we arrange notes roughly one-note-per-string, and then push the pick across the strings in a slow, controlled strum.

In Heavy Metal Lead Guitar, I presented major and minor triads and their different inversions across three strings. We then combined them in different ways to create sequences that outline chord progressions, before expanding to cover two octave arpeggios over five strings. Everything in this chapter will build on those fundamentals of shred vocabulary.

Sometimes the continual up-and-down contour of repeating five-string shapes can be a little too rhythmically predictable, so the following developments will provide variations to experiment with. Also, as shown here, they show how a more substantial lick can be created from a single arpeggio.

It's always important to pay attention to the quality of the final note or phrase, as a confident finish often provides musicality and credibility to some preceding shredding!

Example 5a

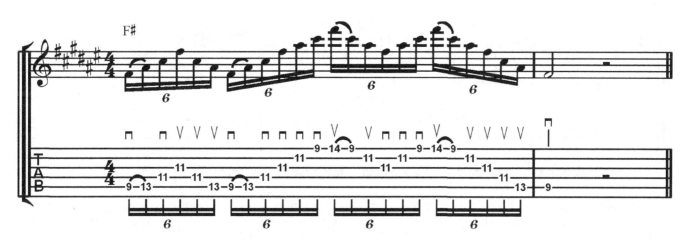

Taking example 5a further, we combine techniques by integrating a tapped note to extend the arpeggio. In the tapping chapter I suggested using the second finger to tap precisely because of licks like these. Keeping the pick ready makes the transition between the two techniques fluid and uncomplicated.

There are several different elements to contend with in this lick, so be sure to isolate each arpeggio shape, the position-shift, and tapped/legato section before trying to run through the whole idea. The rhythmic notation of beat three provides only a rough guide, but so long as the notes are even and you manage to land safely on beat two of the second bar, you'll achieve the desired effect.

As always, the creative benefit will come from inventing your own variations using the different shapes and ideas introduced here.

Example 5b

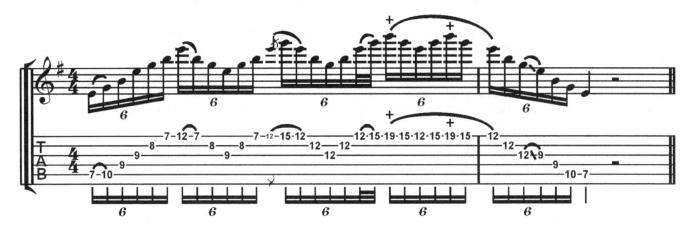

Six-string shapes are less common, but worth investigating if you wish to develop your arpeggio vocabulary.

The goal is to maximize the distance travelled in a single arpeggio. Starting in the fifth position, we move up through several positions using legato and slides. It takes control to break up the sweep pick with legato (rather than just ploughing straight through all the strings), so take your time to really internalise where the hammer-ons occur so the hands remain synchronised.

Example 5c

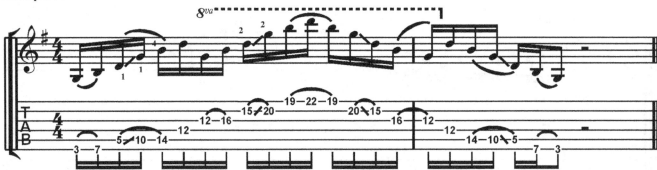

Here's a neat little way to play Diminished arpeggios across all strings. The notes are laid out in such a way that they can be picked while still sweeping from string to string. The quintuplets may feel a little unnatural to start with, but aim to begin each shape on the beat and the notes in between will, with practice, even themselves out.

To help fit this idea into your playing, try starting from different strings, and use just one or two shapes rather than the whole ascending or descending run.

Example 5d

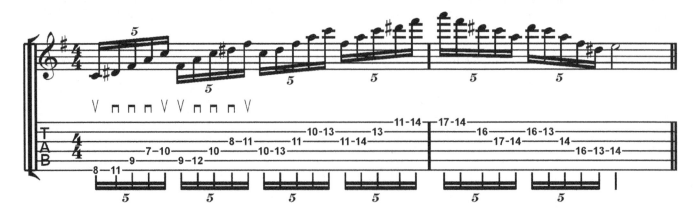

The same picking pattern gets recycled here, and is applied to the notes of the B Minor Pentatonic scale. Experiment with different triad or diatonic 7th shapes across the strings for more licks, and to get more mileage from your sweeping skills.
Example 5e

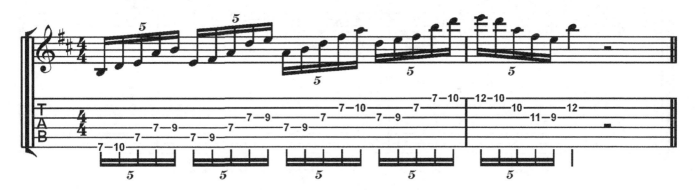

Frank Gambale, although a jazz-rock fusion guitarist, has had a discernible impact on metal lead guitar playing thanks to his frighteningly clean, fast economy picking technique. Economy picking takes sweep picking further by combining it with alternate picking to create a fluid combination of scalic and intervallic movement. The basic rule is to sweep from string to string wherever possible and then continue normal alternate picking while playing on the same string.

Example 5f

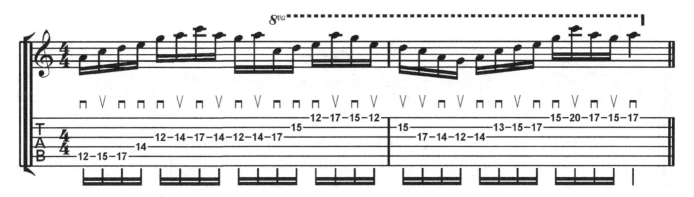

This example shreds its way up through the G Minor Pentatonic scale with a smoothness and rapidity that the standard two note-per-string approach could never match. Follow the picking directions carefully to start with and sweeping to each string should soon become second nature.

Another economy-picked idea here, though this time we use more angular sounding 4ths and 5ths instead of triads. Melodic use of perfect intervals (4ths, 5ths and octave) is still relatively rare, so they are a great source of fresh sounding ideas that will stand out in a solo. Keep the thumb low to help the stretch at the start of the lick and be careful of the barre roll on the 4ths at the end.

Example 5g

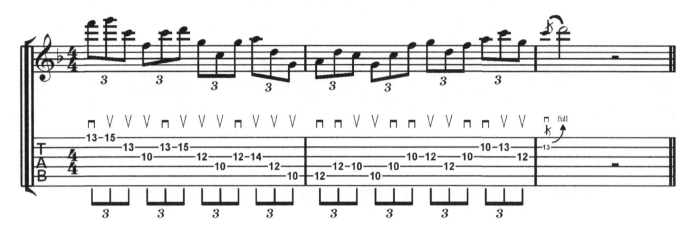

Our final lick is inspired by Cacophony/Megadeth guitarist Marty Friedman and his influence on modern players.

Marty's advanced arpeggio ideas stood out from the crowd in the late '80s and early '90s as being melodic and creative. Here I combine different diatonic triads to create a flowing and harmonically rich line. Try to identify the individual triads I've used and come up with your own licks by applying variations in contour and arpeggios.

Example 5h

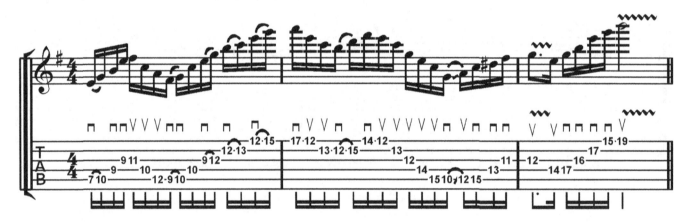

Recommended listening for sweep picking:

Yngwie Malmsteen – *Rising Force*
Megadeth - *Lucretia*
Steve Vai – *For the Love of God*
Slipknot – *Pulse of the Maggots*
Nevermore – The Psalm of Lydia (intro solo)
Animals as Leaders – Wave of Babies (first solo)

Chapter Six: Recasting Pentatonic & Blues scales

I have already emphasised the importance of melody and understanding The Blues influence to the expressiveness of your playing, but in this chapter we'll look at less traditional ways to incorporate the Pentatonic and Blues scales into your music using various modern rock techniques.

Over the previous four chapters we focussed on developing each of the main techniques involved in playing Heavy Metal lead guitar. Now you got a feel for the vocabulary of each technique, we'll use them to create some interesting new licks.

The Pentatonic/blues sound is often heard in conjunction with rather predictable rock phrasing, but when that note choice is heard in a new context (such as a legato or sweep picked run) the results are fresh and exciting. It can be hard to avoid the neoclassical sound when playing with shred-influenced techniques, and this can sometimes create negative associations. Using The Blues scale is a great way to create excitement while using a familiar musical sound.

Much of this chapter deals with rearranging the Pentatonic scale on the fretboard using three or more notes per string, and sliding along strings rather than sticking to the standard 'box' shape of traditional playing. Spreading out Pentatonic scales in this way involves some serious stretches for the fretting hand, so be sure to warm up with some diatonic three-note-per-string playing beforehand, and take a break if any tension develops.

Dream Theater's John Petrucci uses chromatic passing tones in scale-based lines and acknowledges the influence of Steve Morse (Dixie Dregs, Deep Purple) on his playing. The trick to making this technique work is to start and end on strong chord tones. This is best done by approaching them chromatically and trying to place them on the beat.

Our first blues-influenced shred lick uses economy/sweep picking to play a Pentatonic fragment. The high note moves between the 4, b5 and 5 of the E minor blues scale to provide the melodic movement. The lick is rhythmically grouped into sextuplets, although the pattern repeats every four notes, so take time to internalise the resultant cross rhythm before attempting to speed it up.

The picking motion should be relaxed and use very little movement to achieve the speed.

Example 6a

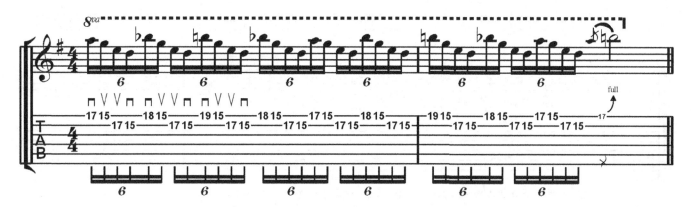

This Paul Gilbert-inspired idea uses a more conventional combination of picking and legato, but the chromatic notes added to the Pentatonic pattern allow for some frightening speed. Mixing the percussive accents of picking into the fluidity of a legato phrase creates a dynamic feel.

Example 6b

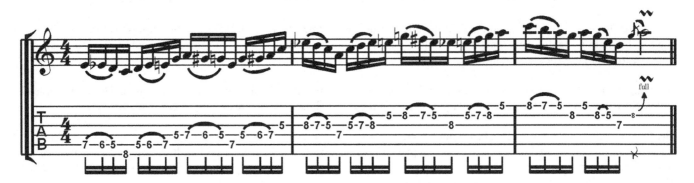

Now for a descending lick that uses the same hybrid scale shape as ex. 6b. The rhythmic combination of 1/16th-note and 1/16th-note triplets is the natural result of the picking pattern and the legato, so you should find that the rhythm sorts itself out.

The top three strings put demands on the ring and pinkie fingers together, so you may find that it takes time to build the strength to sustain these licks. However, once you can manage it, using fragments as repeating licks is an effective tool for building excitement and energy.

Example 6c

Applying bluesy note choices to shapes or patterns from the neoclassical or shred vocabulary is a great way to generate fresh licks, and that is exactly what I've done here. The sextuplet pattern we've used for several diatonic scale licks already has been stretched out to accommodate The Blues scale notes as well. Be aware of the wide stretches, and to make things easier, keep the thumb low on the back of the neck.

Example 6d

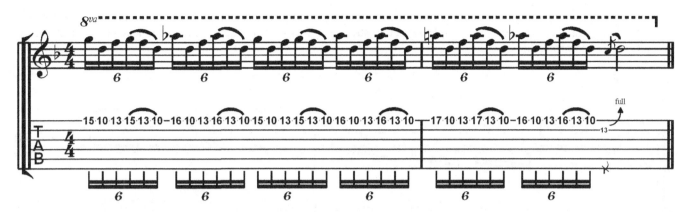

This three-note-per-string Pentatonic lick covers a lot of ground very quickly. Keeping the position shifts under control can be a challenge at first, but imagine trying to play the lick with the same speed and fluidity using two notes-per-string box shapes; the benefit of the alternative fingering is obvious.

Example 6e

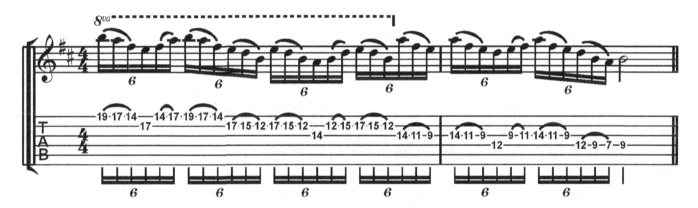

This is certainly not your typical E Minor Pentatonic lick, and isn't for the faint hearted! It comes with a health warning: The stretches involved can be very demanding, so remember to warm up well.

These 3 note-per-string Pentatonic fingerings cover two positions of Pentatonic shapes. Learning to visualise these new licks in terms of the shapes you're already familiar will help you integrate them in a natural and convincing way. To illustrate this, it finishes with a more typical blues phrase.

Example 6f

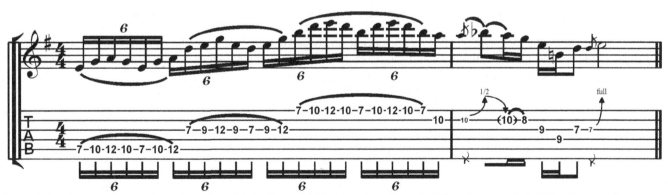

You will notice that the previous shape is not actually a complete Pentatonic scale. There is one note missing from each octave. In the context of these legato runs the wider intervals actually enhance the appeal of these licks. Naming the resultant pool of notes is not really a concern; the sound is a pleasing middle ground between Pentatonic, and minor 7 arpeggio sounds.

Despite the irregularities of the scale shape, we can still apply common sequences like this 'fours' pattern. Being confident with this pattern in a diatonic scale (such as example 3e) before attempting this stretched-out version, will make things much easier as the fingering is transferable.

Example 6g

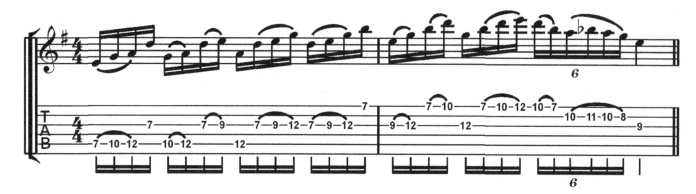

A good way to practice using this scale shape is by running between different notes, rather than rolling across all the notes on each string. This will help you to develop it from a pre-conceived lick into malleable vocabulary. In this line I've played a varied melodic contour within the shape to make the line less predictable.

Example 6h

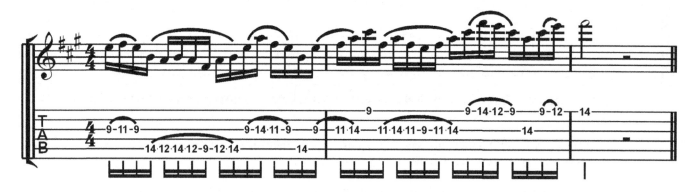

If the idea of incomplete scales offends you, then try this expanded version for size! Using a tapped note to extend along alternate completes the Pentatonic scale; this opens up potential for seamlessly legato playing.

Changing to higher strings involves using a fretting hand tap with the index finger, which you may find weak to start with. This comes as a surprise to some students, so to begin with, aim to hammer down from a distance to generate enough power.

The best way to tackle the rhythm of this lick is to practice it slowly and place emphasis on the notes that land on the beats. Once you can play it cleanly and smoothly, start trying to cram the seven notes between each beat. Your ear will guide you and the notes will space themselves out naturally.

Example 6i

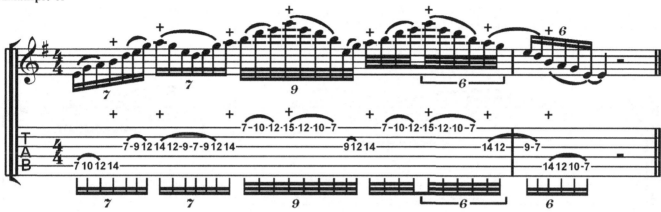

Next we add some chromatic passing tones to enhance the Pentatonic scale. This lick could, at a push, be played just with conventional legato, but bringing an extra finger into play makes the fretting hand's job much easier. Playing 'outside' the key is a topic worthy of its own book, but put simply, you can play any outside note as long as it is followed up with a rhythmically strong 'inside' phrase.

Example 6j

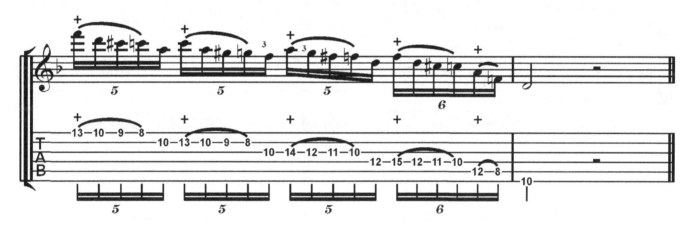

You may need to isolate different sections of the lick and practice transitioning between each string before linking the whole thing up. To hear masterful use of these phrases, listen to anything by Shawn Lane, Michael Romeo or Rusty Cooley, who all have great legato skills using these stretched out shapes.

Keep in mind the different position of the Minor Pentatonic scale as you move up the neck, moving from the 'A shape' at the 12th fret to the 'E shape' at the 17th fret.

Example 6k

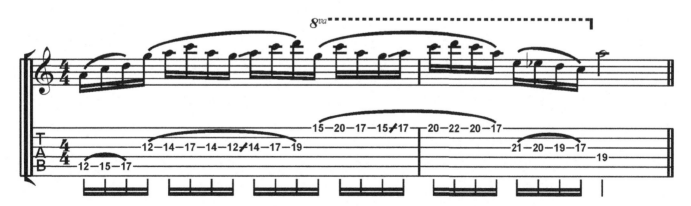

To push the envelope even further, we'll combine everything in this chapter: chromatic passing tones, Pentatonics, tapping and wide stretches. The first section of the lick may prove the hardest due to the stretching low down the neck. If you are really struggling with this, then you may want to use tapping to share the load. Good luck, and remember to get creative!

Example 61

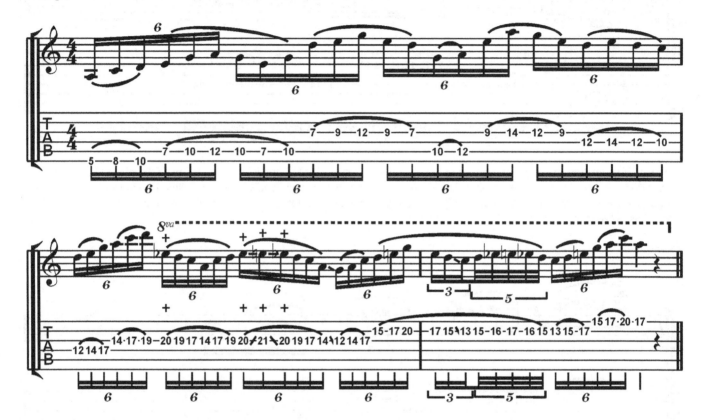

Recommended listening for shred Pentatonic and Blues scales:

Racer X/Paul Gilbert – *Technical Difficulties*
Mr Big – *Colorado Bulldog*
Shawn Lane – *Get You Back*
Pantera – A New Level
Rusty Cooley – *Hillbilly Militia*
The Aristocrats – *Ohhhh Noooo*

Chapter Seven: Exotic Scales, Substitutions & Beyond

This chapter is devoted to exotic scales and harmonic tricks you can use to create new licks, including alternative Pentatonics, symmetrical scales, and unconventional phrasing ideas.

Harmonic Substitution

The substitution of scales is a massive subject that we couldn't do justice to here, but in essence it involves playing a scale or arpeggio over an alternative root note/chord to create a new flavour. In these examples we will limit ourselves to arpeggios and Pentatonics, and with a little theory, begin to understand why the resultant sound changes.

To give a simple example; if we play a major triad over its own root note, the tones would be 1st, 3rd and 5th steps of the Major scale. However, if the triad was played a tone high over the same root note, the three notes of the triad now are the 2nd, #4th and 6th (or 9, #11 and 13) steps above the root, creating a Lydian sound with just three notes.

This means that you could take your favourite sweeping and tapped arpeggio licks and achieve a new sound by playing them over of different harmonies.

We can use the same concept with Pentatonic scales. I'll show you how to derive alternative substitute Pentatonic scales and I've included a table below to act as a handy reference point for the most common substitutions.

At the risk of sounding like a maths teacher, I'll work through one example to illustrate the concept, and leave you to consider the others as much (or as little) as you care to...

Take the Aeolian mode starting on A:

A	B	C	D	E	F	G
R	2	b3	4	5	b6	b7

As well as the Minor Pentatonic scale starting on the root, A, there are two other Pentatonic scales lurking within A Aeolian:

A Minor Pentatonic:

	A	B	**C**	**D**	**E**	F	**G**
	R	2	**b3**	**4**	**5**	b6	**b7**

D Minor Pentatonic:

	D	E	**F**	**G**	**A**	B	**C**
4	5	**b6**	**b7**	**R**	2	**b3**	

E Minor Pentatonic:

	E	F	**G**	**A**	**B**	C	**D**
5	b6	**b7**	**R**	**2**	b3	**4**	

From at the table above you can read off which scale tones the alternative Pentatonic scales provide. Note that the scale formulas all still refer to A as the root.

For example, in the context of A minor, D Minor Pentatonic translates as the intervals 1, b3, 4, b6 and b7 while E Minor Pentatonic provides a 1, 2, 4, 5 and b7. We can then predict that playing D Minor Pentatonic over Am would give a slightly Aeolian flavour due to the b6, while E Minor Pentatonic would be more of a suspended 7th sound because of the 2, 4 and b7.

Thankfully this kind of thinking is not needed in reality, we simply need to remember the distance from the root note the scale needed to be transposed and what sound that will give us. The following table lists popular diatonic Pentatonic substitutions.

Table of Pentatonic Substitutions

Tonic chord	Substitute Minor Pentatonic	Resultant tonality
Major / major 7	1 tone up	Ionian
	Major 3rd up	Major 7 arpeggio
	1/2 tone down	Lydian
Minor / minor 7	1 tone down	Phrygian
	1 tone up	Dorian
	Perfect 4th up	Aeolian
	Perfect 5th up	7sus2/4 arpeggio
Dominant 7	Tone up	Mixolydian
	Perfect 4th up	Dom9sus4 arpeggio
	Perfect 5th up	Mixolydian b6 (Melodic minor mode)

Experiment with each Pentatonic substitution, decide which ones you like the sound of and make a note of them.

Recording a static chord vamp and playing all twelve Minor Pentatonic scales over it with help you decide which substitutions appeal to your taste. Some will sound awful, but others may give you something satisfying that you wouldn't otherwise have thought of playing. After all, the only important judge is the ear.

In the first example, the melody is based around a C major arpeggio, but we hear the combined sound as a richer minor 7 tonality when it's played over Am minor chord,. The C Major arpeggio (C, G and G) becomes the b3, 5 and b7 of the Am chord. The second phrase develops this idea further by using an E minor triad (E, G and B), to target the 5, b7 and 9 of the underlying Am chord.

Example 7a

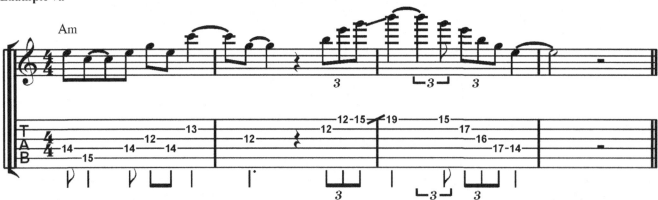

Listen to the audio for example 7a to hear how I vary the articulation to make this simple melodic phrase more expressive. There are some extra slides into notes, and also a pickup change at the end of bar two.

Superimposing arpeggios in ascending 3rds above the root results in extended tonic chords (7th, 9th, 11th, 13th) but moving up or down in 2nds or 4ths result in a more complex sound. In this next phrase we superimpose a minor arpeggio one tone below the tonic minor chord. This creates a Phrygian sound by highlighting the b2.

This kind of restless tension eventually requires resolution, so notice after the C minor arpeggio how we step back 'inside' to the tonic Dm arpeggio.

Example 7b

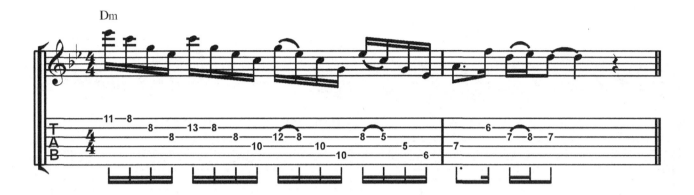

The Minor Pentatonic scale phrasing's inherent bluesiness is paired with the enchanting sound of the Lydian mode thanks to its being superimposed over a maj7 chord. Playing the Minor Pentatonic a half step below the chord provides us with the #4th and major7th steps, the two notes needed to evoke Lydian. Steve Vai is a big fan of the Lydian mode and the slides within the Pentatonic scale here is characteristic of his style.

Example 7c

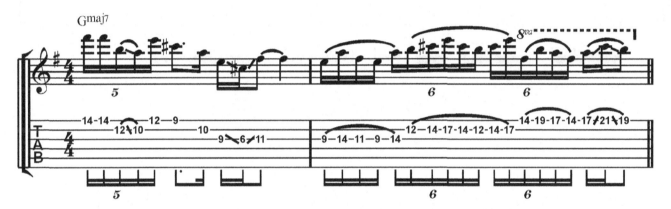

To clearly show the effect of superimposition, a short motif is transposed between the three Pentatonic scales within the Aeolian mode, those formed from the i, iv and v (Am, Dm and Em). Notice how the 'flavour' of the lick changes with each version. In the second phrase I've stayed in the same range but adjusting the notes to fit each scale rather than transposing. This has the effect of morphing between Pentatonics in a smoother manner.

Example 7d

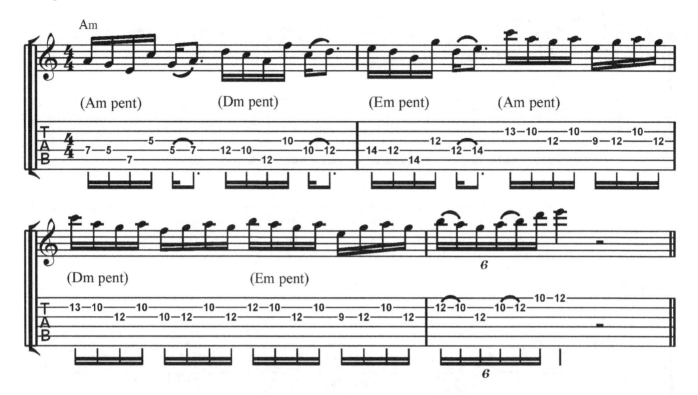

Exotic Scales

Although we tend to think of the Pentatonic scale as the 1 b3 4 5 b7 of The Blues, any group of five notes is a Pentatonic scale. Studies of Indian and Far-Eastern musical traditions reveal that just about any combination of pitches has already been explored by one musical culture or another. Several of these scales are used in the guitar styles of Marty Friedman, Jason Becker and Steve Vai.

We will look at a few named scales in the musical examples, but just as with everything else we've covered, I encourage you to perform your own musical experiments to discover more for yourself. Try taking a seven note scale and remove any two notes to create many different groups of five notes to explore

'Kumoi' Pentatonic scale

The collection of notes in example 7e is known in Japanese music as the Kumoi or Hirajoshi scale. The formula is 1 2 b3 5 b6. It can be more user-friendly to see it as a truncated version of the familiar D Natural Minor scale. Whatever way you choose to look at it, the wider intervals combined with the semitones brings out a distinctly oriental sound not present in the western Pentatonic scale.

Example 7e

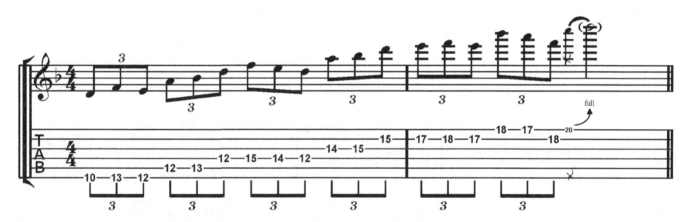

The semitones make fingering the D Kumoi scale with alternating groups of two and three notes per string the easiest option. However, as an interesting blend of the exotic with the familiar it's arranged into two-note-per-string groups below which allows you to apply your favourite Pentatonic patterns easily to the new scale. As a result, some of the shapes can, at first, be a little awkward to get your fingers around. Here we have a typical Zakk Wylde ascending Pentatonic run, albeit with the exotic flavour of the Kumoi scale.

Example 7f

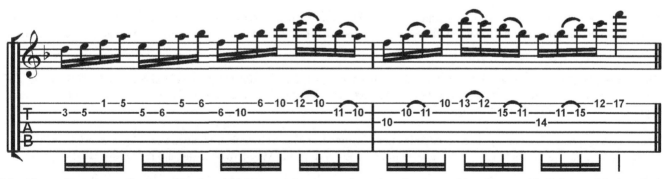

Next is another take on the same idea but this time moving across the strings in one position. You could alternate pick the whole lick for an abrasive sound, but the hammer-on between the first of each group of six notes varies the texture, as well as simplifying the picking.

Example 7g

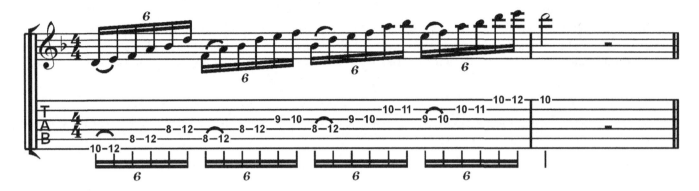

'Indian' Pentatonic scale

The formula of 1 3 4 5 b7 is a more interesting alternative to the Major Pentatonic scale for dominant 7th and major chords where a sense of tension is not required. Known as the 'Indian' Pentatonic, this is not commonly found in rock and pop playing, but provides an interesting alternative to the Major Pentatonic for those rare major chords in metal.

In this lick we start with a hooky melodic fragment then descend through a slippery legato and slide phrase based on an F#7 arpeggio with the addition of the 4th to complete the Pentatonic scale. The bends in bar one should just be a flick of the wrist to give the note a little bounce. These 'curl' bends can be heard in Marty Friedman's playing and are inspired by Japanese Koto music.

Example 7h

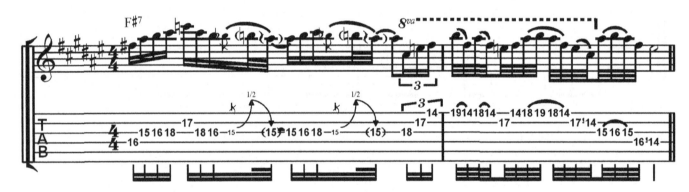

Symmetrical Scales

Finally, some scales are composed of repeating intervals. These are known as symmetrical scales because they contain the same intervals wherever you start in the pattern (unlike the Major scale for example which forms a different mode from each of its notes).

These scales have less "gravitational pull" towards a tonal centre, since in the scale any note could be considered the tonic. This gives them a 'floating' and unsettled quality. For this reason, you will often hear their distinctive tonalities used in film scores to represent unearthly or mysterious themes.

The French composer Olivier Messiaen catalogued many symmetrical scales which are known as his 'modes of limited transposition', but we will only feature the most common ones in rock, the **Wholetone scale**, and the **Diminished** scale.

As the name suggests, the Wholetone scale is a sequence of six whole tones, and as such, can be seen as two Augmented triads a tone apart. This means that there are only two possible scales to learn (A B C# Eb F G, and Bb C D E F# G#), hence 'limited transposition'.

Before we look at some licks, here's the Wholetone scale laid out on the fretboard. This fingering tries to remain at the fifth position across all the strings, but you can also arrange it with three notes per string.

A Wholetone Scale

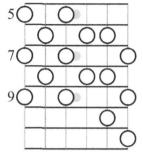

To show how less-conventional scales can easily be integrated into your existing musical vocabulary, the following Wholetone lick derives from a commonly-used metal lick with the fingering adapting to accommodate the appropriate scale tones. If you weren't already acquainted with this scale, you will recognise the sound immediately from dramatic film and video game music, as well as from the work of the more progressive modern metal players.

Example 7i

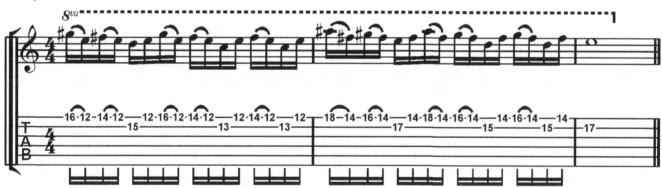

To remain within the Wholetone scale when using a three-note-per-string pattern, we have to keep moving up the fretboard. This continual position shifting adds a challenge to what would otherwise be a straight forward legato exercise.

Example 7j

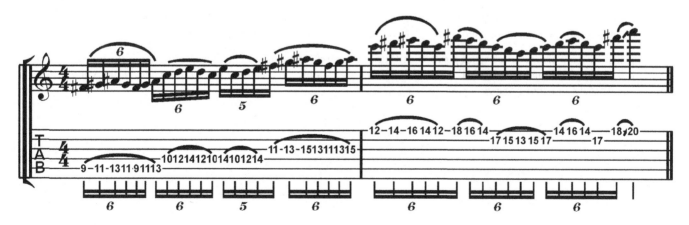

As I said in the introduction to this chapter, the Wholetone scale can be broken down into two Augmented triads (triads composed of stacked major 3rd intervals). A great way to get the Wholetone tonality while using a more 'open' intervallic sound is to alternate between these two triads. This approach offers unlimited variation, so you can adapt any arpeggio approach we've discussed to the Augmented triad, and get creative!

The diagram below shows the Wholetone scale shape with the two triads coloured in black and white. Play all the black notes followed by all the white notes to hear the way the two triads slot together.

Wholetone Triads

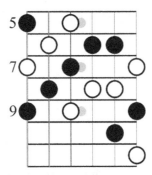

The next phrase moves the same triad shape along the middle strings before developing onto the top strings on beat 2 of bar 2. Analyse the triads used here to help you see how the phrase is constructed.

Example 7k

It's worth noting that due to their strongly recognisable flavour, the Wholetone and Diminished scales can be used over harmony where they may not be 'theoretically' correct. As long as the resolution to a more conventional scale is convincing, the audience can accept almost any temporary departure. This is especially true for metal, where the backing is often power chords or single note riffs.

The Diminished scale is a repeating pattern of semitones and tones. (It's sometimes called 'the Half-Whole scale'). It is symmetrical in minor 3rds, so there are only two different starting notes before the pattern repeats itself.

The Diminished scale also requires some position shifting for the fretting hand, and there are a number of different ways to finger it. I've suggested one option here that remains as static as possible you can assimilate it more easily into your existing knowledge of scale and chord shapes.

A Diminished Scale

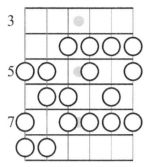

In the following idea, we ascend using a repeating two-string shape before finishing with a string skipping phrase between the G and E strings.

Example 7l

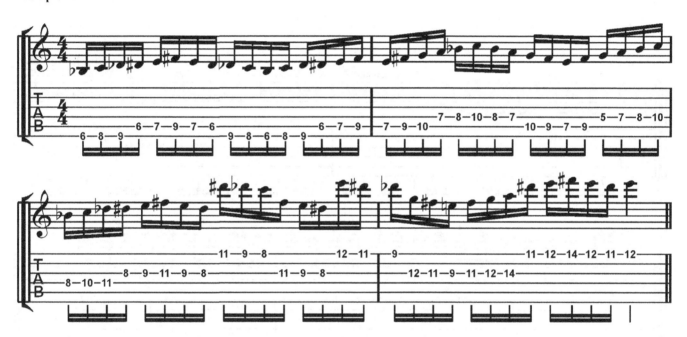

Next, we exploit the repeating semitones found throughout the Diminished scale. In the previous example we started with a tone/semitone, which suggested a Diminished triad, but here we start semitone/tone.

Example 7m

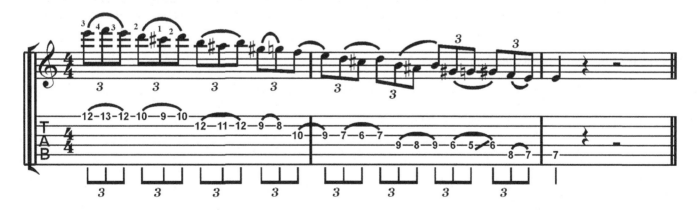

The eight notes of the Diminished scale can be broken down into two Diminished 7th arpeggios a semitone apart. Just as with our Wholetone diagrams, I've illustrated these arpeggios within the scale shape.

Diminished Scale
Triads

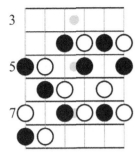

Any phrases that you may use with a single Diminished arpeggio can be shifted up or down by a scale step inside the Diminished scale. In the following example, I move away from predictable patterns by varying the length of time on each arpeggio.

Example 7n

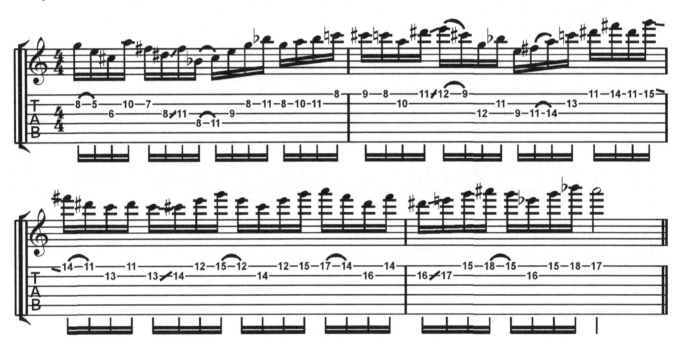

Once again, we use our trend of recycling familiar licks with unfamiliar note choices by incorporating bends and slides from a more traditional blues lick. This time creating the unsettled feeling with first the Harmonic Minor and then the Diminished Scale.

The more bluesy you can make the timing here the better.

Example 7o

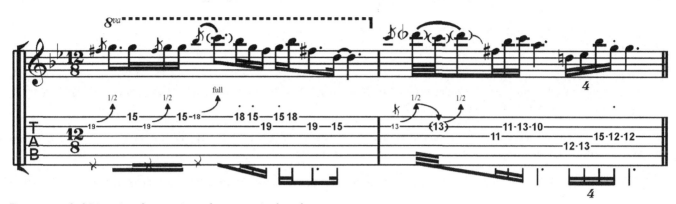

Recommended Listening for exotic and symmetrical scales:

Megadeth - *Tornado of Souls*
Dream Theater – *Octavarium*
Trivium – *Gunshot to the Head of Trepidation*
Opeth – *Eternal Rains Will Come*
Bumblefoot – *Mafalda*

Chapter Eight: Harmony Guitar

After all that soloing, we'll now devote a few chapters to topics that will benefit your writing, arranging and overall musicianship.

We will begin by looking at how to write guitar harmonies. Starting with classic rock bands like Thin Lizzy and Wishbone Ash sharing lead guitar spots, and later with Judas Priest, Iron Maiden and Metallica, there are lots of colourful textures that have been applied in metal song arrangements.

Progressive rock bands that incorporate keyboards have been able to enhance their musical palette even further, often drawing on classical influence too.

We'll move chronologically through a range of musical examples to show different ways that multiple guitar parts can complement each other.

To help us understand what's going on, let's blow the cobwebs off some chord theory. Building common chords always involves stacking notes a 3rd apart from within a scale.

The figure below shows the C Major scale harmonised in triads. C is harmonised by the 3rd (E) and 5th (G) to create a major triad. The note D is harmonised with notes a 3rd and 5th above it (F and A), but the pattern of tones and semitones that make up the Major scale causes this to a minor triad.

The triad harmonisations of the C Major scale are shown below.

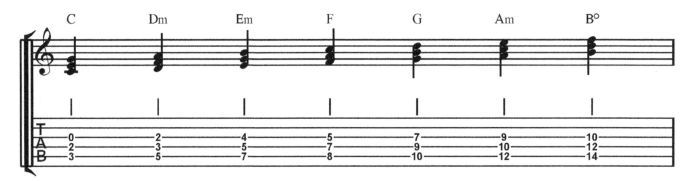

For our first example we're examining the sweet-sounding harmonised melodies of Iron Maiden. In the top line of tablature there is a simple melody in E minor, and in the bottom line we have the harmony part.

To create the harmony part, I moved each note from Gtr A up by two notes in the E Natural Minor (E Aeolian) scale. The top line of the notation contains both parts and you can see that they remain separated by a 3rd throughout.

Each harmony note is either a minor 3rd (three frets) or a major 3rd (four frets) higher than Part A. Your ear will quickly tell you whether you've selected the right note or not when writing parts like this.

To practice the ideas in this chapter, I suggest recording the melody part to a click track and then playing the harmony parts in time with the recording.

Example 8a

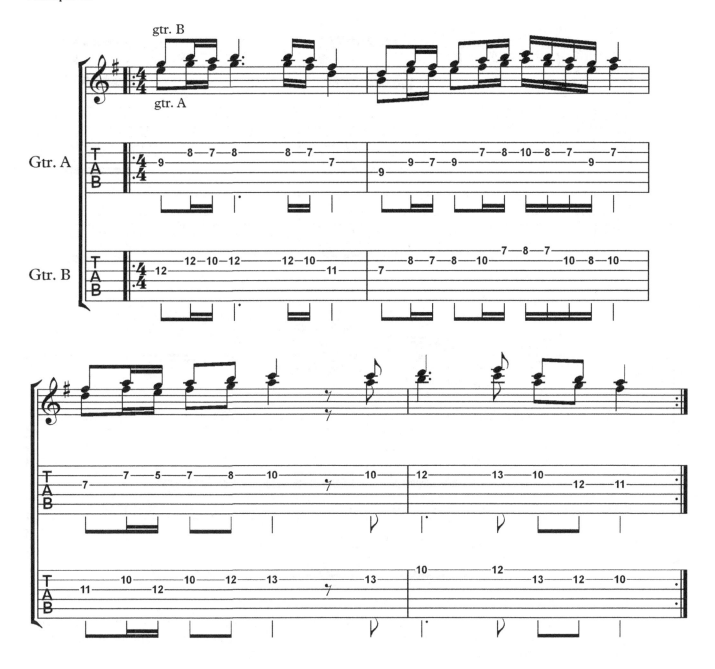

If you are familiar with the different positions of the Major scale and its modes, there's an easy way to work out harmony in 3rds (as well as using your ears!). Start by playing Part A in a three-note-per-string scale shape, and then play the same fingering using the shape two positions higher of the same scale to create the harmony part.

The next example contains more scalic playing.

If you and a fellow guitarist are planning on performing twin harmonies, it's worth setting aside special practice time away from the band to make sure you gel together. Paying attention to the speed of vibrato and string bends will make you sound slick and professional.

Example 8b

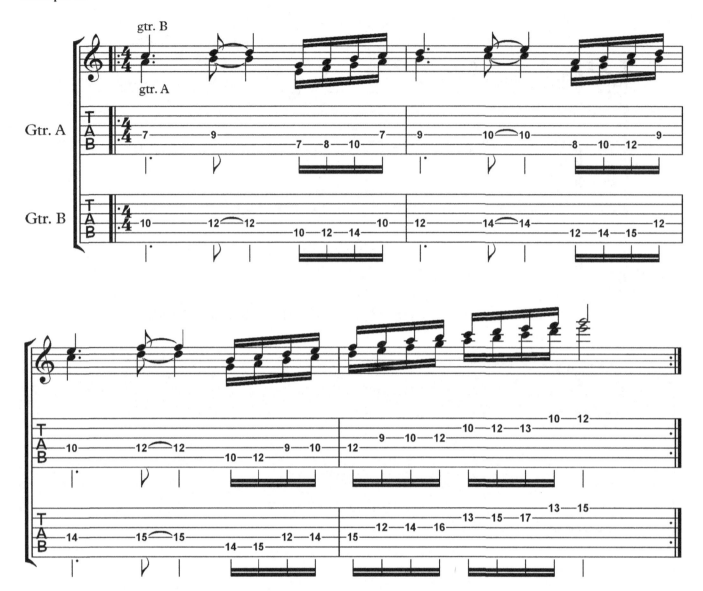

The next passage develops the 3rds harmony by adding a degree of sophistication. Instead of sticking doggedly to diatonic 3rds, we're going to adjust the harmony to better fit the accompanying. Most of the harmony part remains as 3rds but occasionally a 4th or a 2nd is a more appropriate note choice.

For example, in bar two when Part A plays the 5th of the chord, it would be better to have Part B add a 4th above to hit the root, rather than a 3rd which would have given us the less consonant 7th. In bar three we pass over the b7 of the chord, and the harmony is the root rather than the 9th which would be slightly dissonant in this context.

Example 8c

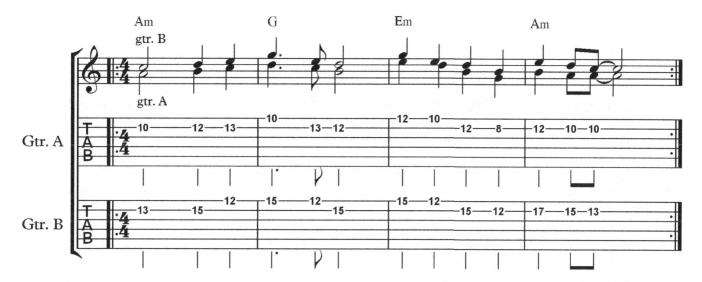

The third example demonstrates how we can invert intervals.

Every interval can be inverted, for example, moving from C to A is a major 6th, but moving from A to C is a minor 3rd. (Top tip: inverted intervals always add up to 9: 3rds become 6ths, 4ths become 5ths and 7ths become 2nds). The inversion of a 3rd is a 6th, therefore playing Part B a 6th below Part A will give us the same notes as playing them a 3rd above Part A.

One advantage of playing your harmony a 6th below is that the original A part will remain the top melody (and therefore more clearly audible), while at the same time being thickened and supported by a harmony underneath.

Feel free to experiment with 3rds below your A part, although this is less commonly done as the harmony part is less likely to compliment the overall harmony. 6ths below does a better job of automatically matching the chords.

Example 8c

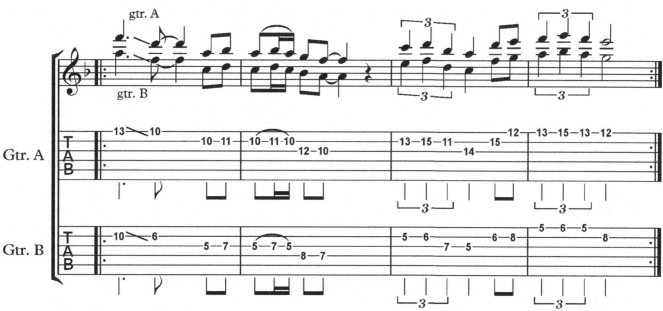

The next passage develops the 3rds harmony by adding a degree of sophistication. Instead of sticking doggedly to diatonic 3rds, we're going to adjust the harmony to better fit the accompanying. Most of the harmony part remains as 3rds but occasionally a 4th or a 2nd is a more appropriate note choice.

For example, in bar two when Part A plays the 5th of the chord, it would be better to have Part B add a 4th above to hit the root, rather than a 3rd which would have given us the less consonant 7th. In bar three we pass over the b7 of the chord, and the harmony is the root rather than the 9th which would be slightly dissonant in this context.

Example 8d

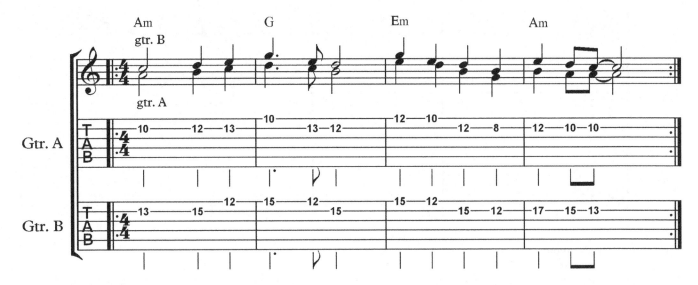

Now for some more technical shred ideas inspired by bands like Racer X, Cacophony and more recently, Trivium.

First we have some fast arpeggios to be harmonised. Trying to synchronise this with another player will really test your rhythmic accuracy. Recording both parts together can be revealing of any sloppy time keeping, but it is a great way to monitor your progress.

We could have harmonised each melody note a 3rd above, however this time I repeated each arpeggio shape in the next inversion up. This way, each one is still limited to the notes of that chord and thus maintains the clarity of harmonic progression initially provided by the use of arpeggios.

Learn each shape slowly to start with, preferably using a metronome that can count individual subdivisions, to help you lock in with the time. Try playing with a friend, or recording yourself when you practice. Record the melody part and then play the harmony part in time.

Example 8e

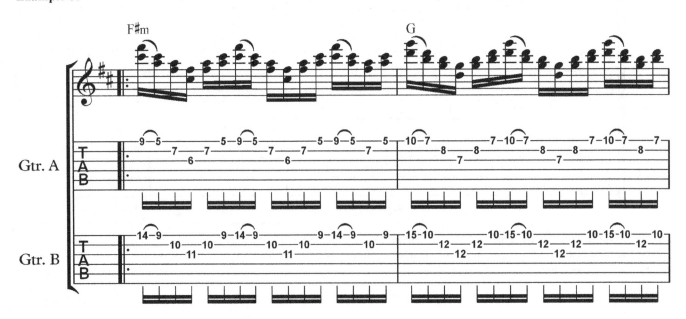

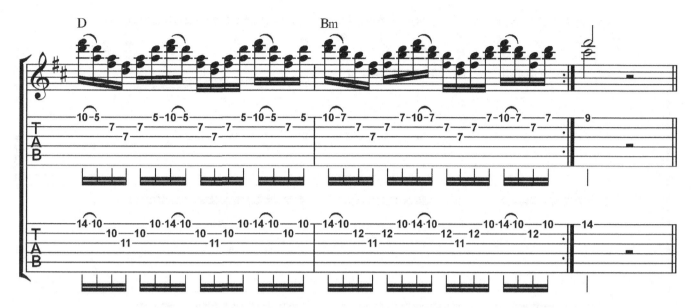

In the next example we combine arpeggios and a scale run to create a more exciting and varied contour. It's impossible to overstate the need for accuracy when playing such material. Practicing with the other player at slow tempos is the only way to really get it properly synchronised. Remaining in time when moving between different picking techniques takes a lot of coordination.

The first bar uses B major and C major arpeggios, but unlike example 8e, the two parts are *contrapuntal* (each line moving in an independent direction) to avoid being too predictable. When coming up with your own arpeggio ideas you can confidently explore different shapes knowing that, with there only being three notes to choose from, it will always be consonant.

The scale run in the second bar begins in diatonic 3rds (just as in example 8b), but then splits into 6ths and ends up a 10th (Major 3rd) apart. Look at the notation to clearly see how the directions of the two lines split.

Example 8f

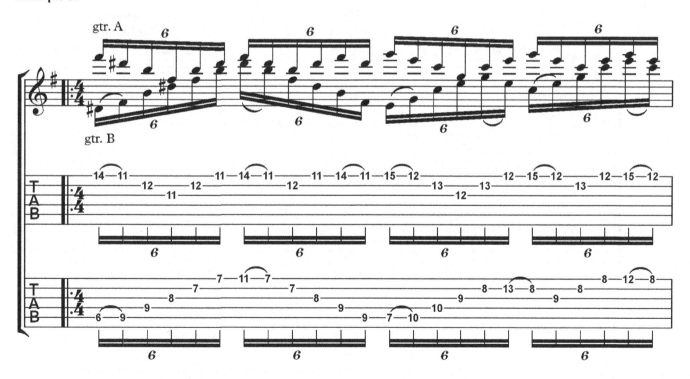

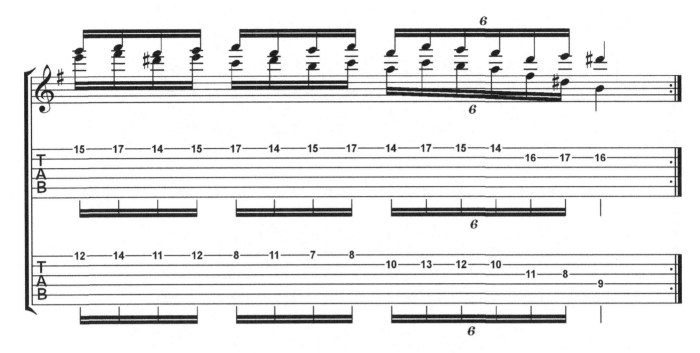

Now we'll move away from the pleasing but rather 'saccharine' sound of 3rds and chord-based harmonies, and look at quartal (4th-based) and parallel harmonies. As I mentioned before, inverting a 4th will give you a 5th which creates a similar sound to harmonising the melody with power chords.

The following example harmonises a melody entirely in 4ths. Listen and compare it with the sound that we achieved when using 3rds. I've kept a perfect 4th between parts A and B, even though the diatonic scale has one Augmented 4th. The Augmented 4th is so dissonant that by comparison the ear accepts the non-scale tone more readily than it does the 'correct' in-key harmony.

Example 8g

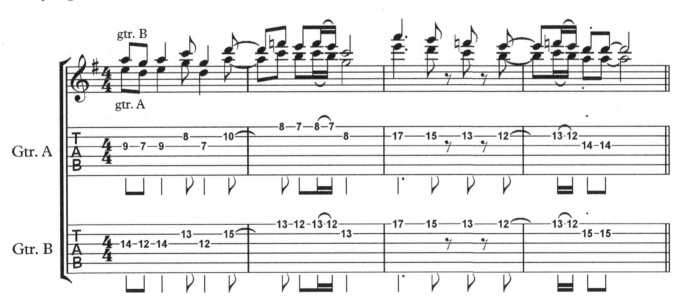

This time we're not going to use the notes of a specific scale to form the harmony part. Instead we will select a fixed interval and stick with it. I've written a harmony part that always stays a major 3rd up from Part A at all times.

The listener is happily lead by the consistency of the pattern whilst the use of non-diatonic notes provides a type of dissonance known as *bitonality*. Bitonality refers to playing in two keys simultaneously. While our Part A lick is in E Phrygian, the harmony, if heard in isolation, would be G# Phrygian. (The same scale a major 3rd above)

Example 8h

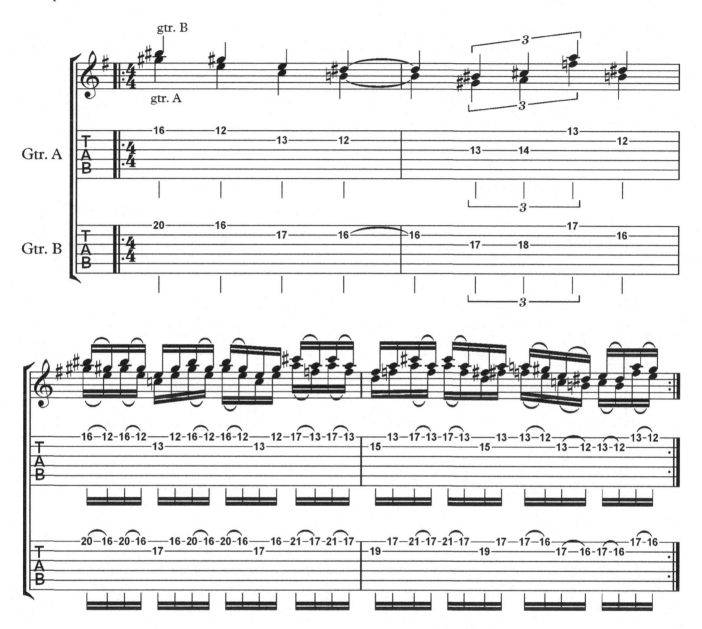

Compared to other styles of music, modern metal's lack of harmonic richness allows us to layer more dissonant note combinations that wouldn't work over conventional pop harmony.

Parallel harmonies can add a quite jarring effect to any passage.

Rhythm Guitar Harmony Riffs

We can take the same techniques and also apply them to rhythm guitar parts.

Drop D tuning is used in the first example to add some extra meat to the low notes. The energy and movement comes from the contrasting bursts of high harmonised notes between the chugging D's and power chords. Listen carefully to the audio to hear how some are palm-muted while others ring out.

This modern-sounding riff is inspired by metalcore bands like Killswitch Engage and The Ocean. This style is characterised by the chunky riffs and huge production. Bolstering the melodic fragments with octaves and then harmonising them guarantees a fatter sound, as does the big open-string power chord made possible by the drop D tuning.

Example 8i

The second harmonised riff is quite intricate, so you may have to slow it right down in order to get the constant 1/16th notes even while balancing the picking and legato. We harmonise within the E Harmonic Minor scale, to give a definite neoclassical slant. The driving rhythmic feel draws on bands as diverse as Megadeth, Yngwie Malmsteen, and Symphony X.

The second bar ends with a Diminished arpeggio that is harmonised by simply moving the same pattern up by three frets. (See Chapter Seven for more detail on symmetrical scales.)

Example 8j

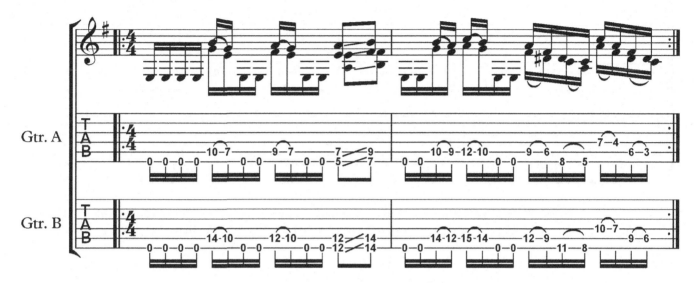

Our third riff uses a much more dissonant harmony. Both guitars bounce off the low E string, but the accented notes are a tritone (b5) apart. The result an alarm bell-like percussive sound effect.

One guitar could play both high notes as a chord, but using two guitars delivers a more focussed result, avoiding the mushiness of playing a chord through a distorted amp.

Example 8k

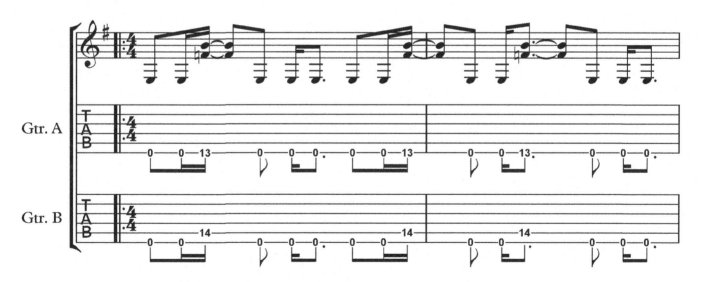

So far, all of the harmony licks have been in rhythmic unison, but the final two riffs give each guitar a contrasting rhythm. The first of which uses a panning trick to make the same phrase bounce back and forth across the stereo field. When playing stop-start rhythmic fragments it is easy rush or delay on the subdivisions, even more so than when playing a constant stream of notes.

The technical music theory term for this shifting back and forth between two musical voices is *hocketing*.

Example 81

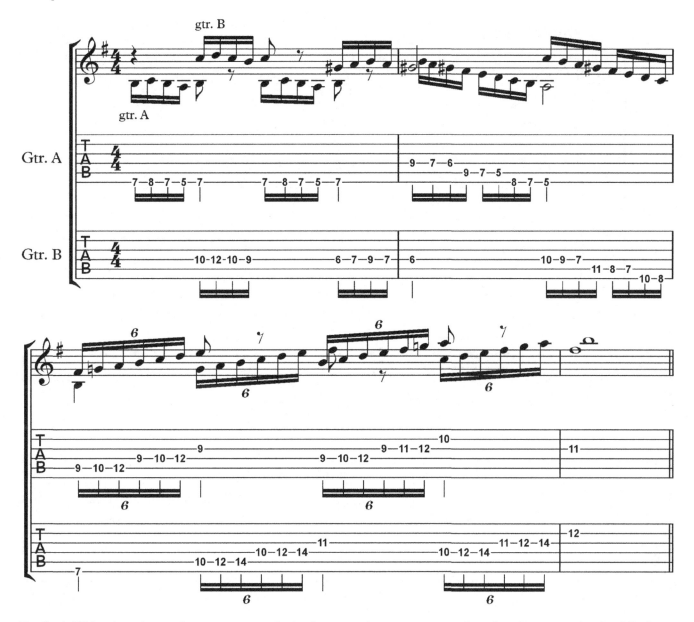

The final riff develops the previous two concepts by having one guitar concentrate on low chugging power chords while the other guitar intersperses with a clashing semitone in between. Break down the syncopated rhythm carefully and listen to the audio.

We're back in Drop-D tuning for a heavier sound and to also make the moving power chords in Gtr. B easier to finger.

In theory, one guitar could once again play both parts, but the sound is much cleaner and relaxed when split between two players: both can focus on making their phrases as clean and detached as possible. To help you both lock in with the rhythm, Part A should listen to the snare drum accents and Part B should focus on the kick drums. The cymbals outline the overall 4/4 pulse.

Listen to Sikth's *Skies of Millennium Night* for a fantastic example of this idea, with each guitar panned hard left and right – the song also ends with a great harmonised tapping riff.

Example 8m

We've barely scratched the surface of how we can orchestrate and arrange rhythm and lead guitar parts. To develop your awareness and creativity in this area, I suggest you experiment writing harmonies using different intervals, both diatonic and parallel. Furthermore, listening to other musicians, starting with the bands I've suggested below, will give you plenty of inspiration.

Recommended listening for creative twin guitar playing:

Iron Maiden – *Revelations*
Judas Priest - Exciter
Metallica – *And Justice for All...*
Racer X – *Technical Difficulties*
Cacophony – *Speed Metal Symphony*
Trivium – *Ascendancy*
Dream Theater – *Never Enough*
Arch Enemy – *Nemesis*

Chapter Nine: Meter and Cross-Rhythm

This chapter introduces some rhythmic concepts found in modern metal that build upon on those discussed in my first book, Heavy Metal Rhythm Guitar. We'll examine more uses of odd time signatures and then we'll look at cross-rhythmic effects that can be achieved by overlaying different meters.

The first group of riffs feature combinations of different time signatures one after another. The way to approach them is to feel the whole phrase as a repeating block. You'll probably need to begin by counting carefully to get your head around their feel, but once you're confident with each meter in the progression, sequencing them shouldn't prove too challenging.

Since the '90s, metal has developed a high degree of rhythmic complexity. Following thrash metal, the Death Metal genre exemplified by Death and Cannibal Corpse often featured dramatic changes of tempo during the course of a song, as well as switching between triplet and straight pulses. A little later Fear Factory and Meshuggah introduced very precise syncopated rhythms, almost always played in unison with the kick drum.

The legacy of these bands, particularly Meshuggah, is clear in many current bands of the so-called 'djent' sub-genre. It's become the norm in this style to use extended range 7 and 8 string guitars, but in the interest of accessibility I've written all the examples for 6 strings, however, these concepts are transferable to any tuning.

I often hear it said that modern metal employs *polyrhythms.* This is slightly incorrect, so before we dive-in I'd like quickly to clarify some terminology. *Polyrhythms* and *crossrhythms* are subtly different methods of combining two or more layers of rhythm, and it is crossrhythm that is commonly found in metal. With the exception of Frank Zappa's compositions, polyrhythmic ideas are rarely used in rock music.

A polyrhythm divides a single length of time in two different ways. If you look at the following figure you'll see we have one bar of 4/4 divided into eight 1/8ths in voice 1. In voice 2 the bar has been divided into six equal notes using 1/4 note triplets which cannot be subdivided to fit into the 1/8th note grid. The audible effect of this is that two tempi appear to be occurring simultaneously, providing a disorientating, ambiguous pulse.

By comparison, the second figure illustrates a crossrhythm, which is easier to play and understand. Here, both voices fit into the same structure of subdivisions, but while the top voice is playing on every second 1/8th note, the lower voice is playing on every third 1/8th note. This means that the pattern does not repeat within one bar. In fact, it takes three bars before the two voices sync up again on the first beat of a bar.

In the second half of this chapter we'll be taking the concept of crossrhythm to more advanced levels. If you're interested in hearing examples of polyrhythm in use, listen to the classical music of Frank Zappa, Charles Ives, or Elliot Carter, as well as traditional African drumming. Charles Ives' polyrhythms are so conflicting that his fourth symphony requires two conductors!

Combining Odd Time Signatures

The first riff links together three bars of 3/4 and one bar of 2/4. Although neither are considered 'odd' on their own, the combined effect may need to be heard several times before you get a feel for what's going on.

Reduce the gain slightly to give clarity to the sustained chords in the first half of the example. The notes should be breaking up without becoming muddy and indistinct.

Example 9a

w/dist

The second riff is built from a fairly straight-ahead 4/4 one-bar riff, interspersed with odd fills that disrupt the groove. The fills are short and constructed from a constant stream of notes, so once the fingerings are memorised they should take care of themselves.

To help to you feel the length of different note groupings, try improvising new fills in the odd-time bars. Either follow the meters I've written here, or just pick one grouping and alternate it with the 4/4 riff.

Example 9b

Next we have an example of *metric modulation*. Metric modulation is when we change between tempi or feels in a controlled way instead of just jumping from one to the other. If the two tempi have something in common then there will be a better sense of flow and continuity to the transition.

In this example we're moving from 140bpm to 105bpm, but the triplets in the first riff are actually the same speed as the semiquavers in the second riff. So in reality we're just changing from accenting every third note, to accenting every fourth note.

Death used this idea a lot to link between contrasting sections of a song, but if you listen to contemporary bands like Tesseract, the music will often shift back and forth between the two feels rapidly, spending only a couple of beats on each.

Example 9c

In the following example, the tempo is constant but the beat is subdivided differently. The main division is straight 1/16th notes but is interspersed with bursts of 1/16th triplets. It can be a challenge to gauge how much to speed up by, in order to get the triplets accurately in time.

It's worth practicing this quite slowly as it'll really help your overall timekeeping and awareness of subdividing the beat. You will probably find it hardest at slow tempos because the longer spaces between notes allow for a wider margin of error.

Example 9d

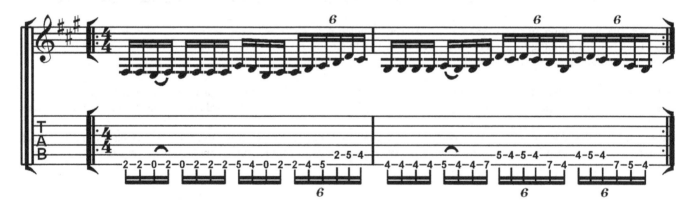

We dipped a toe into 1/16th-based time signatures in Heavy Metal Rhythm Guitar, but next up we have a more daunting example. Although the long notes make the phrase look easier to play, it actually requires much more awareness of the rhythm, this is because we can't simply play a stream of notes and 'meet up' at the finish line as before.

A good way to approach this riff is to count how many 1/16th notes each note is sustained for, and then count in those groupings. Rather than furiously counting numbers, it's easier to have words for different groups. For instance: monkey = 2, elephant =3, alligator = 4 and hippopotamus = 5. You might feel a bit daft, but try them and see if it helps. For colossal sounding riffs in such meters, check out doomy French Prog-metallers, Gojira.

Example 9e

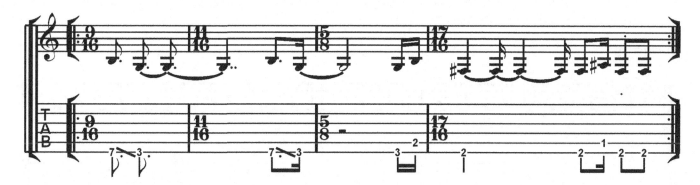

To end the first half of this chapter, here's something a little different.

In this common rhythm, the guitar and bass drums keep a constant tremolo note against a rock beat. The difference is that we cram in five notes per beat (quintuplets) rather than four 1/16ths. Listen carefully to the audio at both speeds to get the sound of fives into your head. This idea will only feel secure once five-note groups feel as comfortable as playing 1/16th notes and triplets

Example 9f

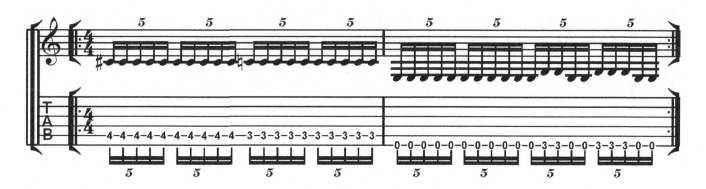

Cross Rhythmic Riffs

By superimposing odd meters over a familiar 4/4 rock feel we can combine interesting, intricate syncopation with a solid sense of groove. Although uneven rhythms can be very effective at the right moment, they can disengage the listener if they're too difficult to follow. The cross rhythmic style that has developed in recent years allows for both cerebral interest *and* the almost-danceable groove that is familiar to most people.

To develop the split sense of time that allows you to be expressive with this technique try clapping the cross rhythm while tapping your foot to the 1/4 note pulse. Tapping your foot is very important because it lets you test whether you are actually balancing both parts.

With practice, you'll start to let the 4/4 pulse carry on subconsciously while you really feel the odd phrase lengths. Once this has clicked, test your skill by moving your foot to half time by only tapping your foot on beasts one and three.

I've used a dotted line to 'box off' each cell in the displaced layer across the main pulse so you can easily observe how the rhythms interact

The first riff uses a feel that you've probably come across before - a three-notes pattern played as straight 1/8th notes. After listening to the audio it should be quite easy to play, but the challenge comes in being able to keep track of the 4/4 pattern and not to get lost in endless repetitions of the 3/8 phrase.

As the displaced part is easy to memorise, you can focus your attention on the drum part when playing along with the track. The cymbals and snare drum remain in 4/4 to help you keep track of where you are. Three bars of 4/4 pass before the crossrhythm returns to start on beat one of the bar again.

Example 9g

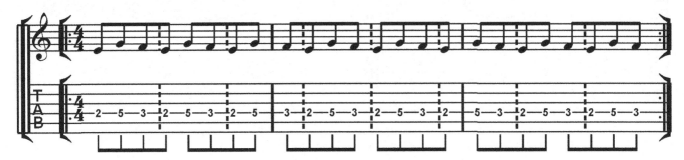

It isn't complicated to explore the possibility of these cross rhythms. If you have a sequencer, program a basic rock beat and try play different odd-note phrases against it. Start by playing every notes, until you can hear the phrase repeating, and then start to include held notes or rests within the phrase.

Example 9h repeats a phrase that lasts eleven 1/8th notes and also includes a more diverse rhythm within the superimposed part. **Example 9h**

Next we up the pace to 1/16th-note-based phrases by essentially halving the phrase-length of example 9g.

To start with you'll find it helpful to keep the picking hand moving in constant 1/16ths, although we're only hitting the first beat of each three semiquaver group. Any repetition of an odd-metered phrase will start on alternate down and up strokes. This can also give you a helpful physical point of reference to keep in time.

Example 9i

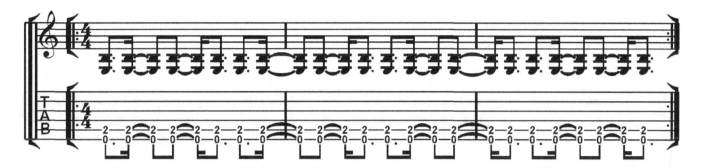

The same advice stands for 7/16, if you keep the picking hand moving consistently throughout. The first cell will be four downstrokes, the second will be four upstrokes and so on.

The first couple of cross rhythms have included enough bars of 4/4 for the downbeats to sync up again, but in reality it's much more common to maintain the familiar structure of four bar phrases, and the melodic and harmonic structure will often remain in 4/4 too. The cross rhythmic texture really provides a way of generating interesting and logical syncopation within a conventional framework. To show this in the next example we allow the 7/16 cell to repeat until four bars are nearly complete, then just add an extra 1/16th note to complete the bar.

Example 9j

Time to stretch ourselves: This next example is inspired by Meshuggah, the kings of this sub-genre. Our overlaid cell is in 25/16. Though this sounds intimidating there are a couple of ways that you can to tackle it. Firstly, try playing the 25/16 cell in isolation, without worrying about the 4/4 element. It is best felt as five straight beats, and then a group of five 1/16ths (i.e. 5/4 + 5/16).

Just as in the previous riff, we use a shorter variation in the final bar to 'close the loop' of the underlying 'standard' eight-bar phrase.

Another approach is to ignore the 25/16, and work through the notated part and memorise each bar of 4/4 in turn, dealing with the syncopated rhythms as they occur. With the riff memorised, try playing along to the audio file. By hacking away at it slowly, the feel of the whole riff will start to make sense.

Using both these approaches together should give you an awareness of how the two parts interact. Perform it accurately and you will be able to step back to observe the repetitions of the cell.

Example 9k

In the following Tool-inspired riff we combine meters with an extra degree of complexity. You can look at this riff as having two parts to it. In the 'bass' part we use a similar 7/16 rhythm to example 9j, while in the top part we play a two-note chord on beat three of each 4/4 bar. This is a real test of how well you're tuned into the underlying 4/4 pulse.

Learn this idea this first as a drumming pattern. Clap out the 7/16 while tapping the 1/4 note pulse with your foot. Next, try counting aloud '1,2,3,4'. When that's okay, catching beat three should be achievable. Otherwise, break it down, bar by bar until you've memorised the whole passage.

Example 9l

All of our riffs so far have been in 4/4, but to inspire you to explore more possibilities, here's a pattern that is overlaid onto 12/8 time. The triple feel gives an added dimension of interest, and helps to keep the imposed 5/8 pattern less predictable than when heard straight.

Finding an appropriate picking pattern can be tricky as down and upstrokes both fall on the beats when playing triplets, so just practice it carefully and be sure to avoid consecutive down strokes without a 1/8th rest between them.

Example 9m

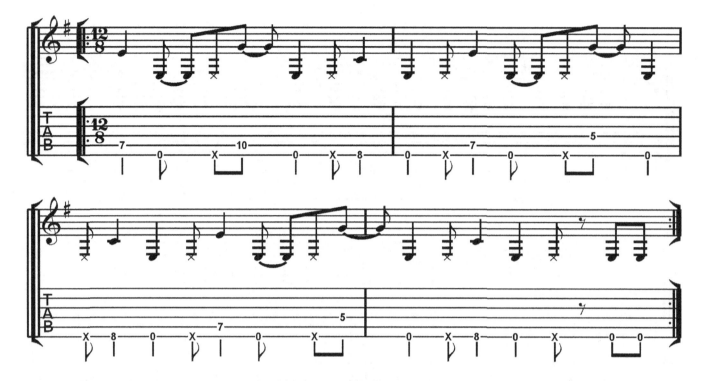

There is boundless scope for experimentation and exploration in this style of music, much of it still untapped. This gives you a good chance of coming up with completely new ideas by combining rhythms and meters in different ways.

The more familiar you are with the sound and 'shape' of each meter, the easier it will be to overlay them. However, there's nothing wrong with programming ideas using a sequencer to 'audition' new ideas quickly. As there is almost infinite scope for experimentation, I advise that you only explore ideas you immediately like the sound of.

Recommended listening for time signatures, groupings and cross rhythm:

Death – *Overactive Imagination*
Cynic – *Textures*
Meshuggah – *Rational Gaze*
Sixth – *Bland Street Bloom*
Tool – *Right in Two*
Panzerballett – *M.w.M.i.O.f.R.*
Animals as Leaders – *Infinite Regression*
Karnivool – *Deadman*
Stimpy Lockjaw – *Shrimpy*

Chapter Ten: Demo Solos

This chapter gives you some longer solo studies to learn, and demonstrates how you can construct solos using some of the ideas we've covered.

I have included four separate solos, each over a different backing track so you can play along as well as writing your own solos.

They cover a range of metal styles from '80s Neoclassical rock to modern Progressive and Death metal.

Example 10a

The first solo study takes its inspiration from the Neoclassical shred movement of the late '70s and '80s by Richie Blackmore, Uli Jon Roth, and of course Yngwie Malmsteen. Many other players explored this style, defined a whole genre of instrumental rock guitar music. Shrapnel Records became the home of many of these artists, and their catalogue of albums shows how populous and diverse the scene became.

The solo is sixteen bars long and follows a common chord progression in the key of A minor. The slow ballad feel is performed using clean picked guitars and synth strings, both of which imply a subtle, classically-influenced feel.

Example 10a – Chord Progression

The solo uses several of the ideas from Chapter One, including pedal point, sequences and arpeggios. I Keep things interesting by varying the tone of the guitar and using a mixture of techniques.

Many of these ideas are technically demanding and combine several different techniques in a single phrase, so be patient and start slowly before building up to performing the entire solo. Alternatively, listen to the audio and cherry pick any licks that you particularly like.

The Neoclassical style creates a strong sense of melody by closely following the harmony. Licks often target chord tones or use arpeggios which help to keep them memorable and musical, even when playing faster licks.

If you listen to different guitarists in this style you'll notice that while they are all very technical, each will favour different techniques and patterns. Becoming a unique, individual musician can be as much about missing things out as including everything. So, while pushing yourself to learn more and more, it's also important to play to your strengths and focus on the ideas with which you really connect. For example, if you favour legato or tapping rather than sweep picking or alternate picking, then go ahead and modify the solo to suit your style. After all, don't waste time learning things you would never want to use!

Bars 1-2: The opening section of the solo features an Am arpeggio, but with each of the notes embellished with a chromatic passing tone. The second phrases begins in the same way an octave higher but is interrupted with a tapped bend before descending to target the D note in the next chord...

Bars 3-6: As expected, we now play a D minor arpeggio. Hybrid picking could help you here if you are struggling to alternate pick all string crossing in the pattern.

After the slippery legato embellishment, slide up to a held string bend. Sliding into a bend gives the impression of a much wider and more dramatic change in pitch. You'll frequently hear this type of articulation at the end of licks in Malmsteen's playing.

One of Yngwie's trademarks is his floating and expressive sense of rhythm when playing fast runs. Rather than sticking to strict 1/16ths, he will float across the beats, before landing in time on the downbeat.

The descending arpeggio over the F major chord will take some time to get clean as it's very fast. The speed will only come when the shape feels completely familiar and effortless at slower tempos. The 11-tuplet rhythm may look daunting on the page, but the important thing is to land on the next beat in time; the notes are just crammed in as needed.

Bars 7-8: As the solo builds to its first climax over the E7 chord, we hit the first of our long scalic runs drawn from E Phrygian Dominant. I've used alternate picking throughout, but you could try economy picking or legato according to your taste and technical strengths. The second bar of the run accelerates from sextuplets to demisemiquavers (1/32nd notes, or 8 notes per beat). However, given that our tempo is a sedate 70bpm, this is not quite as scary as it looks.

Bars 9-12: As we resolve back to A minor, we keep the intensity of the speed picking but apply it to a melodic phrase down through the arpeggio.

The second bar is a pedal point lick and was examined in detail in our Neoclassical chapter. Vinnie Moore in particular is known for pedal point licks, executed with spellbinding speed and accuracy. However, to give the solo a sense of pace and dynamics, this one is much slower, with a bluesy, staccato articulation at the end.

After that short lull, the gas is reapplied with an ascending three-note-per-string legato sequence reminiscent of Randy Rhoads. The nine-tuplets are fast, but again it's a case of cramming in the notes and landing on the beat. The picking hand only plays the first note on every string, so actually picks 1/8th note triplets. With repeated listens trying to hear the underlying triplet, the '3x3'ness of the full nine-note grouping might be easier to play than you think.

Bars 13-14: The next dose of shred calls upon Tony MacAlpine and Greg Howe, both of whom possess a wide range of legato and tapping licks that make use of tapping. Familiarity with fretting-hand tapping enables us to be free from clichés by being able to start on any note.

Muting with both hands wherever possible will help to ensure a clean execution, as unwanted ringing can happen when tapping with both hands. When performing the two fingered tap with the picking hand at the end of the run, I actually flatten my fretting hand across all the strings slightly before it's needed again, to fret the last three notes.

Bars 15-17: Finally, we 'unleash the fury' with a long E major and Diminished sweep arpeggio phrase typical of the mighty Swede! Yngwie has absolute fluency with this vocabulary, and rather than simply ascend and descend through the E arpeggio, we take a more varied and interesting contour that also draws on the occasional scale tone. This lick is fast and technically challenging so be disciplined in ironing out any technical issues to reach the level of control demanded by this style.

To finish, we have a descending A Harmonic Minor run. The timing is free here, so aim for a gradual and expressive slowing down towards the last note.

Example 10a – Lead Guitar

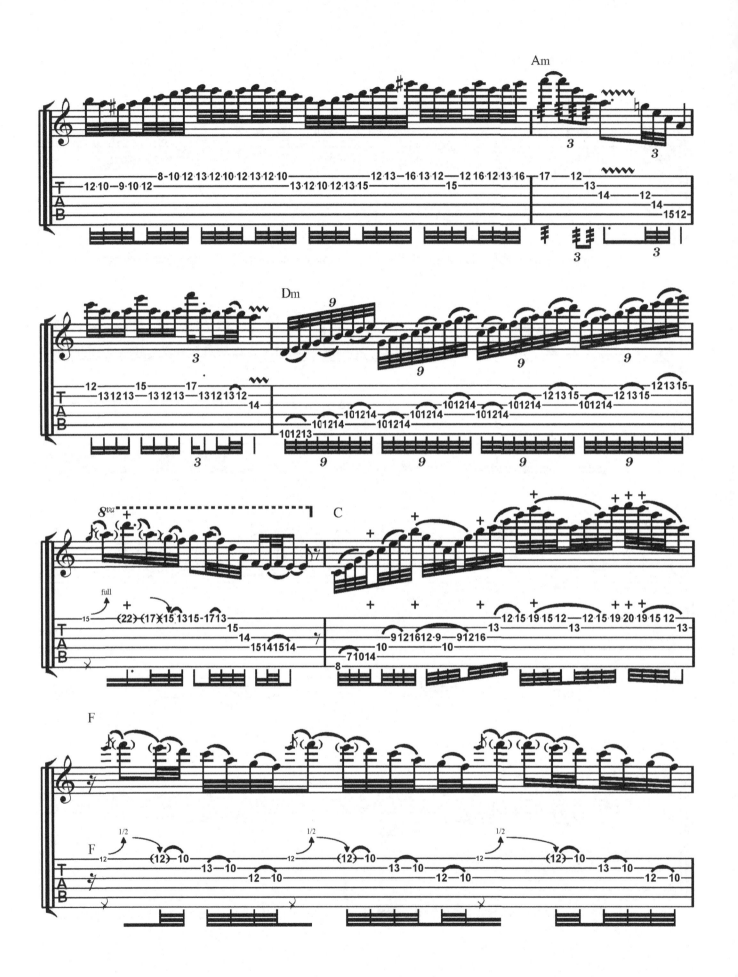

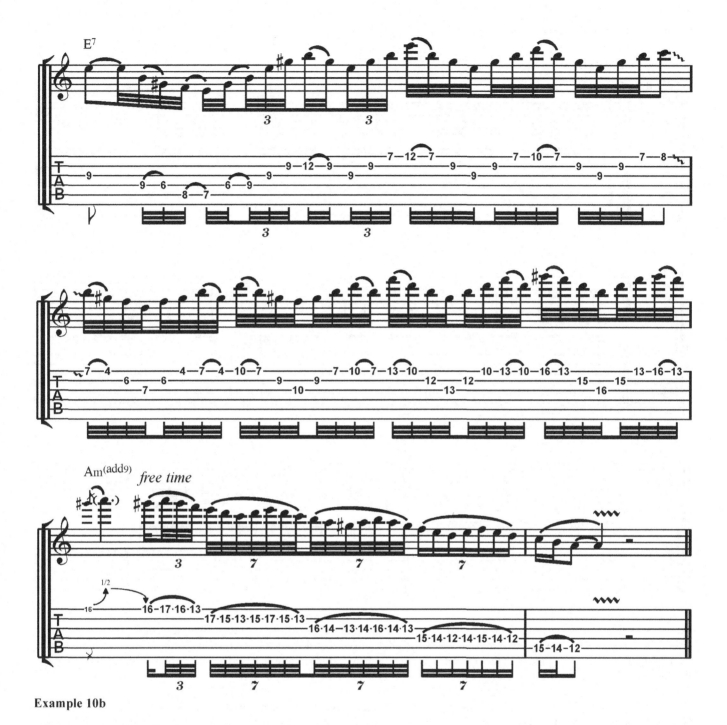

Example 10b

Our second solo features a more contemporary backing part based in F# minor and draws on the F# Phrygian mode to create a dark tonality. This is more reminiscent of the more Progressive Death Metal bands like Cynic or modern acts like Nevermore and Between the Buried and Me.

Although the licks aren't any faster than the first solo, the technical challenges are a little more involved as we're drawing on a combination of advanced techniques, including hybrid picking, wide legato stretches, string skipping, alternate picking and sweep picking. The melodic phrasing is a lot less blues influenced and owes more to angular jazz fusion.

Example 10b - Rhythm Part

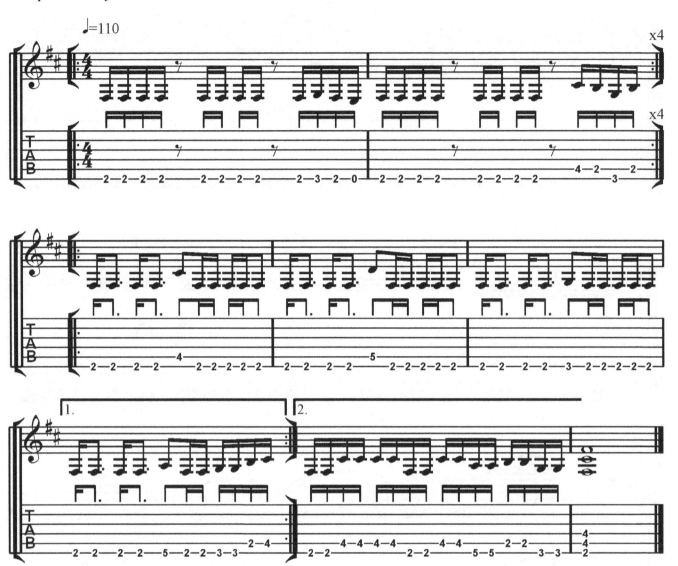

Bars 1-4: Although metal soloing had shaken off much of The Blues and hard rock influence by this period, we start with some unison bends. Listen to the way the first bend is articulated. I purposely released the bend slightly to produce a jarring effect as the bent note moves out of tune with the other. The melody in bars three and four is based around semitone intervals found in F# Phrygian (F#-G, and C#-D) to bring the dark Phrygian tonality to the fore.

Bars 5-8: Use hybrid picking to play the mutated country lick. It begins with a banjo roll pattern applied to a Dsus2 shape. The A# comes from Phrygian Dominant, which can be used interchangeably with the normal Phrygian mode here. The descending lick again picks out diatonic semitone pairs and alternates them with the open strings to get an appealingly dissonant result. Country guitar is usually played with a clean sound so notes can ring together, but with a high gain distortion it's worth applying some palm muting to give the notes more definition and prevent them becoming a sloppy mess. John 5 imports bluegrass ideas seamlessly into his shred metal solo albums.

Bars 9-12: Here the underlying groove changes and the solo uses some longer notes to allow the music to breathe again for a moment. 5ths give an angular modern sound compared to 3rds and 6ths. Here we have two perfect 5ths a tritone apart, resulting in two consonant intervals dissonant with one another. The fast sliding melody in bar ten requires accurate timing in the fretting hand, but makes the solo more expressive and varied. The disjoined phrase in bars eleven to twelve works against the rhythmic flow of the music, but confident execution and a solid sense of time will make it convincing.

Bars 13-16: Here's a long picking run in the style of Chuck Schuldiner or Andy LaRocque. It starts off in straight 1/16ths but then accelerates to 1/16th-note triplets. I've notated the groupings exactly as played, but aim to keep your sense of pulse and simply land in the right place. The final two bars are quite demanding and use some Diminished arpeggios and an F#7 arpeggio (with both the 5 and b5).

The majority of bar fifteen uses legato and picking combined, but the speed and the note choice give it a new flavour. We looked at a longer version final sweep picked Diminished arpeggio lick back in Chapter Six.

Example 10b – Lead Guitar

Example 10c

Our third solo is in the style of progressive metal bands like Dream Theater and Symphony X. There are several technical moments in this solo, but the main feature is the time signature. Even when you've played many riffs in 7/8 or other odd time signatures, phrasing the lead guitar melodically can still pose a challenge.

When creating your own ideas in odd meters the best approach is to set up a loop and improvising simply with only a few notes per bar, then gradually explore different rhythmic permutations. Try off-beat ideas too, to give yourself the most freedom, but remember to focus on the underlying pulse.

It's common to mix several different meters to enhance the musical impact of passages such as this. Unbalancing the rhythm can provide a sensation a bit like dissonance in harmony, which can be 'resolved' to a more regular time signature. However, for the purposes of this study, we remaining in 7/8 throughout.

After the first section of alternating G minor and Eb major chords, there is a short unison riff shared between organ, synth, bass and guitar which is common in this style. Rhythmic precision is of concern in all aspects of heavy metal, but never more so than unison parts, which should all sound like a single voice to blend the different timbres seamlessly. When repeated, this is transposed up an octave to add intensity. In the final two bars we use the tense F Diminished scale (half/whole) to bring the music to a climax before landing on a big Fsus4 chord.

Example 10c – Rhythm Part

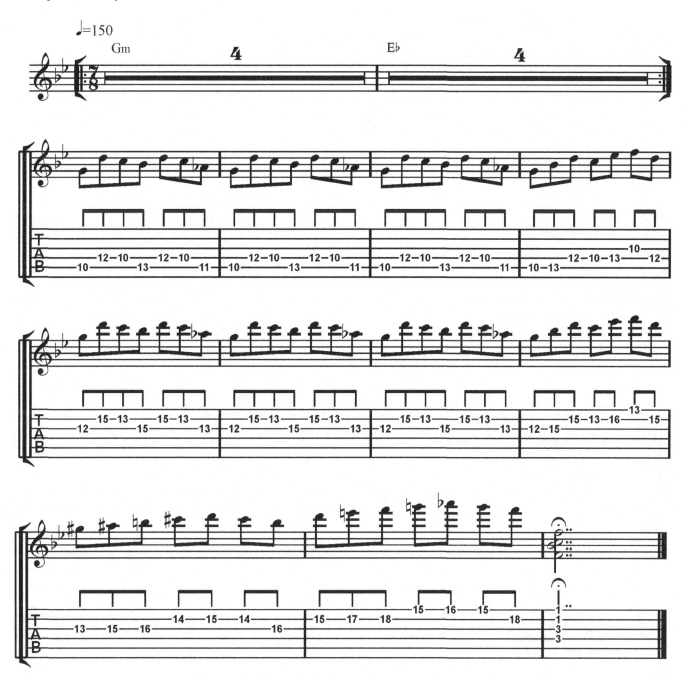

Bars 1-4: We kick things off with an intervallic idea that slides up the fretboard. Notice how the intervals get bigger over the course of the phrase, starting with 3rds, and then 6ths, and finally a minor 7th. Use the second finger for the first bar, with the first finger muting behind it to prevent unwanted noise.

Keep the same fingering for each section of the descending lick starting in bar three. The bends should be a quick curl rather than being strictly in time as notated.

Bars 5-8: The harmony has now moved to Eb with a more melodic phrase that involves tapped bends. Although the use of odd time in rock was mostly inspired by 20th century classical music, the origin is in the folk music of Eastern Europe and North Africa; so explore music from those cultures to get more inspiration for melodic ideas in meters in five and seven.

More intervallic ideas next, starting with ascending 5ths which lead into a fast sus2 arpeggio. Prog keyboard players like Keith

Emerson and Jordan Rudess can often be heard using sus2/4 arpeggios in their solos, as they create an exciting modern tonality and work over both major and minor harmony.

Bars 9-12: A defining feature of John Petrucci and Dimebag Darrel's playing styles (which helped them both stand out from the rather bloated shred scene in the early '90s), is a bluesy slant to their solos. This was in part influenced Stevie Ray Vaughan and Steve Morse. This four-bar phrase makes a nod to that approach with Hendrix-esque sliding doublestops and a chromatic passing tone.

Bars 13-16: We conclude with a long alternate picking run. After using Ab's in the preceding the solo to imply G Phrygian, we switch here to A naturals, giving the more colourful sound of Eb Lydian. Notice how the run is divided into groups of seven notes. Accent the first note of each seven note grouping, every other one of which will begin with an upstroke.

Example 10c – Lead Guitar

264

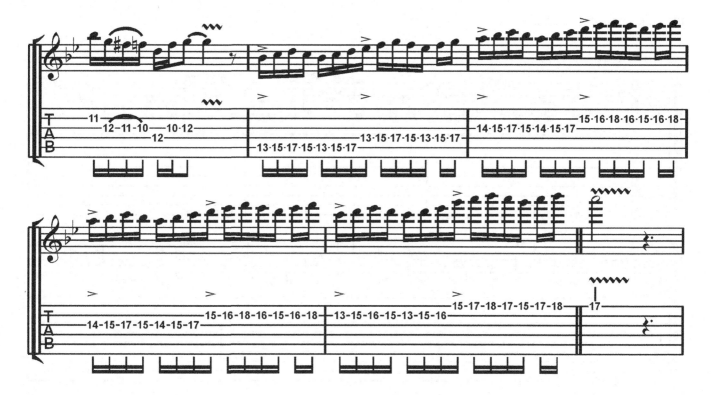

Example 10d

Our final metal solo study draws on the most experimental avant guard players in heavy music such as Buckethead, Bumble Foot, Ron Jarzombek and Mattias Eklund. These players often use unusual and dissonant note choices, odd rhythmic groupings, and complex combinations of various rock techniques to push the boundaries of metal and make original and individual music.

The rhythm part here is inspired by bands like Meshuggah and Animals as Leaders. It is a chromatic vamp around a B pedal tone. (To get a modern heavy sound I tuned down to B for the riff, but you could get a similar result by playing an octave higher.) Rhythmically, the guitar is divided into five semiquaver cells, and repeats a sequence of five groups of five notes, followed by a group of three before repeating. This cross-rhythm played against the main pulse of the track creates a constantly changing syncopation.

The second half of the track follows the same rhythmic grouping, but with a constant stream of notes. If you're learning the rhythm guitar part, then tackling this part (after working through the examples in the cross rhythm sub-chapter) is easier than the A section riff, as getting the notes in the right order means the rhythmic phrasing takes care of itself.

In an attempt to escape clichés, a lot of experimental metal is atonal, or contains great dissonance. Your note choice when soloing is therefore wide open. All twelve notes add a different colour over the B tonal centre, but we still have a sense of tension and release if we see these colours in a spectrum from consonant to most dissonant.

As a creative listening exercise, try ordering all twelve notes against a held drone in what, to you, sounds like increasing dissonance.

Example 10d – Rhythm Part

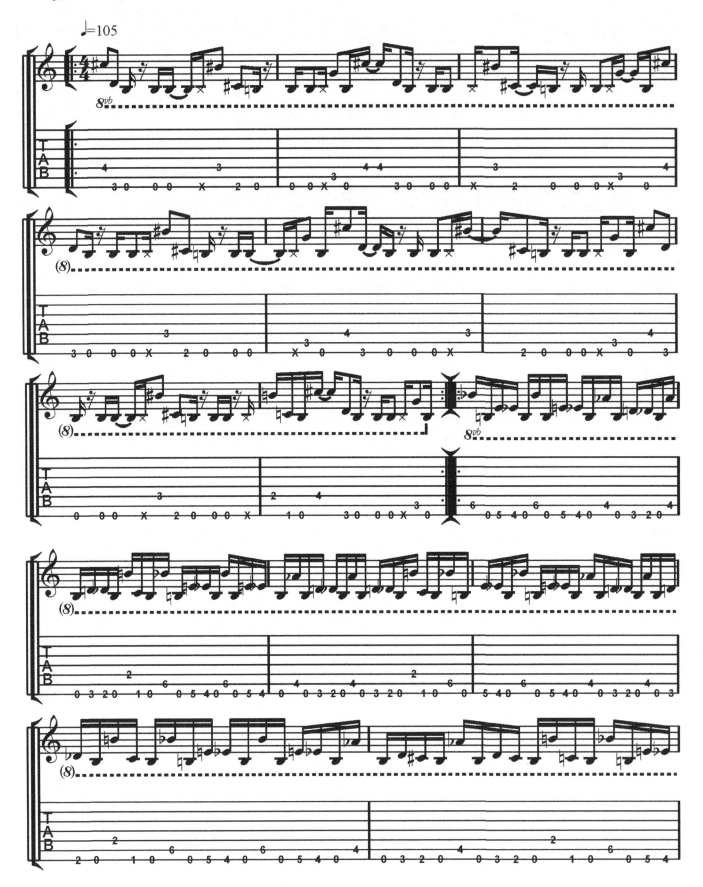

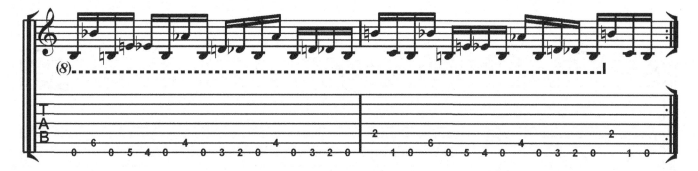

Bars 1-8: The first section starts with a slow melody comprising several tritone intervals, before developing into short bursts of legato. The long slide in bar five gives the effect of a whammy pedal. The position shift for the fretting hand should be made during duration of the tapped note. If you need to look at the fretboard, keep your eyes ahead of your hands by looking at the destination fret.

The legato phrase in bar eight loosely targets the notes of D minor with a lot of chromatic notes surrounding them. Jazz fusion guitarist Allan Holdsworth has had a great influence on metal guitarists. His virtuosic legato technique and outside note choice has been approximated by many metal guitarists, introducing a fusion influenced sound to their lead licks. Players as diverse as Van Halen and Frederik Thordendal have acknowledged his influence.

Bars 9-12: An atonal backing track doesn't dictate any particular mode or key as being 'inside'. So it is entirely down to you to use your ear to find melodies that sound 'correct' to you. Any note is fair game any groups of different intervals can be put together or transposed to help give your ideas more cohesion.

To illustrate this, our next line expands the legato texture to include both tapping, and open strings to achieve longer arpeggio-like contours. We start with a D Augmented triad, before repeating the same note cluster on the B string. The intervals along each string are then altered but the repetition of the overall shape gives the listener something to hang on to.

There is more fusion-influenced vocabulary as we continue, with an ascending and descending line of perfect 4ths. Cleanly articulating the 4ths takes a careful barre-roll with the first and second fingers of the fretting hand. This phrase concludes with a mixture of perfect 5th and 4th intervals and a short sliding melody.

The 4ths and 5ths still have a recognisable flavour even in the dissonant context. Superimposing a line with some internal logic will work even when they are 'wrong notes', so long as they are resolved tactfully.

Bars 13-16: Accent every fifth note in the first part of this lick to help convey the cross-rhythmic pulse. The string-skipping octaves will probably take some slow practice to master, but will really help your overall picking dexterity.

Bars 17-20: These four bars all follow the same two-beat sextuplet tapping pattern. If this is new to you, get confident with the first two beats before moving on to the different positions. Many players use a hair band or string mute to prevent unwanted string noise, but keeping the noise down is manageable by carefully placing the heel of the picking hand over the lower strings and muting the B string with the tip of the fretting hand's first finger.

Bars 21-25: Here's where things get a little more unorthodox. If you've ever experimented playing with a bottleneck, or making sound effects by tapping the strings with the whammy bar a la Tom Morello, you'll know that notes can continue up the string after the fretboard ends. Inspired by Ron Thal (aka Bumblefoot) I used a thimble on my picking hand pinkie to tap notes over the neck pickup area. Use the lower part of the neck to reference the lower octave to find the accurate pitches and remember where they occur over the pickups. For example, on my guitar the G natural ('28th fret') is just higher than the middle of my neck pickup)

Again, take each section of this lick very slowly so you can be sure that the thimble tapped notes are in tune and in time. You'll need to be use the bridge pickup here so that the pickup is still behind the active portion of the string.

Some sound effects round of this piece: The cascade of slides is done by alternately sliding up the fretboard, hand over hand. The second part is done by rubbing the thimble across the strings starting on the high E close to the bridge, and moving towards the lower strings over the neck. Finally, we end on a ringing dissonant semitone interval. To get some more interest into the sustaining notes, I rapidly switched between the two pickups to give a filter-sweep effect.

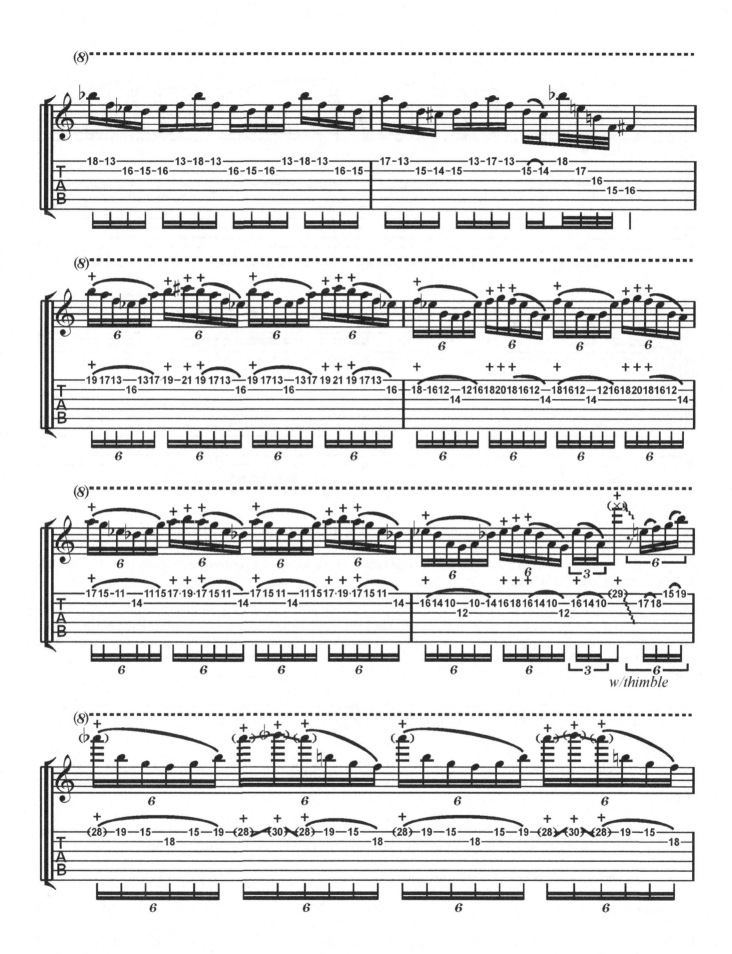

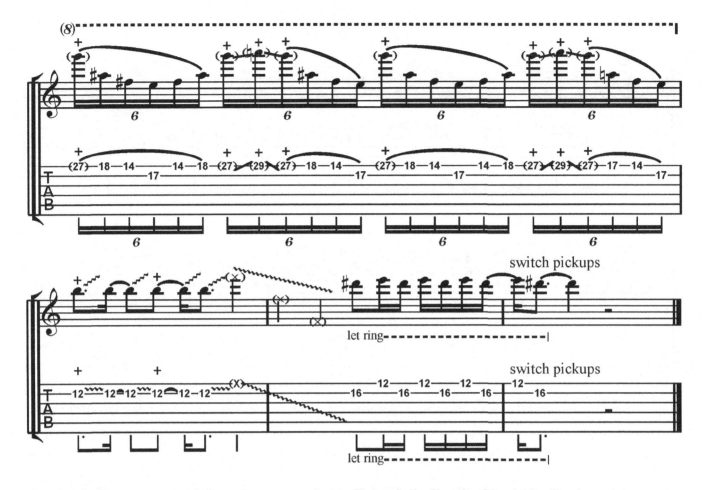

Neoclassical unaccompanied performance piece – Paganini's Caprice No. 16 in G minor

Among violin virtuoso Nicolo Paganini's (1782-1840) best known compositions are a set of twenty-four caprices. Here we'll be looking at the 16th Caprice in G minor.

The final study is a transcription of Paganini's Caprice No. 16 originally composed for unaccompanied violin. Adapting such pieces provides us with the rare opportunity to play a rewarding and highly musical solo item. Violins are tuned in 5ths which, coupled with the much shorter scale length, allows for wider intervallic leaps to fall easily under the fingers. To keep up with 'The Devil's Violinist' the transcription uses a mixture of several advanced rock guitar techniques including sweep picking, hybrid picking, legato and two-handed tapping.

Paganini was one of the main sources of inspiration for the neoclassical shred movement as a composer, but also because of his reputation as a virtuosic instrumentalist and flamboyant performer, just like his contemporary, the pianist Franz Liszt, and of course the master, J.S. Bach.

As well as being internationally known as a master of the violin and a flamboyant performer, Paganini also played guitar, and I'd like to think he'd approve of the direction in which electric guitar playing has developed to be able to perform his violin music.

We don't have room to analyse the whole of this piece from a harmonic perspective so to get the most out of learning this work you should keep track of the compositional devices used as you work through the music phrase by phrase.

Paganini's masterful use of arpeggios and chord tone targeting allows the solo melody to clearly imply a chord progression. Visualising the chord shapes that each phrases draws upon will help you to memorise it and also carry over the ideas into your own vocabulary.

Before playing, listen to the audio and isolate any sections that particularly appeal to you and work on those first. Come up with different versions and practice using them over metal backing tracks to really develop your neoclassical style. Of course, learning the whole piece will give you a beautiful and impressive piece of solo guitar music to add to your repertoire.

Bars 1-8: The opening section covers many of the ideas that recur throughout the piece so it's worth spending a good period of time memorising and practicing this chunk before tackling the rest of the tune.

If you've been practicing your arpeggio shapes, then the patterns will be recognisable. The first bar outlines the tonic G minor triad with a short embellishment around the root before descending. Bar two moves to D7, and, after a short pedal point lick, the line leaps up to start a descending dominant 7 arpeggio from the root, before switching to a Diminished idea in bar three.

After another brief recycling of bar two's pedal point motif on beat one of bar five, the harmony changes direction towards Cm, setting up the change with a G7 arpeggio to signal C as the new tonic. However, this is immediately undermined by the following arpeggios which outline F and Bb chords, revealing a II-V-I sequence in Bb major, the relative major of G minor. This might sound like a lot of theory but the musical effect is a confounding of our expectation as listeners as to where the piece is heading, all done by the use of chords shared by two keys.

Bars: 12-13: After more hybrid picking, we reach one of the fiddliest moments in the whole piece. We are juggling two note fragments in different registers of the instrument - similar to some of the twin guitar ideas we looked at towards the end of Chapter Eight. Follow the picking directions very carefully to ensure you have the most economic approach, and memorise the shifts slowly. Combining sweep and hybrid picking like this requires a compromise of hand position, so experiment until you find a comfortable balance.

Bars 15-20: This passage uses a lot of chromatic notes to target different chord tones, but should prove technically easier than the gymnastics of the previous few bars. Using legato here can provide a nice break from the pick attack, both for you and for the listener!

Bars 21-26: Back for more sweep/hybrid picking action. Paganini has combined an arpeggio with some chromatic passing notes and answered it with a pedal point lick over the next chord. We're moving from Bb – F7 then Adim back to Bb in the second two bars. The A Diminished triad functions here as an F7 which resolves to Bb.

Bars 46-49: A flurry of descending chromatic notes finishes the piece. I've kept things as legato as possible from the start of the section to help transition into the tapping used at the end. Damping the strings will be an issue when making such wide string skips as this. The wide jumps up to the high D and F# in bars 48-49 are best handled by tapping with the middle and ring fingers.

Bars 50-51: The motif we saw introduced in the previous bars of jumping to a pair of high chord tones in D major is now recycled on the tonic chord of G minor in order to resolve harmonically. Both hands are tapping here. Keep the fingers of the fretting hand flat against the strings in between hammering onto the low G notes to clean up the left hand tapping.

Bar 52-End: If you're playing this track with distortion the final chord will sound unclear, so during the preceding legato phrase leading use your picking hand to roll off the volume pot a little. This will bring out a pleasingly warm G minor chord, and will leave the listener with a much nicer final impression than if you ended on a muddy distorted noise.

Niccolò Paganini (1782-1840)

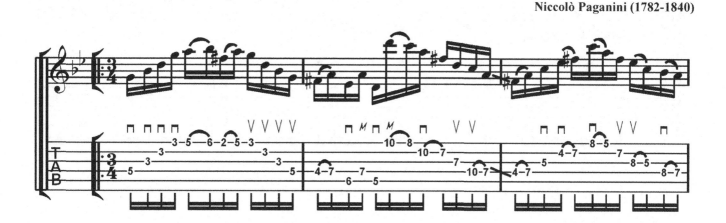

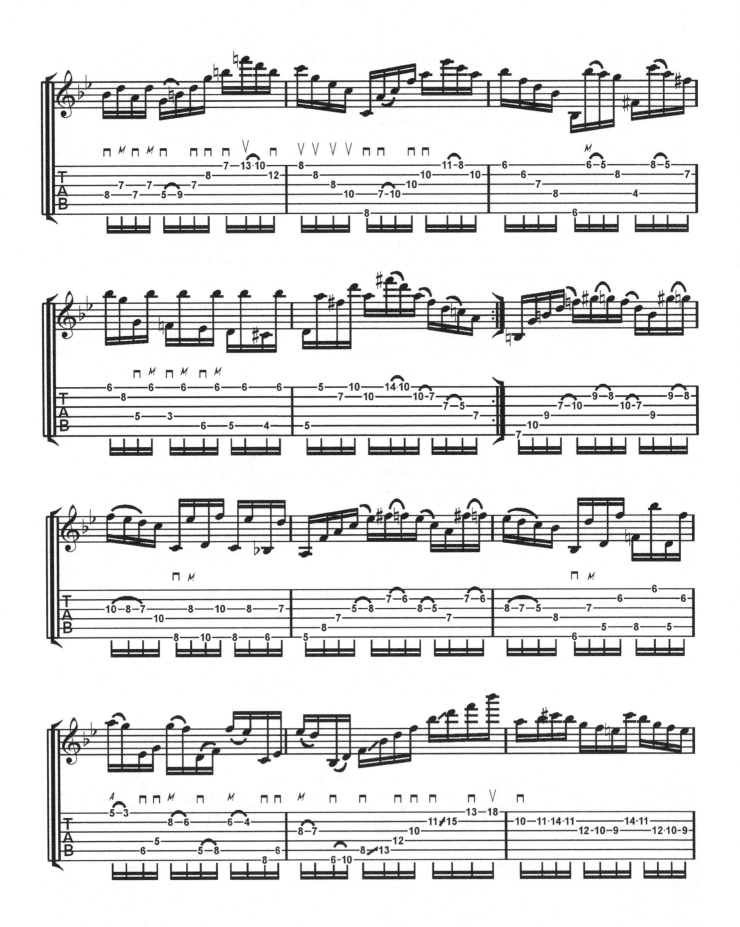

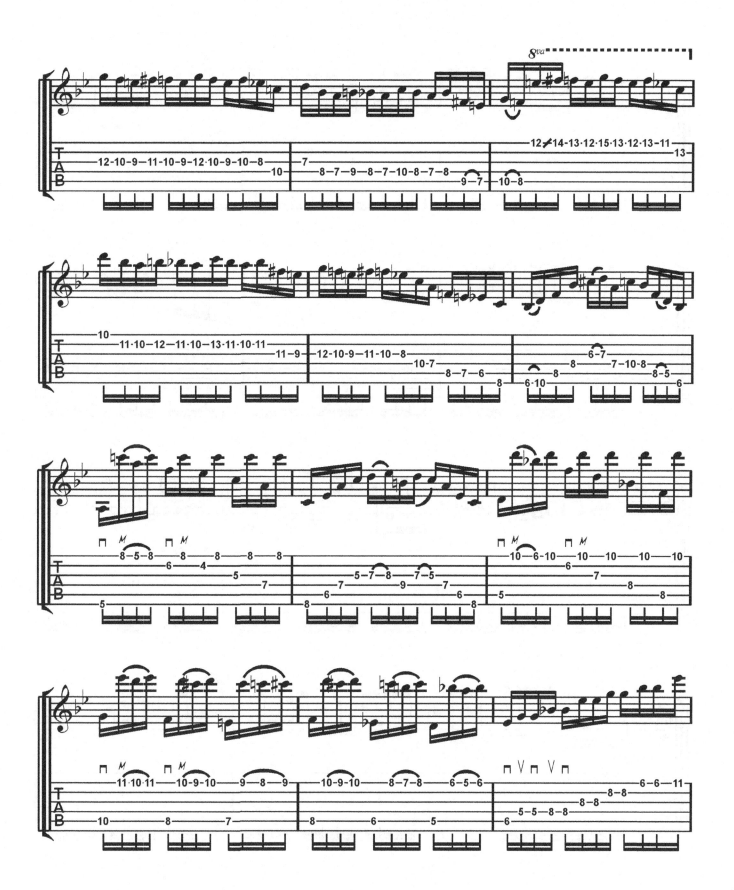

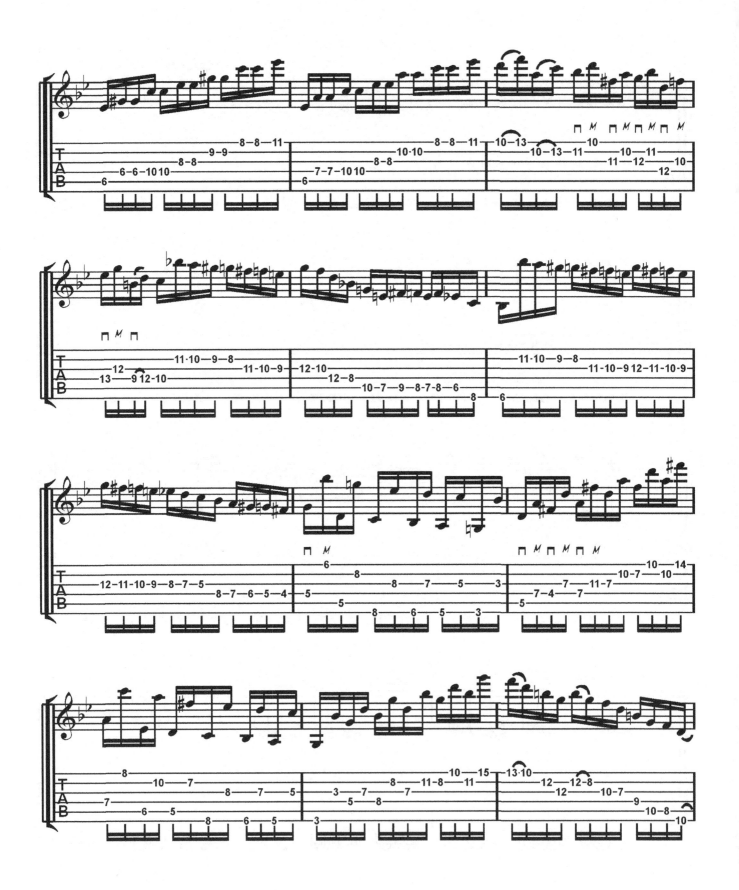

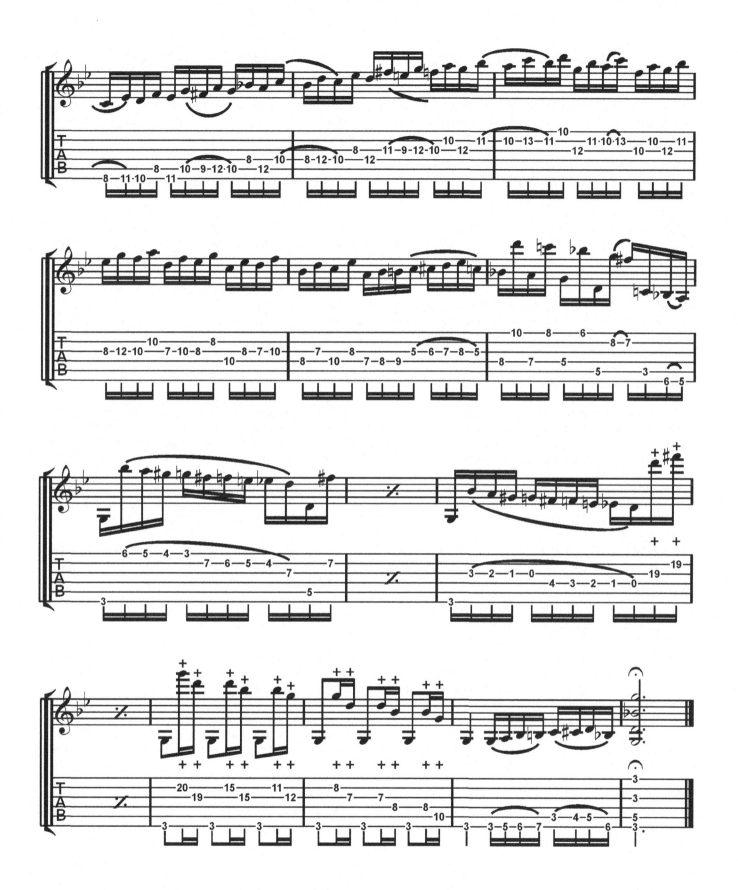

Chapter Eleven: Forging Your Own Style - You Can Do It!

To close, I'd like to offer some suggestions to help you develop your own unique voice on the instrument. As creative musicians the ultimate goal is surely to be expressive on the guitar. All too often however, we feel that our progress is sluggish, or that we are just regurgitating the ideas of other players without saying anything new.

It may be a lofty dream to achieve the mastery of the most famous and respected players (and unrealistic as we all have busy lives in which practice is limited) but I believe there are some logical steps you can employ to help drive your playing in a more personal and expressive direction.

A player with a strong individual musical identity can usually be recognised from hearing only a few phrases. For many of these players, their style is defined as much by the ideas they don't use as by those they do. By narrowing the focus of their vocabulary they are highlighting those elements of their playing that are unique to them.

It's worth noting that while some players distance themselves from the pack by employing unusual or very complicated ideas, (Buckethead and Ron Thal spring immediately to mind) an expressive voice can be a fresh or slightly progressed take on the conventions of the style. After all, many clichés end up such because they are great! Think of Kirk Hammett's solos on the early Metallica recordings – he is employing mainly bending and repeating Pentatonic licks, but with his own patterns, phrasing and wah pedal use, it is recognisably 'Kirk Hammett'.

Expanding Your Vocabulary

All of us draw inspiration from other people's music in the same way that language is learnt by listening to, and copying others. There is no shame is taking the licks of players whose style resonates with you, but after imitating them the creative guitarist will take those inherited ideas and break out of the gravitational orbit of their heroes to become an individual. The process by which you can start to achieve this is straightforward, although it takes creative thinking and hard work!

Isolate a lick that particularly appeals to you, maybe one of the licks we've looked at in this book, or something gleaned from learning a solo. Once you're reasonably comfortable with playing the lick in its original form, try to transpose it to different keys. To do this you'll have to be able to visualise it in terms of the tonic note, or better still, a familiar chord shape.

The next thing you could try would be work out a version of the lick using a different scale. If, for example the lick used the Phrygian mode, you could adapt it to fit the Lydian or Aeolian modes. If the lick uses three note-per-string scale shapes this should be an easy process, otherwise you may need to work out how each pitch needs to be changed, using your ear as a guide.

Change the length of the phrase. If the lick moves through positions – keep going for twice as long, or perhaps practice shorter versions of the lick which can be inserted more easily into solos.

Analyse what makes up the lick and what it is that made you choose it. Is there an interesting sounding interval, sequential pattern, or perhaps the smooth flowing sound of legato and tapping piqued your interest? Whatever the DNA of the lick, set yourself the challenge of writing five licks that use that specific sound or technique. Don't worry if you feel like they are too similar, any reinterpretation of the material will enhance your creative thinking and musical understanding.

If you keep repeating this process, and record the results of your experimentation in a notepad, audio recording or tab/score editor on the computer, then you will soon develop a library of original ideas that have moved away from the style of whoever's lick you used as a launch pad.

This is only half the battle though, and the remaining task is to load this new vocabulary into your instinctive muscle memory so that it comes out in your natural playing. To stretch the well-worn language metaphor, you can usually tell when someone has consciously 'dressed up' their language with elaborate vocabulary to seem intelligent, as compared to when it is has been naturally acquired by osmosis.

The key to succeeding is reassuringly fun, after all the study and repetition. Look for a backing track with a feel that suits the licks you've been working on (there are plenty of 'jam tracks' for sale or on YouTube). Make sure that you can play your new licks in that key - then just play! You should pay attention to how you transition between phrases, and aim to link the new ideas into your existing playing. Given time, they will stop being new licks and become assimilated into your unique voice, especially if you use different variations interchangeably.

Taking Unusual Influences

One way to stand out is to take inspiration from different instruments and styles of music. Most guitarists listen to guitarists, copy their licks, and thus sound like guitarists! However, there are many who've managed to distinguish themselves by taking ideas from keyboard, violin, saxophone, banjo or instruments from other cultures like the koto and sitar.

The way notes are arranged on different instruments and the limitations of size or breath, mean that certain musical ideas are more accessible on some instruments than others.

While the guitar will always sound like a guitar, thinking about how we can copy the attributes of other instruments will lead us down new roads. Great examples include John 5 who's incorporated country licks derived from banjo and pedal steel into his metal vocabulary, Marty Friedman for his koto influenced bends, and guitarists like Paul Masvidal (Cynic) and Frederik Thordendal (Meshuggah) whose fusion influenced legato ideas come from saxophone players like John Coltrane and Michael Brecker, via jazz-rock legend Allan Holdsworth.

Building a Cohesive Style

While a good player can draw on the different textures and techniques to be expressive and maintain interest during a solo, a truly great player combines them seamlessly. This takes time and effort after first being comfortable with each technique individually. There are plenty of players who prove that speed and virtuosity are not prerequisites for great metal playing and little dashes of flashiness in an otherwise melodic and well thought-out solo can be much more effective than endless histrionics!

So, as a final thought, work on your technique, tone, theory and of course power stance!... but remember that the real goal is making powerful and emotionally engaging music. Regardless of the science behind the music, always ask yourself, 'does this move me?' and follow your ear!

Made in the USA
Las Vegas, NV
15 December 2023

82943597R00155